LEARNING FROM COMPARIN

new directions in comparative educational research

Volume 1. Contexts, Classrooms and Outcomes

LEARNING FROM COMPARING
new directions in comparative educational research

Volume 1. Contexts, Classrooms and Outcomes

Edited by
Robin Alexander
Patricia Broadfoot
& David Phillips

SYMPOSIUM
BOOKS

Symposium Books

PO Box 65, Wallingford, Oxford OX10 0YG, United Kingdom

Published in the United Kingdom, 1999

ISBN 1 873927 58 4

Typeset in Melior by Symposium Books
Printed and bound in the United Kingdom by Cambridge University Press

Contents

COMPANION VOLUME

LEARNING FROM COMPARING:
new directions in comparative educational research
Volume 2: Policy, Professionals and Development
ISBN 1 873927 63 0   Symposium Books, 1999

Introduction

ROBIN ALEXANDER

Contexts, Classrooms and Outcomes is Volume 1 in a two-volume set with the overall title *Learning From Comparing: new directions in comparative educational research*. With Volume 2, *Policy, Professionals and Development*, it re-assesses the contribution of comparative educational research and theory to our understanding of contemporary educational problems and to our capacity to solve them.

The books are the outcome of a programme of seminars funded over the period 1997-1999 by the Economic and Social Research Council (ESRC). The programme was initiated by Robin Alexander, and was organised jointly by three university research centres: the Centre for Research in Elementary and Primary Education at the University of Warwick (Robin Alexander, Michele Schweisfurth and Rosemary Preston), the Centre for Curriculum and Assessment Studies at the University of Bristol (Patricia Broadfoot and Marilyn Osborn), and the Centre for Comparative Studies in Education at the University of Oxford (David Phillips and Colin Brock).

During the late 1990s a number of developments combined to make this initiative desirable: indeed, in our view, the corrective function of what we had in mind became increasingly urgent once the slogan 'education, education, education' had been coined to urge the British electorate into the polling booths for the 1997 general election.

First, and most evident to those outside as well as inside education, the economic and technological globalisation of the 1980s led to a globalisation of educational discourse during the 1990s. Its most prominent feature was the use of international comparisons, both spurious and genuine, to legitimate government claims about the condition of national systems of education and to justify radical changes in educational policy. This condition was not confined to the United Kingdom (UK): to varying degrees and with differing consequences other countries in Europe, the Americas and Australasia found themselves caught up in the game of international league tables and policy borrowing. For most, the focus of concern was the dramatic rise of the 'Asian Tiger' economies of the Pacific Rim, while the conjunction of economic evidence and test score data from the surveys provided by the International Association for the Evaluation of Educational Achievement (IEA) and the International Assessment of Educational Progress (IAEP) suggested a cause-effect relationship which many, throwing caution to the winds, found irresistible.

Second, the link between educational and economic performance appeared to be consolidated by developments in pedagogic research, which by the early 1990s had also moved into the international arena. Thus, in the UK, the parallel traditions of largely-quantitative pre-test/post-test sampled studies and more intensive qualitative and ethnographic investigations were being used as the springboard for ambitious cross-cultural comparisons of teaching and learning involving two or more countries.

At the same time, a new research paradigm, that of 'school effectiveness', was being marketed as the means of cutting through the equivocations of established research methods to the 'best buy' pedagogies which would at a stroke improve schools, transform teaching, and deliver national targets of educational attainment. This paradigm, too, had an international dimension, constituted partly of reviews of the international research literature and partly of new studies in which classrooms in the more successful Asian and European economies featured prominently and thereby seemed to provide the vital 'process' ingredient which would link the test and economic data and could then be translated into practical strategies to drive up educational standards.

Third, the richer nations' preoccupation with educational league tables contrasted starkly with the condition of the developing countries, the more so as similar processes of data aggregation, extrapolation and comparison were being used to shape the donor agencies' calculations about what quantities of aid, and what intervention strategies, would yield the best and quickest return on their grants and loans, given the widespread assumption that education provides the key to both economic development and political stability. Among comparativists and analysts of education and development, however, the economic and political subtexts of these calculations were coming in for close scrutiny; as were, in an ostensibly post-imperialist and post-colonial era, the attitudes of the donor nations and agencies themselves.

Finally, and partly as a consequence of the intellectual turmoil generated by developments such as these, the academic discipline of comparative education was experiencing on the one hand a renaissance and an influx of new recruits, but on the other a crisis of identity and purpose.

The seminars were conceived as a relatively intimate forum for taking stock of all these developments. They brought together representatives from two key constituencies: researchers (mainly from universities), and 'users' (from government departments, public bodies, international agencies, and the press). Incidentally, though the seminars adopted the term 'users' – it has become a standard requirement of research grant applications – and responded directly to the imperatives of research communication and relevance which it signals, there were many in both constituencies who found it not entirely helpful. To them, 'users' unnecessarily compartmentalised the processes of research, policy and action, and discouraged the reflexive and interactive relationship between these domains which they felt was appropriate to the particular character of educational problems.

Indeed, in planning the seminars, it was felt that the matter of how comparative research is initiated and used was no less important than questions of theory and methodology: the series, after all, had been prompted in part by an awareness that if international comparison of educational processes and outcomes is intrinsically problematic, international borrowing of educational practices of the kind being commended by government advisers during the mid-1990s can be downright dangerous, because it can affect the educational and employment prospects of millions.

Thus, the seminars as planned combined attention to a series of substantive topics with the exploration of a number of recurrent, cross-cutting themes. The topics were as follows.

- Comparative education in the 1990s: theory, method and context: an overview of comparative education as a field of academic enquiry, set against the background of its development over the past century or so (May 1997, Oxford).
- Comparing classrooms and schools: an examination of different ways of researching and analysing educational processes, including pedagogy, in a crosscultural context, of the strengths and limitations of each, and of the problems of the enterprise as a whole (November 1997, Warwick).
- Comparing pupil achievement: an assessment of the evidence from international achievement studies and the problems which these raise, especially once applied in the context of policy (March 1998, Bristol).
- Research, development and education: what research has contributed, and can contribute, to education in the developing country context, and how the relationship between education and development can best be understood (June 1998, Warwick).
- The comparative study of educational policy: how in an international context national educational policies can validly be researched and

compared, how their impact can be assessed, and the lessons which they offer (November 1998, Oxford).

- Education professionals compared: comparing the work of teachers and other education professionals across national and cultural boundaries, the conditions within which they work, and the relationship between their work as defined and as undertaken (March 1999, Bristol).

The generic or cross-cutting themes running through the series as a whole were as follows.

- Theoretical issues: changing accounts of the theory and rationale of comparative education.
- Methodological issues: cases and problems from specific research paradigms such as survey and ethnography, together with generic issues such as sampling, generalisabilty, language and culture.
- Policy issues: the various policy contexts in which comparative research and analysis is or might be used – for example, economic strategy, development education, school improvement, inspection and quality assurance, curriculum change.
- Practice/practitioner issues: the applications of comparative research in the context of educational practice; the ethical and other challenges of involving practitioners in such research.
- Strategic issues: funding for comparative research; comparative education and disciplinary/ departmental boundaries.
- Phase-specific issues: the conduct and application of comparative research in, for example, pre-school, primary/ elementary and secondary education, in teacher training and higher education, and in lifelong learning.
- Regional issues: the conduct of comparative research, and the lessons it offers, in different regional, national and cultural contexts – for example the European Union, Eastern Europe, the countries of the former Soviet Union, North America, and developing countries in Africa, Asia and South America.

In addition, because for funding reasons seminar numbers had to kept fairly low, the planning group decided to round off the programme with an open conference for a much larger membership. At the time of writing this is still being planned, though it is likely to be held at the University of Warwick in late 1999.

Now to the structure of this book. It arises, as will be evident, from the first three seminars in the list above, but it is not merely a collated set of seminar proceedings. All the papers have been revised, some extensively so, and in undertaking their revisions authors have been able to reflect on or respond to the transcripts of the taped discussions which their papers provoked. In addition, the main issues from each seminar have been summarised. Each section opens with an editorial note setting the scene.

There are also additional papers (from Maurice Galton and Michele Schweisfurth) specially commissioned for this volume, and Part One starts with a section introduction by David Phillips on the use of cross-national comparisons in education.

We hope that the two volumes of *Learning From Comparing* will prove topical, challenging, interesting and useful – to 'users', naturally, no less than to researchers and research students. We hope, too, that at a time when educational research is under attack on the grounds of 'bias' and 'irrelevance', and under pressure to address only those questions which are acceptable politically (as good a definition of bias as any), the seriousness of our attempt to bridge the worlds of research, policy and practice will be recognised. And we trust that the catholicity of the collection – in terms of both perspective and nationality – will be appreciated, for we have taken care to locate contrasting viewpoints on each topic, and each also includes a contribution from outside the UK.

Finally, we record our thanks to all those who participated in the seminars, and to the Economic and Social Research Council, which funded them.

PART ONE

Comparative Education in the 1990s: theory, method and context

On Comparing

DAVID PHILLIPS

At a time when we are seeing a decline in comparative education in some universities in some countries and a growth in others – the patterns are very varied – it is perhaps necessary to step back from what we are doing and to postulate defences of it. At the present time there is arguably an unprecedented interest in what is happening in education systems outside our own, especially with the growth in importance for politicians and the media of the findings of large-scale international studies of pupil attainment. We are also witnessing the – I think refreshing – involvement of researchers who are not, professionally speaking, comparativists but who bring to the discussion of issues in our subject new perspectives from their backgrounds as sociologists or political scientists, as economists or statisticians.

Those involved in the wide range of scholarly investigations subsumed under 'comparative education' should not need to be reticent about defending what they do. It is, after all, in the very nature of intellectual activity to make comparisons. Comparing is a fundamental part of the thought processes which enable us to make sense of the world and our experience of it. Indeed, it can be argued that *only* by making comparisons can we properly defend our position on most questions of importance which require the making of judgements.[1] Comparing causes us to make statements to the effect that *p* is intellectually or morally preferable to, or more efficient or effective than, or simply in some general sense 'better' than *q*. And where might comparison serve us better than in the sphere of education, where the quest for improvement, for 'doing things better', is always so compelling?

But if we are called upon to provide a checklist of arguments in defence of the study of educational issues in a comparative context, then such a list would surely include the following. The comparative study of education:

- shows what is possible by examining alternatives to provision 'at home';
- offers yardsticks by which to judge the performance of education systems;
- describes what might be the consequences of certain courses of action, by looking at experience in various countries (i.e. in attempting to predict outcomes it can serve both to support and to warn against potential policy decisions);
- provides a body of descriptive and explanatory data which allows us to see various practices and procedures in a very wide context that helps to throw light upon them;[2]
- contributes to the development of an increasingly sophisticated theoretical framework in which to describe and analyse educational phenomena;
- serves to provide authoritative objective data which can be used to put the less objective data of others (politicians and administrators, principally) who use comparisons for a variety of political and other reasons, to the test;
- has an important supportive and instructional role to play in the development of any plans for educational reform, when there must be concern to examine experience elsewhere;
- helps to foster co-operation and mutual understanding among nations by discussing cultural differences and similarities and offering explanations for them;
- is of intrinsic intellectual interest as a scholarly activity, in much the same way as the comparative study of religion, or literature, or government, is.

The 'comparative method' is of course a cornerstone of sociological investigation. The classic description is to be found in Durkheim:

> *We have only one way of demonstrating that one phenomenon is the cause of another. This is to compare the cases where they are both simultaneously present or absent, so as to discover whether the variations they display in these different combinations of circumstances provide evidence that one depends upon the other. When the phenomena can be artificially produced at will by the observer, the method is that of experimentation proper. When, on the other hand, the production of facts is something beyond our power to command, and we can only bring them together as they have been spontaneously produced, the method used is one of indirect experimentation, or the comparative method.*
> *(Durkheim, 1982 [second edition, 1901], p. 147)*

Comparativists investigating educational issues have precisely the advantage of being able to look at situations in other countries which could not be set up experimentally in their own. indeed, 'indirect experimentation' is a term which might be utilised more widely to describe the processes which many comparativists follow. Investigating comprehensive education has been one good example. The Swedish comprehensive schools were the object of considerable interest in the 1960s (not least on the part of British educationists and politicians [3]); later the English comprehensive school was to become the focus of investigation by observers from other countries contemplating reform.[4] In each case it was possible, before going so far as to introduce wholesale reform, to examine by 'indirect experimentation' the experience elsewhere.

Another simple example might serve to test the efficacy of a comparative dimension in an educational investigation. Our understanding, within the context of any one country with which we are intimately familiar, of the issues surrounding a subject like pupil grouping, might be as complete as could reasonably be expected. It might be the case – though probably unlikely in this particular instance – that research studies have demonstrated that a particular form of grouping (mixed-ability/setting) produces better academic outcomes for some or all age groups in some or all types of schools. But before relying too much on accumulated knowledge from observation and experience and from research results at home, it would be as well to look at the lessons which various pupil grouping arrangements in other countries offer.

We might, for example, look at what was the situation in the countries of Eastern Europe before the changes of 1989, where undifferentiated classes were the norm up to age 14 or 16. The former German Democratic Republic provided what could be called the 'purest' form of comprehensive education, with only mixed-ability classes, with teachers trained to cope with undifferentiated groups, and with a general acceptance that this was unquestionably right. Similarly, we might look at Japan, where – especially in the junior high schools – there is no differentiation by ability, and where there is an expectancy that all children will reach the required standard (as most do).

If we wished to examine the advantages and disadvantages of a differentiated education system, then the models currently in use in the various *Länder* (states) of the Federal Republic of Germany would provide a wealth of evidence both for and against the provision of separate schools for children with different abilities and aspirations.

Such observations of foreign practice would be subject to all the caveats – to do with cultural, social, religious, political, and economic context – which have been rehearsed by comparativists since the days of Michael Sadler.[5] Often too, in looking at the particularities of educational provision in other countries, it proves to be the case that the very aspects attracting our attention are being subjected to close scrutiny in those countries; sometimes, indeed, we might find that there is reciprocal interest in what might be learnt from the features of our home system which we are desirous to reform.[6] Policy-makers contemplating reform might learn much from such external interest.

Learning from others' experience is far removed from simplistic notions of 'borrowing' – itself a curious term in the context of comparative education, since literally it implies a temporary arrangement. The adoption of policies and approaches in education which might be extracted from a foreign situation, as argued above, is very unlikely to succeed in a quite different context, but the weighing of evidence from other countries in such a way as to inform and influence policy development at home should be a very natural part of any efforts to introduce change. In Sadler's terms:

> *The practical value of studying, in a right spirit and with*
> *scholarly accuracy, the working of foreign systems of*
> *education is that it will result in our being better fitted to*
> *study and to understand our own. (Sadler, 1979 [1900], p. 50)*

And herein lies one of the principal contributions that comparativists can make. By bringing their detailed knowledge of the workings of foreign systems of education to bear on policy issues at home they can provide new perspectives on those issues which can be of enormous benefit to our understanding of them. In this context the recent series of studies of aspects of education in other countries undertaken by Her Majesty's Inspectorate is to be welcomed; such studies would be strengthened if independent specialists with long-standing knowledge of the target systems were to be involved, as is the case with OECD studies.

Insight into the potential of comparison can also be gained from other 'comparative' disciplines or fields of inquiry. 'Comparative anatomy' is a branch of medicine with an important historical role in the development of medical understanding;[7] 'comparative religion', from the time (1890) of Frazer's *The Golden Bough*, has thrown light on the nature and origins of religious belief through careful description and classification; 'comparative law' attempts "to [discover] generalisations applicable to law generally, or a group of systems generally, with a view to law reform, or with a view to the unification of law and the achievement of a universal law shared by all civilised humanity" (Walker, 1980, p. 261);[8] 'comparative literature', first established as a field in universities in the 1890s (Clements, 1978, p. 978), seeks *inter alia* to identify commonalities between literary approaches and traditions in various countries and cultures.

The burgeoning fields of 'comparative politics' and 'comparative government' are also of interest. "Comparative politics is everything – or it is nothing" (Roberts, 1972, p. 7). So begins one study of comparative politics, highlighting a problem which is of concern to those running courses in 'comparative' anything: such courses can be seen to attempt what is impossible – namely to cover all aspects of an often complex inter-disciplinary subject as it is manifest in all countries throughout all time. This daunting universality causes Debeauvais (1985) to declare that "comparative education covers a vast field which does not correspond to any strict normative definition".

But what is important in other 'comparative' disciplines is the acceptance of the need to compare, of faith in the advantages to be gained from the processes of comparing for the development of the field of knowledge in question. It is in this spirit that papers of this section should be read. They attempt to take the debate about the value of the comparative dimension in education forward and serve as background to papers in other parts of this volume. They are followed by an account of a recent survey of comparative and international education at United Kingdom universities, undertaken by Michele Schweisfurth.

Notes

[1] As one French philosopher puts it: "All judgement is comparative: every comparison an interpretation of diversity by way of identity" (Masson-Oursel, 1926, p. 31).

[2] Halls (1990, p. 22) calls this an 'educational morphology'.

[3] For an account of interest (positive and negative) in the Swedish reforms, see Torsten Husén (1989) 'The Swedish school reform – exemplary both ways'.

[4] See, for example, Karl Heinz Gruber's report for the Austrian ministry of education on reform in the English education system, *Entwicklungen und Reformtendenzen im englischen Bildungswesen*, Bundesministerium für Unterricht und Kunst, Vienna, n.d. [1974].

[5] We would do well, in defending comparative studies in education, to recall a classic passage from the writings of Michael Sadler, one of the most important of the first wave of British comparativists and someone who made a significant impact on British educational policy in the early years of this century. In a now much quoted lecture delivered in 1900 he said:
In studying foreign systems of Education we should not forget that the things outside the schools matter even more than the things inside the schools, and govern and interpret the things inside. We cannot wander at pleasure among the educational systems of the world, like a child strolling through a garden, and pick off a flower from one bush and some leaves from another, and then expect that if we stick what we have gathered into the soil at home, we shall have a living plant. A national system of Education is a living thing, the outcome of forgotten struggles and 'of battles long ago'. It has in it some of the secret workings of national life. (Sadler, 1979 [1900], p. 49)

[6] This appears to be the case at present (1998) with Japan, where the reform discussions reveal interest in such matters as more flexible approaches to teaching and learning in England, while British interest in Japan has recently focussed on the perceived advantages of whole-class teaching and more formal teaching styles. See: Kingston (1998); HMI (1991); DFE (1992).

[7] According to the eleventh edition of the *Encyclopaedia Britannica* (1910) the term was "falling into desuetude, and lingers practically only in the titles of books or in the designation of university chairs". The entry on 'Comparative Anatomy' continues: "From the point of view of structure, man is one of the animals; all investigations into anatomical structure must be comparative".

[8] Walker, interestingly for our purposes, distinguishes between 'comparative law' and 'foreign law', the latter being "simply the study of any system of law other than the one with which the student is primarily concerned, and ... not necessarily [involving] any element of comparison" (Walker, 1980, p. 261). This reminds us of the distinction between *vergleichende Pädagogik* and *Auslandspädagogik* ('comparative education' and 'education abroad').

Bibliography

Clements, Robert J. (1978) Comparative literature (field of study), in Asa S. Knowles (Ed.) *The International Encyclopedia of Higher Education.* San Francisco: Jossey-Bass.

Debeauvais, M. (1985) Documentation in comparative education, in Torsten Husén & T. Neville Postlethwaite (Eds) *The International Encyclopedia of Education.* Oxford: Pergamon.

DFE (1992) *Teaching and Learning in Japanese Elementary Schools.* London: HMSO.

Durkheim, Emile (1982) [1901] *The Rules of Sociological Method and Selected Texts on Sociology and its Method*, ed. Steven Lukes. London: Macmillan.

Gruber, Karl Heinz (n.d.) [1974] *Entwicklungen und Reformtendenzen im englischen Bildungswesen.* Vienna: Bundesministerium für Unterricht und Kunst.

Halls, W.D. (Ed.) (1990) *Comparative Education: contemporary issues and trends.* London: Jessica Kingsley/Unesco.

HMI (1991) *Aspects of Upper Secondary and Higher Education in Japan.* London: HMSO.

Husén, Torsten (1989) The Swedish school reform – exemplary both ways, *Comparative Education*, 25, pp. 345-355.

Kingston, Peter (1998) East meets west, *The Guardian*, 12 May.

Masson-Oursel, Paul (1926) *Comparative Philosophy.* London: Kegan Paul, Trench, Trubner.

Roberts, Geoffrey K. (1972) *What is Comparative Politics?* London: Macmillan.

Sadler, Michael (1979) [1900] How far can we learn anything of practical value from the study of foreign systems of education, in J.H. Higginson (Ed.) *Selections from Michael Sadler: studies in world citizenship.* Liverpool: Dejall & Meyorre.

Walker, David M. (1980) *The Oxford Companion to Law.* Oxford: Clarendon Press.

Not So Much a Context, More a Way of Life? Comparative Education in the 1990s

PATRICIA BROADFOOT

My choice of title for this chapter echoes a paper which I wrote some 20 years ago as part of a special issue of the journal *Comparative Education* on 'The state of the art'. In my contribution I argued that "the comparative study of education is not a discipline: it is a context" (Broadfoot, 1977, p. 133). Writing from the point of view of a policy researcher rather than as a comparativist *per se*, I argued that comparative studies had three important potential roles to play:

- by providing internationally consistent data on the effects of different educational practices – if indeed these exist;
- by providing case-studies of the internal dynamics of education systems and how these influence the idiosyncratic effects of educational practices in any particular context. By so doing, I suggested, policy-makers could be provided with guidance as to the likely outcomes of any particular innovation.
- by questioning the most basic and taken for granted assumptions under which any educational system operates.

Taken together, I suggested, these arguments for comparative studies were overwhelming. In practice, however, the development of comparative education as a field of study during the last 20 years has been oddly mixed. On the one hand, our field has enjoyed something of a renaissance as its potential contribution appears once again to be being recognised by policy makers, scholars and even some practitioners. But this welcome growth of interest in our field has also brought with it its own challenges. Like any popular orthodoxy, it has attracted its share of popularisers, and even charlatans. On the other hand comparative education continues to be marginalised as a taught subject in many higher education institutions and is still bedevilled by a reputation as "an esoteric, even arcane pursuit, far removed from the mainstream of educational research" (Watson & Williams, 1984).

An ESRC-sponsored seminar on comparative education – perhaps in itself a significant new vote of confidence in the field – invites us to consider the current situation of comparative education research and, in the light of this consideration, to adduce some guidelines for the future development of the field. In particular I want to address three key questions that I think we need to be able to answer with a degree of consensus if we are to achieve that degree of vision I believe to be essential to sustaining the quality of scholarship to which we have traditionally aspired in the field. I shall argue that only by having a clear sense of what comparative education is, and hence, what it is not, can we hope to fulfil the potential for the development of the field which is inherent in the interest now being shown in it by educational policy-makers and practitioners as a potential source of guidance and insight in an increasingly international world.

Thus, the questions that I will address are deceptively simple ones:

- What is comparative education?
- What is not comparative education?
- How should we seek to develop our field in the future?

What is Comparative Education?

Comparative education has found it more difficult than many other specialisms to define precisely what its boundaries are. A relatively cursory review of articles in leading comparative journals reveals that contributions can range from single country studies of almost any aspect of educational provision at one extreme, to relatively decontextualised, international comparisons such as the International Association for the Evaluation of Educational Achievement (IEA) studies at the other. In between are a range of explicitly international comparisons of particular aspects of provision such as special education, or levels of the education system such as universities or of themes such as multi-culturalism or post-modernism. Add to this the possibility of *intranational* comparisons and it seems that almost anything can be included within the ambit of comparative education.

This diversity is well illustrated by the range of contributions typically presented at comparative education conferences. For example, the periodic World Congresses of Comparative Education Societies. The submissions cover diverse topics and esoteric methodological debates as well as a host of other concerns.

It would be hard indeed for an outsider to detect what it is that distinguishes comparative education apart from its very obvious international character. It is almost equally difficult to deduce the boundaries and defining concerns of the field from its specialist publications. To illustrate this, Figure 1 provides an analysis of the types of 'comparative studies' published in the journal *Comparative Education* since 1993.

One country study	Comparative study	Theoretical/ thematic study
31	29	21

Figure 1. Articles published in *Comparative Education*, 1993-1996.

A more detailed classification might be as set out in Figure 2 which organises the range of approaches in terms of a hierarchy of theoretical generality.

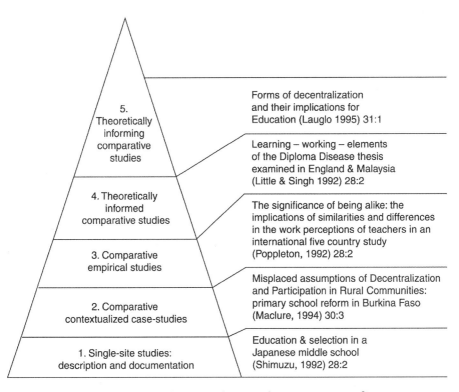

Figure 2. A hierarchical classification of types of comparative studies.

1. Studies which provide detailed empirical documentation of educational phenomena in a particular, typically national, setting.
2. Studies which provide (1) above but which are contextualized in terms of the broader international debates/theoretical frameworks/empirical accounts of the issue.
3. Studies which are designed as explicitly comparative, based on a coherent rationale for their selection in order to illuminate 'constants and contexts'.
4. Studies in which the contexts being compared are themselves theorised as part of wider social science debates on, for example, the relationship between system and action, power and control, culture and the creation of meaning.
5. Studies which use comparative research to inform theory.

Clearly, then, there are a number of different answers to the question: what is comparative education? The long history of comparative education provides some clues to this diversity. Like other specialist fields, comparative education has had its share of 'paradigm wars'.

Writing in 1992, on the scope, problems and potential of comparative and international research in education, Michael Crossley and I identified some of these different traditions. The detailed documentation approach of Jullien is one that established at an early stage of the development of comparative education a respect for careful description of the different ways individual systems have for providing for the organisation and delivery of education. This empiricist approach may be contrasted with another significant body of comparative educational research which has taken place within the ambit of a positivist epistemology, driven by the desire to apply the scientific method in the search for generalisability (see for example Holmes, 1981). A third identifiable strand is the more holistic approach of Sadler – one of the earliest scholars in the field and his student, Kandel. The latter well expressed this approach in his 1933 book *Studies in Comparative Education*:

> *The comparative approach demands first an appreciation of the intangible, impalpable, spiritual and cultural forces which underlie an educational system; the forces and factors outside the school matter even more than what goes on inside it.*
> *Hence the comparative study of education must be founded on an analysis of the social and political ideas which the school reflects, for the school epitomises these for transmission and for progress. In order to understand, appreciate and evaluate the real meaning of the educational system of a nation, it is essential to know something of its history and traditions, of the forces and attitudes governing its social organisations, of*

*the political and economic conditions that determine its
development. (p. xix)*

Crossley & Broadfoot link Kandel's perspective to the more recent and
highly influential work of Edmund King but suggest that "King's cogent
arguments in support of cultural integrity within comparative education
have yet to be extended into a more explicit link with those of
anthropology and interpretative sociology" (p. 105).

I believe it is this latter integration of comparative education as a
field of study within social science debates more generally that I was
groping towards in 1977 when I argued the need for an
ethnomethodological approach which could reveal the dynamic
workings of the educational system as "the whole living organism rather
than the skeleton" (p. 135). Many other writers since than have
recognised that it is epistemological questions that lie at the heart of the
question: what is comparative education? That the debate can never be
simply one of methodology or focus but must rather be centred on the
more general project of explaining and exploring the nature of social life
and conceptualising this in a way that provides both insight and
guidance concerning how learning may best be facilitated and provided
for in a particular time and place.

We have now come close at least to answering the question of *what
is not comparative education*. Postlethwaite (1988) offers some further
clues:

*Strictly speaking to 'compare' means to examine two or more
entities by putting them side by side and looking for
similarities and differences between or among them. In the
field of education, this can apply both to comparisons
between and within systems of education. In addition,
however, there are many studies that are not comparative in
the strict sense of the word which have traditionally been
classified under the heading of comparative education. Such
studies do not compare but rather describe, analyse or make
proposals for a particular aspect of education in one country
other than the author's own country. (p. xvii)*

Postlethwaite refers to these latter studies as 'international' rather than
comparative.

To be clear about the future development of comparative education
as a field of study, we have to be clear what its mission is; what we are
trying to achieve and what is unique about the nature of this particular
quest in the general territory of both social science in general and of
educational research in particular. Does it matter where we draw the line
in Figure 2 in classifying what is and what is not comparative
education? I believe that it does.

I suggest that the goal of comparative education is to build on systematic studies of common educational issues, needs or practices as these are realised in diverse cultural settings in order to enhance awareness of possibilities, clarify contextual constraints and contribute to the development of a comprehensive socio-cultural perspective.

This assertion of what comparative education both is and is not brings me to my final question which, in attempting to answer, will allow me to justify the position taken above. It will also explain my perhaps rather esoteric choice of title. If in 1977 I believed that comparative education was a 'context rather than a discipline', I now believe that it is not a context but 'more a way of life'.

> *not so much a programme,*
> *more a way of life;*
> *and a way of looking at the world;*
> *one eye open wide, one eye closed,*
> *and between the two the picture gets composed ...*

This song was the theme tune to a satirical 1960s television programme entitled 'That Was the Week That Was' in which recent events were subjected to alternative depictions and interpretations. Without wishing to stretch the metaphor too far, it seems to me that this song highlights the essence of what comparative education must be. On the one hand, there is the challenge to 'make the familiar strange' – though this is arguably one of the *raisons d'être* of all social science. On the other, comparative education is 'not so much a context, more a way of life' in being the means of highlighting the multiple levels of cultural perspective and ideological and institutional constraints that constitute the territory for social science. Archer, sums up this perspective well:

> *Imputation dispenses* with analysis of social interaction *and the interests actually salient in it at the time. For these are the real processes which drive the system – which are responsible for structuring it and for its re-structuration ... to deal only with abstract interests (eg parents seek the best for their child, the State has an interest in a minimum level of civil disobedience within the total population) prevents interests from (a) ever being seen as* vested interests in a particular structure t*hat is firmly anchored in time and space and conditioned by that specific educational reality and (b) as elements whose results depend exclusively upon* interaction *taking place in that context. (Archer, 1981, p. 213, emphasis in original)*

Archer's argument concerning the need to extend the comparative perspective may usefully be illustrated by a recent research project, in which I was involved, which compared English and French primary school pupils' attitudes to school, their experiences of it and their learning outcomes (Osborn et al, 1996.) The findings of this study showed clear and significant differences in the orientations of these two groups of pupils. These differences can be traced back to differences in the national cultural context which informed both educational values and practices. I suggest that insight into such differences in pupils' perspectives is an essential precursor to the formulation of both successful policy and pedagogic decisions.

Comparative Education: the way forward

In the late 20th century the focus of educational debate is moving increasingly towards learning and how it can best be facilitated, rather than on teaching; towards a concern with the outcomes of education rather than the inputs. But whether the debate is at the level of policy or of practice, the underlying concern ultimately remains the search for insights to guide the more effective provision of education. In this context, socio-cultural studies have gained an increased prominence in their capacity to provide a conceptual link between individual perspectives and the broader social context; to link culture with both individuals and institutions in an intellectually coherent way that provides guidance for the facilitation of learning.

The notion of a 'learning society' presents new challenges for education. It makes it imperative to understand the various building blocks of learning, not just issues of educational delivery. Traditional preoccupations in this latter sense have included issues of educational

- provision (buildings, teacher supply, control, quality assurance, exams etc) i.e. quantity;
- process (teaching method, curriculum content, teacher expertise, pupil attitudes), i.e. quality;
- effectiveness (tools and attitudes for learning, diverse contexts/learning to learn).

The OECD indicators (INES) project for example, has generated an enormously complex set of such indicators, yet its model is almost entirely detached from culture (OECD, 1992).

Now, increasingly, it is *learning itself* that is providing the starting point for analysis and with it the socio-cultural context which defines the way in which individuals make sense of their natural and social context.

As Wertsch (1991) suggests, this perspective assumes that individuals construct their personal, group and national identities through a stock of narratives which are the result of particular historical and cultural contexts. Such 'mediated action' is the product of the interaction of a range of mediatonal means – cultural tools which both facilitate and constrain how individuals engage with the situation in which they find themselves. Such tools are associated with power and authority and as such are potential sources of individual and social control.

These broad cultural differences as they are reflected in notions of citizenship and 'the good society' provide the informing principles of school culture and organisation. In particular they influence both the goals imposed on schools either through central directions or through consumer pressure. These expectations are in turn mediated through the particular organisational culture and ethos of the school to shape the environment in which individual learners develop a sense of themselves socially and intellectually.

It follows that teachers too are the product of a particular socio-cultural setting and their values and understandings concerning professional activity reflect this. The cultural tools, which are available to them to promote pupils' learning include crucially language – 'the master tool' for learning other tools (Cole, 1985) but also a whole range of more specific educational tools embedded in curriculum, pedagogy and assessment practices. Teachers' different ways of using these tools illustrate their interpretation of general educational priorities within the system; the constraints they experience within the particular organisation of the school and the culturally-derived and specific perceived needs of pupils both as class groups and as individuals. The contemporary development of new mediatonal means such as computer-based learning and new forms of educational assessment, as well as the more general pressures for change in the purposes of education already referred to, present a new and exciting territory for comparative educational research.

The adoption of a comparative perspective establishes the socio-cultural organisational setting of the education system as the starting point to explore the way in which different approaches to the formal organisation of education impact on the development of individual identity and learning. By the same token it is essential that comparativists should recognise the importance of culture at every level of the system. The cultural perspective of the individual actor such as teachers and pupils mediates the reality they experience both to give it meaning and to provide them with the 'tools' they need to act effectively within it.

Equally important, however, is the culture of the organisation within which this education is delivered – both at the level of the institution and of the system itself. But, as Ouchi & Wilkins (1988) suggest:

> *rarely do (studies) attempt to explain the relationship between an organisation's internal culture and its larger cultural or socio-economic environment.(Ouchi & Wilkins, 1988, p. 237)*

Marceau 1977 makes a very similar point:

> *Culture is not only a set of symbolic goods but also a picture*
> *of the world; it involves a hierarchy which is normative as well*
> *as 'factual' and people who 'own' (or control in the sense of*
> *understanding in particular) most of the cultural goods have a*
> *moral worth denied to those who 'own' least. (Marceau, 1977,*
> *p. 176)*

Power to define the way issues are conceptualised is embodied in the key cultural tool of language. Discourse analysis of this kind offers a potentially rich harvest for comparative scholars who can use it to explore the different formulations of educational priorities in different cultural settings and hence the constraints influencing who gets what in what form for what purpose within the education system. The recent advent of the discourse of the market in a number of Western counties provides a very clear example of the power of discourse to constrain thinking.

Cultures reflect small and large social groupings – families, gender, social class and ethnicity are some of the more significant. The importance of such mediated realities is highlighted in the now extensive comparative literature on postmodernity including a special issue of *Comparative Education*. Postmodernism highlights the significance of this cultural diversity by challenging the hegemony of any one culture – especially at national level.

Disciplines are characterised by specialist theory and often their associated language and terminology; they are likely to develop a particular set of concepts, methodology and subject-matter. Comparative education is not, in this sense, a discipline but rather needs to be seen as the expression of a more generally conceived social science perspective. Its particular contribution, if we take the pervasive influence of culture as a starting point, is to document the salient cultural features in a given context, to compare cultures in order to generate insights about variables whilst recognising the integrity of the cultural whole.

Comparative education is definitely *not* travellers' tales, nor the basis for unsystematic policy-borrowing. Neither is it descriptive accounts of 'what is', however carefully done. It is not de-contextualized comparisons of particular dimensions such as educational achievement. Whilst many of these latter studies are high profile and well-funded compared to more esoteric studies, they lack the theoretical framework that is essential to justifying the drawing of any conclusions from the data gathered.

Social science in general is now at last recognising the importance of inter-disciplinarity as the basis for an adequate understanding of how people learn. In this paper I have suggested that a comparative perspective is essential to a comprehensive conceptualisation of this process in providing for the influence of different cultural contexts to be identified.

By the same token, a social science perspective which can articulate the relationship between system and action, between the individual perspective and external reality is equally essential to comparative education. As Bourdieu says:

> *An adequate model of reality must take into account the*
> *distance between the practical experience of agents (who*
> *ignore the model) and the model which enables the*
> *mechanisms it describes to function with the unknowing*
> *'complicity' of agents. (Bourdieu, 1989, p. 34)*

Or, in the words of our theme tune 'one eye open wide, one eye closed and between the two the picture gets composed'. Surely the way ahead is not internecine warfare between paradigms, methodologies or disciplines. Rather it is a passion to explore the constituents and significance of culture as the driving force of experience using the unique potential of' the comparative *way of life.*

References

Archer, M. (1981) On predicting the behaviour of the educational system: extended review, *British Journal of Sociology of Education*, 2, pp. 211-219.

Bourdieu, P. (1989) Towards a reflexive sociology in Wacquant, LA Workshop with Pierre Bourdieu, *Sociological Theory*, 7, pp. 26-63.

Broadfoot, P. (1977) The comparative contribution: a research perspective, *Comparative Education*, 13, pp. 133-137.

Cole, M. (1985) The zone of proximal development: where culture and cognition create each other, in J.V. Wertsch (Ed.) *Culture, Communication and Cognition: Vygotskian perspectives*, pp. 146-161. Cambridge: Cambridge University Press.

Crossley, M. & Broadfoot, P. (1992) Comparative and international research in education: scope, problems and potential, *British Educational Research Journal*, 18, pp. 99-112.

Holmes, B. (1981) *Comparative Education: some considerations on method.* London: Allen & Unwin.

Marceau, J. (1977) *Class and Status in France: economic change and social immobility, 1945-1975.* Oxford: Clarendon.

OECD (1992) *Education at a Glance.* Paris: OECD.

Osborn, M., Broadfoot, P., Planel, C., Sharpe, K. & Ward, B. (1996) Being a pupil in England and France: findings from a comparative study, paper presented at 17th CESE Conference, Athens, Greece.

Ouchi, W.G. & Wilkins, A.L. (1988) Organisational power, in A. Westoby (Ed.) *Culture and Power in Educational Organisations*, pp. 223-255. Milton Keynes: Open University Press.

Postlethwaite, T.N. (Ed.) (1988) *The Encyclopaedia of Comparative Education and National Systems of Education.* Oxford: Pergamon.

Watson, K. & Williams, P. (1984) Comparative studies and international awareness in teacher education: the need for reappraisal, *Journal of Education for Teaching*, 10, pp. 249-255.

Wertsch, J. (1991) *Education and National Systems of Education.* Oxford: Pergamon.

Coping with Complexity in Comparative Methodology: issues of social causation and processes of macro-historical globalisation

JÜRGEN SCHRIEWER

Section I: the formulation of comparative methodology out of the spirit of experimental science

Few readers may be aware of the fact that it has been just over a century since one of the seminal works of modern social science appeared, in which comparative method takes an extremely prominent place. The work referred to is Emile Durkheim's *The Rules of Sociological Method*.[1] It is well known that Durkheim, in close connection with the founding, intended in the *Rules*, of a social science that was to be equally theoretically oriented and empirically based, introduced comparative method as the "rule for the demonstration of sociological proof" *par excellence* and discussed it as the social sciences' equivalent of the natural sciences experiment.

In the development of comparative social research, Durkheim's *Rules* were a turning point. On the one hand, they linked with the guiding ideas which in the late 18th and early 19th centuries accompanied the emergence of what later became the comparative social and human sciences, translating them into a strictly scientistic methodology. Durkheim's often cited thesis, that "comparative sociology is not a special branch of sociology, it is sociology itself, in so far as it ceases to be purely descriptive and aspires to account for facts" [2], confirmed the wide-ranging expectations both of the methodical positivisation and of the differentiation, along disciplinary lines, of emerging fields of study, made possible through comparative research, i.e. expectations which around 1800 the harbingers of the comparative study of language, law, religion, education and (later, in the 19th century) government had derived from the success of comparative anatomy and transmuted onto their respective subject areas.

On the other hand, one finds formulated in Durkheim's *Rules* methodological principles of theoretically oriented comparative social research, the validity of which, up to the recent past, have remained essentially uncontested. Continued in the framework of epistemological positions rooted in the orthodox philosophy of science [3], Durkheim's characterisation of the comparative method as the 'high road' of macro-social research delineated the starting point for the numerous comparative methodologies which developed in increasingly sophisticated forms, especially after World War II. It was not by chance, then, that these developments ultimately flowed into methodologies by which comparative social research became committed to turning, to the greatest possible extent, social science knowledge into nomothetic statements.[4] Initially worked out within the framework of comparative sociology and political science [5], this mainstream methodology of comparative social inquiry met with general acceptance in other fields of study as well, such as cross-cultural psychology, cultural anthropology [6], and comparative education.[7] Despite the internal ramifications of this methodology – the further development of which was fostered by reiterated interactions of the practice of comparative inquiry and the general logic of scientific discovery – some essential principles, formulated in the framework of this tradition and held in common by different strands of comparative research, can be emphasised [8]:

(i) The first of these principles is related to the explanatory claims implied by comparative method. Notwithstanding other aspects of knowledge facilitated by comparison – such as description, contextualisation, and classification – the explanation of macro-social phenomena describes the essential epistemic achievement and, therefore, the *raison d'être* of comparative research in the social sciences. It is in this sense that Durkheim's characterisation of the comparative method as a "rule for the demonstration of sociological proof" was to be understood, namely as a rule of providing evidence for causal explanatory arguments. And it is in this same sense that Adam Przeworski's paradoxical formulation, asserting that "a consensus exists that comparative research consists not of comparing but of explaining" [9], emphasises a conviction common to present-day methodologies, as well.[10]

(ii) These explanatory claims unfold in a guiding problematique distinctive of the comparative social sciences, one which transcends the differences between varying strands, themes, and disciplines. The research-framing basic assumptions interwoven in this problematique imply:

- that (a) societal (national, cultural, etc.) settings have a decisive impact on intra-societal (intra-national, intra-cultural, etc.) phenomena – such as processes, organisational models, and patterns of thought, behavior, or social relations – as well as on resultant social effects and problems;
- that (b) the societal (national, cultural, etc.) settings purported to have such an impact can be deconstructed, according to varying issues that are of theoretical interest, into individual contextual variables;
- that (c) the broadening of the inter-societal (inter-national, inter-cultural, etc.) knowledge basis obtainable through comparative research offers an evolved field of social observation which encompasses these contextual variables in varying forms, and facilitates, accordingly, by way of investigating relevant relationships between societal (national, cultural, etc.) variables and social phenomena – or, technically speaking, between "system-level variables" and "within-system variables"[11] – the systematic ascertainment of these variables' explanatory power.

This guiding problematique does not only unfold in the form of the cros-sectional designs so characteristic of comparative research aiming at explanation, just because they are tailored for the study of connections between varying features of societal settings – hence for establishing relationships. It also corresponds to the research-framing significance which this guiding problematique has had for comparative social sciences, if individual authors identify as the decisive criterion defining a comparative discipline, not the particular method of comparison, as is usually the case, but the specifically analytical use made of societal (national, cultural, etc.) settings: "what distinguishes comparative social science is its use of attributes of macrosocial units in explanatory statements".[12]

(iii) On the other hand, these research-framing basic assumptions of comparative research came toward meeting with the elaboration of comparison into a social scientific method. All comparison – to make clear the scope of this methodological transformation carried out in the Durkheimian tradition – is *Relationserkenntnis*, or relational thinking [13], and to that extent an active mental operation, framed by specific problems, theoretical perspectives, and expectation-generating schemes. It is necessary to distinguish, then, between operations that set the objects of comparison as such in relationship to one another (with regard merely to their factual aspects), and those operations which are concerned with relationships between varying object areas or system levels and with setting these in relation to one another. It is this differentiation between 'simple' and 'complex' comparative techniques or, more pointedly formulated, between 'establishing relations between observable facts' and 'establishing relations between relationships', that determines the difference between comparison as a *universal mental operation* embedded in everyday social life and comparison as a *social scientific method*.[14] It is only in the latter form, and as a consequence of its distinctive operation geared to analytical abstraction, that comparison could be used to investigate, informed by certain hypothetical assumptions, different societal (national, cultural, etc.) settings with respect to recurring macro-social relationships and with a view to determining these relationships' causal regularity.

(iv) The logical foundations of these procedures are rooted in the logic of scientific induction worked out by John Stuart Mill [15] and the logic of scientific experimentation successfully demonstrated by Claude Bernard.[16] From Mill, Durkheim adopted the rules of inductive reasoning – the method of difference, the method of agreement, and the method of concomitant variations (given special emphasis) – which were built into later comparative methodologies to varying degrees. From Bernard, Durkheim borrowed more than the epistemological approach of a hypothetico-deductive life science. Together with the transfer of this approach from living nature to social life, or from physiology to sociology, he also transformed the natural sciences experiment into the only substitute form that seemed to him appropriate for macro-social research, the comparative method.

This transformation had considerable consequences. From that point on, social scientific comparison was insufficiently defined if it was merely labelled as a 'method.' Durkheim's transformation, worked out further by his successors, made something different of comparison than a 'method' in the sense of a specific technique of data collection or empirical research. The merging of the principles sketched above – a research-framing guiding problematique, an elaborated technique of establishing relations between relationships, and an analytical logic equivalent to experimentation – resulted, rather, in a distinctive research approach tending toward acquiring, structuring, and analysing data in a creative way. According to varying theoretical orientations, then, this research approach was introduced into subsequent methodologies as a 'meta-method' [17], as a 'quasi-' or '*ex-post-facto-*' experiment [18] or – more open – as a 'complex research approach' or 'strategy'.[19] And these methodologies usually went on to discuss the comparative approach with respect to its analytical power, and to a certain extent also to relativise it against the backdrop of the 'real' experiment, that of the natural sciences.

(v) In two key phases of their development, thus, the comparative social sciences have adopted fundamental methodological ideas from the natural sciences (or, more precisely, the life-sciences): first, in the take-off phase of the late 18th century, from comparative anatomy (represented by the work of George de Cuvier, who, in his time, enjoyed a Europe-wide audience); second, in the phase of deliberate scientification characteristic of the late 19th century, from physiology (represented by the no less sensational success of Claude Bernard). Clearly, these successive receptions entailed a corresponding change in the types of comparison that were adopted. Thus, in the period around 1800, comparison was essentially used as a procedure for determining proportions, *rapports*, or relations of analogy, and this particularly with a view to ordering the newly discovered masses of empirical knowledge according to typological patterns or morphological features. Around 1900, by contrast, due to its elaboration into the social sciences substitute for experimentation, comparison took an uncomparably more abstract character. Accordingly, comparative research changed into the theoretically oriented analysis of the dynamics of societal processes, or – rightfully using Durkheim's term – into the "physiology of the social".[20]

This twofold borrowing of epistemological and methodological models from the natural sciences also explains, then, the long-lasting commitment of the principles underlying the comparative approach to the understanding of causality prevailing in the sciences. Just as Durkheim declared in the *Rules*, and as present-day methodological considerations do not fail to confirm, comparison as a quasi-experimental mode of analysis makes sense only under the condition that the validity of the principle of causation is taken for granted:

> *If therefore we wish to use the comparative method scientifically, i.e., in conformity with the principle of causality as it arises in science itself, we shall have to take as the basis of the comparisons established the following proposition:* To the same effect there always corresponds the same cause.*[21]*

Not only is the fact that the commitment of comparative research to explanatory results is grounded on the postulate of the validity of unambiguous and regular causal relationships between causes and effects taken for granted in the systematic social sciences, it can even be traced back into comparative history. Comparative method alone, in the words of Marc Bloch, can "grasp, in the thicket of imaginables causes, those that have had a general impact, the only real causes". For, according to the quasi-metaphysical worldview underlying such reasoning [22], "a general phenomenon can only be the result of equally general causes".[23] And like a confirmation coined directly on this, half a century later, came Fritz Ringer's formulation: "The generality of causes is related to the generality of their effects".[24]

Now, after several decades of 'normal' science, i.e. the practice of comparative research oriented on the above-mentioned principles both in Education and the social sciences, experience with the application and the refining of particular methods of comparison as well as experience with varying explanatory models is available. What emerges in the present situation, in the late 20th century, on the basis of such experience, but also in view of fundamental theoretical alternatives, is a more or less radical questioning of the basic theoretical-*cum*-methodological assumptions of (neo-)positivist mainstream comparative social science. In this sense, a twofold theoretical and methodological challenge with which mainstream comparative methodology is confronted will be sketched in the following. I will address, on the one hand, the challenges which have emerged from unfulfilled expectations of comparative explanation. These are challenges related to the causal schemes underlying the commonly used explanatory models (Section II). On the other hand, I will deal with challenges which have grown out of the emergence of world society – i.e. the "evolutionarily unprecedented" contemporary situation of increasing global interconnectedness [25] – as well as corresponding theory developments. These are challenges working towards undermining the distinctiveness of comparative investigation's units of analysis and hence a form of experimental reasoning built on exactly the assumption that there exist units of analysis which are independent from one another (Section III).[26]

Section II: the complexity of causal networks

It is an often-highlighted advantage of comparative research that it in certain ways compels the making explicit of its theoretical assumptions. Thus, a convincing explanation produced by comparative analysis should match certain statements of social-scientific theory with the inter-national (inter-cultural, etc.) empirical data by means of the comparative operations of establishing relations between relationships. A look at the results of comparative research, however, invites scepticism.

In the following, I will summarise some findings of comparative studies which are mainly related to comparative education, to the intersecting fields of comparative historical research on education, on education and development, and on modernisation processes, as well as to industrial sociology. In so doing, I will accentuate studies concerning societal problem areas which have been or continue to be interpreted in pronouncedly universalist terms within the framework of relevant social theories; problem areas, in other words, which have been assumed to be ruled by almost deterministic macro-social causal or functional relationships. Contrary to such assumptions, however, comparative research has unearthed an impressive range of international variation regarding the problem-solving patterns and strategies that have been realised in diverse historical, socio-cultural or political settings.

In any case, such is the principal insight offered by an increasingly extensive body of comparative research dealing with the interconnections between vocational education and training, qualification structures of the labour force, and work organisation in large-scale manufacturing units. Such studies have taught us to thoroughly distrust the thesis – posited by industrial sociology and the economics of education – stating that qualification-requirements and educational structures are largely determined by technological change, economic development, and the exigencies of a universal rationality purportedly intrinsic to industrialism.[27] The pertinence of deterministic relationships of this kind has been called into question, by way of historical comparisons, not only with regard to modern educational systems in their entirety.[28] Comparative research has also denied such relationships in fields where their validity had been most readily accepted, namely in the shaping of vocational education and training structures.[29] Relevant studies have insistently shown – especially when extended to the historical process dimension – that vocational education and training as well as the utilisation of human labour are, even within the ranks of technologically advanced industrialised societies, to a large extent defined by social and cultural factors.[30] What the findings of comparative research tend to express, moreover, are, in contrast to the claims of validity made by exogenous explanatory models, the relative autonomy of educational systems (as of socio-cultural systems more generally) and processes of change largely steered by those systems' internal dynamics.[31]

Largely similar findings have been produced by international comparative research with regard to the connections between education, modernisation, and development. An assessment of the extensive body of research shows that these connections are considerably more complex than the assumptions of modernisation theories – based on the economics of education, political science, or social psychology – would lead one to expect.[32] This applies all the more to models suggesting linear causal links between *modernising institutions* (such as the school or factory), *modern values, modern behaviour, modern society* and *economic development* as they have been constructed with a view to suggesting developmental policies.[33] The connections between "education, economic growth and employment", "education, modernisation and quality of life", and between "education, political mobilisation and development" are neither direct, nor linear, nor do they produce the same effects in different societies. Instead, they are as a rule not very pronounced, only partially effective, basically disfunctional, or simply counter-productive. In any case, they are "highly problematic" and can only be understood as interrelationships.

> *"Education" [in the sense of Western type organised mass schooling] is both determined and a determinant of the society in which it is located; ... both an agent of change and in turn is changed by society; ... both a producer of social mobility and an agent for the reproduction of the social order.[34]*

Interrelationships of this kind are for their part embedded in, and re-shaped by, more encompassing social relation networks. Thus, the impact of schooling that is observable in different countries, as well as the structures of modernity attained in each of them, are the consequences of the varying contextual conditions dominant in different societies and in turn impinge upon these contextual conditions in varying ways.

What these strands of comparative research have in common, then, is that their findings flow together, resulting in a multiplicity of interrelationship networks and developmental paths. Although these networks and developmental paths may be conceptualised, at a general level, within the framework of system models and systemic typologies, the elucidation of their distinctive complexity remains the task of comparative-historical process analyses. Such insights do not only recall the findings of comparative-historical modernisation research.[35] The tone sounded here is further echoed in assessments of research carried out in fields such as the comparative sociology of organisations and comparative politics. Such assessments do indeed diagnose the dissolution, in the face of comparative evidence, of concepts based on a supposedly universal rationality of industrialism [36] and of conceptions which assume a uni-dimensional logic of development.[37] More generally, theories which claim universal validity and, in *intra*-national investigation, are (nearly) always flexible enough to match the data, break down when confronted with the breadth of variation of socio-cultural relationship patterns that is obtainable through *inter*-national analysis.[38] In other words, empirical evidence brought to light in comparative research leads less to the confirmation of purportedly regular macro-social relationships than to the necessity of their modification.[39] Consequently, the "crisis of universalism" established by scholars in comparative politics, who have argued that "there are no universal determinants; individual historical processes are too numerous, too complex, and, in effect, too independent of one another" [40], corresponds to "the failure of the grand theories" that has been concluded from international research on the relationships between education, modernisation, and development.[41] Rather than serving – as posited by Durkheim – as a "rule for the demonstration of sociological proof" for theoretically assumed macro-social cause-effect relationships, the social-scientific method of comparison has shown itself to function more as a procedure of theory-critique. Instead of convincing explanations, comparative research has tended to produce falsifications. Inevitably, then, one of the most prominent theoreticians of comparative inquiry committed to causal analysis felt led, in an overview of the recent state of research, to raise the sceptical question:

> *Can a hypothesis that X is,* ceteris paribus, *a cause of Y in the real world ever be confirmed? [42]*

Does, however, the obviously successful pursuit of comparative theory critique – which fully corresponds, incidentally, to the 'logic of scientific discovery' [43] – mean that, on the other hand, the claims of comparative social sciences for providing substantive explanations should definitely be called into question? Does, in other words, the state of comparative social inquiry outlined above justify proclaiming the "victory of history over comparison and analogy", hence over theory and explanation, as Erich Rothacker once did in precisely the idiographic and historicist tradition of the philosophical-*cum*-hermeneutic human sciences?[44]

Rather than endorse an epistemological scepticism of this kind, though, I would be more inclined to argue:

- that (a) it is the *universalist form* (viz. in terms of general causal relationships, or of functional relationships interpretable in causal terms) in which social theories and models have stated their explanatory claims that will again and again be denied when confronted with the "dreadful variety"[45] of socio-cultural processes and organisation patterns uncovered through comparative research;[46]

- that (b) it is, moreover, the *"exogenous" structure* of the most commonly used explanatory models which is being called into question, i.e. the type of reasoning suggested, as if it were the most natural way of thinking, by the research-framing problematique of comparative fields of study, and which localises the decisive starting point for explaining the forms, functions and processes of change of social phenomena (such as education or law) in – socio-cultural, political, and economic – contextual conditions;[47]

- that (c), finally, it is precisely the advantage of comparative analysis to actually throw into relief, in contrast to the reductionism inherent in many of the macro-social models, the full *complexity of causal networks*, the "complexity of human affairs" as MacIntyre has called it in a critique of nomothetically oriented comparative politics.[48] The reason is that social causation – to take up a graphic phrasing coined by Niklas Luhmann – leads "into endless horizons, not only appearing in linear succession (i.e. in a temporal sense), but at the same time cascading in any number of co-origins and side-effects".[49]

Section III: the complex interweaving of socio-cultural unities and global interdependencies

Complexity of causal relationships is, however, not the only result which puts certain basic assumptions of (neo-)positivist mainstream comparative social science in question. Similar challenges appear in consideration of an obvious eclipsing of societal (national, cultural, etc.) settings by intensifying international exchange and cooperation networks, and by the resultant crystallisation of structures proper to an emergent world-society.

Recent research and theory developments do indeed amount to the unravelling of the largely unquestioned subject-matter of Comparative Education: the world conceived of as a multitude of separate regional or national societies which, as autonomous entities, as historically distinct configurations, constitute one another's environment. The immediate consequence of such an epistemic elimination of the field's subject-matter is that its defining methodological procedure as well – comparison applied to a multiplicity of independent units of analysis – is deprived of its meaning. Comparison, then, is replaced by historical reconstructions of wide-reaching processes of cultural diffusion or by global analyses of transnational interdependence.[50] Finally, two different strands of theoretical reasoning, namely retrospectively construed theory critiques and prospectively fashioned 'World system' models, interlink in such conclusions.

The kind of theory critiques referred to have been presented by, among others, Friedrich H. Tenbruck.[51] The title of his study, 'The birth of society out of the spirit of sociology' [*Die Geburt der Gesellschaft aus dem Geist der Soziologie*], contains his theses in a nutshell. According to Tenbruck, if the formation of a specifically sociological communication network can be conceived of as an intellectual response to the radically novel social reality that emerged, at the end of the 18th and the beginning of the 19th century, from the dissolution of the corporative, estate-based, social structures of early modern Europe, then the conception of a 'society' subsequently favored by that sociological discourse – i.e. the abstract concept of a multiplicity of mutually independent, quasi-autarkic, and to that extent comparable societies – is context-bound in several respects and, therefore, of questionable theoretical validity. Not only had this concept of society, Tenbruck further relates, the imprint of the theoretical requirements of a discipline patterned on natural-science models, it also took as immutable a certain, merely transient,

> *contemporary state of affairs, namely the self-image of*
> *19th-century nations concerned about their cultural*
> *individuality and political autonomy for which ... the identity*
> *of the people, culture, nation and state was an obvious lesson*
> *of history.[52]*

But, Tenbruck continues, a concept of society with that pretension should have been, in fact, empirically disproven long ago by internationalisation phenomena and large-scale processes of transcultural diffusion.

While critical reconstructions of social theory have thus historically relativised, not merely the basic assumptions regarding its specific subject-matter, but, in so doing, the comparative social sciences project proper, this project is currently being overtaken – in terms of evolutionary theory – within the framework of 'world-system' analyses. And just as classical sociology saw itself as a response to the altered social reality of the 19th century, 'world-system' models for their part claim that social macrostructures in the late 20th century can be adequately grasped only by taking into consideration the global context of world-wide relations of interdependence which have intensified in novel ways. This idea can be further explained with reference to a theoretical version of the 'world-system' paradigm that can be traced back to the Wallersteinian tradition and its grounding in economic history. The selected text, authored by Albert Bergesen, particularly exemplifies the history-of-science dimension of the replacement of the perspectives predominant in international social and educational research by the world-system paradigm.[53]

In this text, Bergesen recapitulates the fundamental paradigm shifts that, since the 18th century, have successively gained acceptance in the history of social theory. In so doing, he demonstrates that each of these theory shifts has corresponded to an inversion in the basic model of social order. Thus, he draws parallels between, on the one hand, the transition from (i) the individual-based interactionist models characteristic of late 18th-century utilitarianism to (ii) the holistic conceptions of order characteristic of the sociological systems developed in the late 19th century and, on the other hand, a theoretical revolution that is due to occur at the end of the 20th century. Bergesen indeed claims that (iii) the early forms of the world-system paradigm, which had been developing since the 1950s within the framework of dependency-theory, still conceived of the disproportionate world division of labor as a result that had gradually emerged from the interactions – the exchange relations and economic processes - between the core states and peripheral areas, i.e. between a small number of highly developed industrial nations and a large number of more or less developing, dependent countries. It is time, however, according to Bergesen, to proceed to yet another radical change in the conceptualisation of global order, and to conceive of the world-system as (iv) an emerging reality *sui generis*, as a "collective reality exogenous to nations":

> *The final paradigm revolution will come when we invert the parts-to-whole framework of the world-system outlook and move to a distinctly whole-to-parts paradigm which posits* a priori *world social relations of production which in turn determine the core-periphery relations of trade and exchange.*

The world-system, consequently,

> *has its own laws of motion that, in turn, determine the social, political, and economic realities of the national societies it encompasses.[54]*

'Sociology', the science of society, is therefore to be replaced by 'Globology', the science of "the collective reality of world order".[55]

Does this mean, then, that "the light of the central issues of civilisation" has – to take up an impressive formulation coined by Max Weber – irrevocably shifted?[56] Has, in other words, the right to represent scientific modernity to which the comparative social and human sciences quite rightfully laid claim at the beginning of the 19th century passed, at the end of the 20th century, to analyses of the single world-system as a global network of interrelations and interdependencies that have intensified in hitherto unknown ways?

A view of the state of empirical – i.e., in this instance, comparative-historical – research invites the relativisation of such wide-ranging conclusions. For research has, in this respect as well, broken down the definiteness of theoretical models and in their place allowed an interweaving of partly contrary, partly overlapping, partly reactively related structural elaborations to step forward: an interweaving both of the global spread of transnationally institutionalised ideologies and models and of the persistence of varying socio-cultural interrelationship networks.

An examination of major trends of comparative research concerning the development of higher education, the sciences (particularly the social sciences), and the international states-system should further deepen these general findings. Thus, on the one hand, comparative analyses show, indeed, a considerable increase in the international alignment of expansion processes and a marked homogenisation of organisational features. Furthermore, it becomes clear that the European university is the one institution whose world-wide dissemination has been more self-evident and has taken place with a greater "lack of alternatives" than is the case for most other institutions characteristic of societal modernity.[57] In contrast, however, to global alignment processes at the organisational level, recent research has demonstrated that it is precisely the global expansion of universities into large-scale systems that results, not in growing convergence, but in further national differentiation. To the extent that higher education systems lose their elite character, the evidence suggests, their concrete integration into the varying nation-specific patterns of social stratification, labor force qualification structure, administrative regulation, and public policy is strengthened.[58]

Contrary developments appear, likewise, in the social sciences. Comparative sociology-of-knowledge analyses have shown the persistence, in spite of the claim to universal validity intrinsic to scientific rationality, of social interpretations couched in national language and of 'academic cultures' imprinted by tradition.[59] They demonstrate, additionally, how particular disciplines – despite the intensification of international communication between scholars – continue to draw, and even renew, their major paradigmatic orientations out of the spirit of their respective theory traditions.[60] Furthermore, in reaction to the global Anglo-American dominance in the area of scientific research and dissemination, controversial debate has recently appeared concerning the conflicting tendencies of 'internationalisation' versus 'indigenisation' in the social sciences, and the development of culture-specific 'indigenous sociologies' in contrast to a 'universal social science'.[61]

Analyses from comparative politics, finally, turn up findings which point to an almost 'dialectical' interlocking of supra-national integration and intra-national fragmentation.[62] They demonstrate how attempts at supra-national integration, primarily European, parallel not only the maintenance but also the strengthening of the nation-state and the extension and intensification of its powers of penetration and mobilisation.[63] By the same token, they support the idea that increased efforts at transnational integration go hand in hand with the dynamisation of processes of regional – linguistically, ethnically, or culturally imprinted – diversification.[64]

As comparative research in higher education, in social sciences developments, and in the international states-system makes clear, therefore, the contrary phenomena of internationalisation and nation-specific structural elaboration do not simply occur side by side, unrelated. Rather, they are connected to one another as challenges and responses, as processes and unintended consequences. They illustrate equally concatenations constituted over time and the potential for diversification inherent in such concatenations; overarching developmental processes and the complexity generated by such processes. They emphasise, in other words, the macroperspective regarding large-scale area-encompassing historical processes which is characteristic of the world-system approach; in so doing, however, they disabuse us of any notion of a unilinear, let alone evolutionistic, goal-determined rationality that might be attributed to such processes.

> *It would ... be inaccurate to conceive of globalisation as some kind of teleological process. The idea that globalisation incorporates some predetermined historical logic which is leading inexorably either to the creation of a world society or to some form of world government is simply not tenable. The historical evidence is ranged against it. For globalisation stimulates forces of opposition which may just as readily lead to an increasingly fragmented world, since greater mutual awareness and interconnections between different societies may simply sow the seeds of conflict and tension.[65]*

Equally fruitful are the insights arising from analyses of the transnational processes of migration (of scholars and experts) and diffusion and reception (of ideas and models) which pervade with increasing intensity the European – and later the world-wide – history of education from the 19th century on. Beyond illuminating the conflict-laden character of internationalisation and globalisation processes, the particular advantage of such analyses is that they show the mediating steps, taken by individual actors and/or social groups, of which these processes are composed. They underscore, moreover, in contrast to the assumptions of a supposed world-historical developmental logic, both the non-linear, contingent nature of globalisation processes and the impact recurringly provoked in such processes by deviation-generating potentials. Characteristically, the transcultural diffusion of knowledge, organisation models, problem-solving patterns, or policies is met by the receiving cultural or national groups with specific reinterpretation and adaptation procedures. As a consequence, models offered transculturally are, in the new environment, selected according to prevailing interests, adapted to specific situations and needs, reinterpreted along cultural lines, and – to historically varying degrees – transmuted into structural re-formations.

The world-wide dissemination of the European-style university, the history of the social sciences, and the spread of Western principles of political order and state organisation all provide a multitude of examples of these adaptive procedures. Comparisons, for example, of Brasil and Japan show that the reception and institutional implementation of the European university model in non-European countries has followed quite different patterns despite similar modernisation challenges. Individual preconditions in these countries, such as the respective political system's power of penetration, the varying presence of modernising elites, the dominant patterns of social stratification, and the structure of existing educational institutions have figured decisively in this process.[66] Findings from the history of science support similar conclusions. Even a superficial overview of this research – from the spread of 19th-century German philosophy and philology throughout Western Europe;[67] to the adoption of Weberian sociology in France, the United States, and Southeast Asia;[68] to the genesis of modern pedagogy in Japan (introduced by a Herbartian theorist since forgotten in Germany)[69] – shows the reception of philosophical and social theories and innovations to form an endless series of interpretations and re-interpretations, filtered by prevailing interests and channelled into pre-existing discourse constellations. The same holds true for the dissemination of Western democratic principles and political institutions throughout non-Western countries.[70] As, once more, the Japanese example may attest, these merely formally adopted institutions are interwoven with previous layers of political behavior, social meanings, and culture-specific patterns of the exercise of authority and, in the resultant process of restructuring into a "system without a core", change their significance and the way they function.[71]

The multitude of 'adaptation logics' hinted at by such examples, as well as the underlying multitude of – repeatedly deviation-generating – cultural deep structures, differing notions of time and truth, and collective experiences sedimenting in the course of history

> *unmask the highly ideological visions proclaiming the end of history [due to a supposedly irresistible convergence toward the Western model of liberal capitalist society] as purely illusory. Such a claim can at best refer to surface-level phenomena and to the impression of Westernisation looming in certain processes of transmission. Behind this front, in reality, is dissimulated a complex play of importations and appropriations, and also of resurging popular modes of political action and ancient cultures which the comparativist is obliged to take into consideration: the Chinese, Indian, and Japanese trajectories are made just as much of pure overlay as of measured appropriations and the re-actualisation of millenial cultural traditions.[72]*

Theoretically-informed investigations of diffusion and reception processes which do not marginalise this interweaving of structural overlapping, refraction, and reactive elaboration but place them in the center of analysis, could then link together with research and modelling processes focusing on the global spread of patterns of state organisation and modern ideology.[73] The general conclusions to be drawn from this combination of different strands of research would result in the hypothesis that there is an abstract universalism of trans-nationally disseminated models which fans out into multiform structural patterns wherever such models interact, in the course of institutional implementation, with different state-defined frameworks, legal and administrative regulations, forms of the division of labour in society, national academic cultures, context-bound social meanings, and religious world-views. Institutionalised schooling, for example, which in a world-system perspective has been distinguished as an "evolutionary universal" of the socio-cultural development of modernity [74], turns out to be not so much universal as socio-culturally particular as soon as one systematically analyses the multiple interrelationships between systems of examination and certification and the entitlements they bestow; between school achievement and professional careers; between the structure of educational qualifications and the occupational structure of the labour force; between selection in schools and stratification in society; between the organisational structure of educational systems and systems of public administration; between university training and mental structures in society; between education and social change; and between scientific rationality and the self-evolutive momentum of accumulated social interpretations.[75]

Such references to state, law, culture, and collective experiences, to world views mediated through religion, national language, and social meanings, indicate deviation-generating and deviation-amplifying potentials which give rise, historically, to ever new socio-cultural configurations. Moreover, the very interweaving of contrary currents, resulting from previous research,

- of *internationalisation* and *indigenisation*;
- of *supra-national integration* and *intra-national diversification*;
- of *"evolutionary universals"* and *socio-cultural configurations*;
- of *global diffusion processes* and *culture-specific reception processes*;
- of an *abstract universalism of trans-nationally disseminated models* and of *deviation-generating structural elaboration*; as well as
- of the *global spread of a world-level developmental and educational ideology* and the *persistent diversity of socio-cultural interrelationship networks*,

marks out the full dimensions of the problems of empirical analysis and theoretical explanation which comparative research in education and the social sciences is called upon to resolve.

Section IV: reconciling history and comparison

If both lines of reasoning, that focusing on issues of social causation and that related to processes of macro-historical globalisation, are drawn together, the full extent of the fundamental challenges with which classical comparative methodology in the late 20th century sees itself confronted – not least due to the very insights of comparative research itself – is revealed. Not only is the problem of the complexity of causal networks (already discussed with respect to the social sciences by, e.g. John Stuart Mill, yet methodologically reduced in positivist epistemology) put back on the agenda, but quite another strand of issues of complexity (not entirely novel, but acquiring unprecedented weight) appears in the object domain of comparative social science proper. Nations, societies, and cultures – i.e. the largely unquestioned units of analysis used in comparative research – lose their empirical and thus their logical definiteness and are eclipsed by the complex interweaving of socio-cultural unities and global interdependencies or, in other words, of historical configurations and world-level processes of civilisational interpenetration. Against this background, threefold consequences arise:

(i) Comparative educational research that intends to throw fully into relief the complexity of its domain has no choice but *in perspective* to conceptualise its subject-matter equally in terms of societal modernisation trajectories, socio-cultural configurations, and trans-cultural diffusion and reception processes.[76] As a consequence of this dovetailing of perspectives, comparative inquiry can be linked to, and becomes pertinent for, a broad array of varying strands of theory-building and research. Quite particularly, comparative inquiry can be related to the theses of the world-system theoreticians and, by the same token, contribute to the empirical elucidation (by way of detailed historical reconstructions) of the encompassing character of globalisation processes, and the critical examination (by way of methodical comparisons) of evolutionary universalism's claim to validity.

(ii) To the extent that comparative educational research takes up the challenges of the macro-historical perspective, which has taken shape both in response to globalisation processes and in the wake of world systems analysis, it is called upon to *in method* relativise the contrasts between historical and social scientific – or between idiographic and nomothetic – types of comparative analysis. Instead of confirming what Rothacker called the "victory of history over comparison and analogy"[77], the aforementioned dovetailing of perspectives, rather, aims at the "reconciliation of history and comparison" which looms in the shape of insights from historical sociology.[78] This reconciliation is not merely the merging of cross-cultural comparison and historical process analyses into comparative-historical research.[79] It also implies an approach which transmutes comparison's explanatory claims into the conceptually informed reconstruction of the developmental paths taken by distinct socio-cultural configurations.

(iii) Finally, such consequences stress the need for comparative educational research *in concept* to rely on theoretical orientations and conceptual systems that are capable of incorporating the considerable array of methodological points of view and analytical perspectives, and of informing corresponding research; which is to say, are capable of integrating the insights generated in the various fields of comparative research into interrelationship networks and systems dynamics, deviation-amplifying mechanisms and complex causality, and into structural elaboration and the dependency of recurring structural change on previous structures.

Theories that both incorporate and elaborate such insights have been developed on the basis of research in the natural sciences, the life sciences, and the social sciences throughout the past two decades or so. Under headings such as 'self-organisation' and 'morphogenesis', they delineate an inter-disciplinary research program of growing importance.[80] Significantly enough, self-organisation models appearing in the sphere of the social sciences – not unlike the late 18th-century *grand programme* of comparative study patterned on anatomy, or the late 19th-century scientistic methodology of comparative social science patterned on physiology – represent yet another theoretical innovation taken from the life sciences. Yet it is the distinctive achievement of major authors whose works deal with these theory developments – such as Margaret S. Archer, writing in English [81], Edgar Morin, in French [82], and, in German, Niklas Luhmann [83] – that they take up the fundamental ideas of general systems theory, cybernetics, neurophysiology, and communication theory and that, at the same time, they reformulate these concepts with reference to the specificity of the social sphere. In so doing, Luhmann for instance precisely elaborates the differences between 'living systems' and 'meaning-generating systems' and, among the latter, between 'psychic systems' (constituted on the basis of consciousness) and 'social systems' (constituted on the basis of communication).[84] Moreover, self-organisation theories respond to the erosion, which has become apparent in recent decades, of the prevailing models of scientific theory-building and explanation based on nomothetic epistemology. This is a consequence of the fact that the natural sciences have also been increasingly confronted, through ever more sophisticated research designs, with an unstable and unpredictable world, a world characterised by the predominance of "nonlinearity over linearity [and] complexity over simplification", by the impossibility of removing the measurer from the measurement and, most importantly, by the crucial role played by the "arrow of time". To the extent, then, that the natural sciences have come to see "the universe as unstable and unpredictable, thereby conceiving of the universe as an active reality ... in which future developments are the outcome of temporally irreversible processes", to the extent, in other words, that they embark upon post-Newtonian paradigms, the purported distances between the "two cultures" – that of the natural sciences and that of the social sciences and humanities – are called into question. Consequently, the major lesson that has to be drawn from developments in the former, for theoretical progress in the latter, is that:

> *the complexity of social dynamics needs to be taken more*
> *seriously than ever.... The conceptual framework offered by*
> *evolutionary complex systems as developed by the natural*
> *sciences presents to the social sciences a coherent set of ideas*
> *that matches long-standing views in the social sciences,*
> *particularly among those who have been resistant to the forms*
> *of nomothetic analysis inspired by the science of linear*
> *equilibria. Scientific analysis based on the dynamics of*
> *nonequilibria, with its emphasis on multiple futures,*
> *bifurcation and choice, historical dependence, and, for some,*
> *intrinsic and inherent uncertainty resonates well with*
> *important traditions of the social sciences.[85]*

In the following, two distinctive features displayed by self-organisation theories of the social will be emphasised; for they are directly related to the twofold complexity issue that, according to our examination of major strands of comparative and international educational and social research, has turned out to be of crucial importance for the field's analytical capacity and explanatory power.

It is thus first of all an advantage of the theories developed in this context that they deliberately introduce the "arrow of time" into the structure of theory itself as a decisive factor. This applies equally to Archer's emphasis on the temporality of all processes of structural elaboration and to Luhmann's interweaving of systems theory with evolutionary theory, or, more specifically, of a theory of social communication with a theory of social differentiation. In order to avoid misunderstandings, one feels invited to recall a distinction – the theoretical significance of which has been worked out with reference to the writings of Max Weber – between philosophies of history in the Hegel-Marx-Toynbee tradition and more recent reformulations of evolutionary theory as undertaken by, among others, Luhmann. The former are rooted in the idea of 'necessary causation' and construe universally valid sequences of developmental stages. The latter are based on 'contingent' or 'attributed causation' and recognise only sequences of stages reconstructed a posteriori; they renounce, accordingly, general criteria of development and the possibility of a universally valid periodisation of socio-historical change. Differentiation theory constructed upon this model not only provides, then, the conceptual tools for grasping both the specificity of socio-cultural fields of action (such as education) and their relations to the societal environment; it also offers the conceptual options for making understandable these fields of action (or sub-systems) in their evolution within the context of more encompassing socio-historical differentiation processes – including the contemporary world-societal intensification of specialised communication.[86]

The second important idea, particularly emphasised by Morin and Luhmann, is related to their efforts to take into consideration, in theory construction itself, the complexity of causal relationships so conspicuously demonstrated through comparative analyses. This is where concepts such as 'self-reference' and 'meaning', 'attribution' and 'contingency', or 'function' and 'functional alternative' play a role.

Section V: from concomitant variation to functional equivalence

It is with reference to such concepts that, in the remaining sections of this chapter, a theoretical-*cum*-methodological alternative to the nomothetic mainstream model of explanation will be developed. This attempt to reconstruct the claims toward explanation of comparative method takes as its point of departure above all the reconceptualisation of the term 'function' characteristic of Luhmannian theory-building. This presupposes taking into consideration the terminological differentiation between 'function' conceived as a relationship purported to exist in the object domain of theory and 'function' conceived as an observation attitude specific to science. Statements which make use of the term 'function' in the former sense are common in social scientific literature. The statement, e.g. that (a) "something *is* a function *of* something else ..." denotes a genetic or dependency relation. The statement that (b) "something *has* a function *for* something else ..." refers to the production of effects or to the achievement of input and output performances. (Moreover, the type of analysis commonly described as 'functional' in the relevant literature is related, as a rule, to statements of the latter kind, i.e. to statements that emphasise the performances achieved for the maintenance of whole entities or systems by elements of such entities or component parts of such systems.) If, on the other hand, the variant of systems theory elaborated by Luhmann is characterised as 'functional', this does not refer primarily to the fact that it includes, *inter alia*, statements about the existence of functional relations in social reality. Rather, Luhmann's 'functional' theory emphasises a specific observation attitude, a generalised perspective which calls into question the apparent definiteness of the production of effects, or of the achievements of performances, and which claims, by way of this relativisation, to take into account the complexity of causal relationships that is so insistently confirmed through advancing research.[87]

The "emergence of complex causality" has been described by Edgar Morin on the basis of a highly diversified state of research, particularly as regards self-organising systems.[88] Systems of this type – such as organisms, individuals, and, a fortiori, social systems – when confronted with effects coming from their outer environment, with heteronomous orders, or external constraints, are not simply at their mercy. Due to their distinctive internal operations and their capacity for systemic processing, such systems unleash, rather, counteractive forces of their own (*endo-causalité*) which neutralise, break down, and transform the external factors' impact and aggressiveness (*exo-causalité*). Thus, *exo-causalité* and *endo-causalité*, external impact and internal processing, a system's openness to its outer environment and its operative closure, overlap in an intertwining of at once antagonistic and complementary forces.

In such an intertwining, then, not only do the phenomena originate, which are so impressively described as systemic inertia or momentum in Fritz Ringer's or Thomas P. Hughes's comparative-historical analyses of different types of complex social systems; it is also in this intertwining that the intricate simultaneity of both the global spread of trans-nationally institutionalised ideologies and the persistence of varying socio-cultural interrelationship networks – the most significant result of the broad array of comparative social and educational research examined above – has its origin. It is, moreover, with reference to insights of this order that self-organisation theories provide explanatory models that avoid the pitfalls of the "exogenous" nature of explanation found to follow both from mainstream social theory and from the guiding research-framing problematique of most of the comparative social sciences. Finally, it is this intertwining of *exo-causalité* and *endo-causalité*, external impact and internal processing, which is involved in generating the complex or "tissue-like" causality which is assumed to prevail – e.g. in the form of "differentiation-amplifying heterogenising mutual causal processes" – in the social arena in general.[89] 'Complexity of causal relationships' means, then – in direct contradiction to the basic assumptions of the comparative social sciences as mentioned above with reference to Durkheim, Bloch, and Ringer – that:

(a) Like causes can give rise to different and/or divergent effects.
(b) Different causes can give rise to like effects.
(c) Minor causes can entail quite major effects.
(d) Major causes can entail quite minor effects.
(e) Some causes can give rise to opposite effects.
(f) The effects of antagonistic causes are uncertain.

Complex causation is not linear: it is circular and interrelated; cause and effect have lost their substantiality; causes have lost their all-pervading power, effects their all-embracing

*dependency. They are relativised by one another and are
transformed each into the other. Complex causation is no
longer just deterministic or probabilistic; it creates, rather, the
improbable.[90]*

It is against this background that the theoretical meaning of the
concept 'function' – as conceived in the framework of functional systems
theory – has to be understood. It is aimed at contingency or, more
precisely, at the broadening of contingency. The meaning of 'function' is
not aimed, in other words, at establishing purportedly invariant
relationships between particular causes and particular effects. The
distinctive perspective implied by the functional approach, rather, seeks
to compare such relationships with alternative ones, with relationships
that may substitute for one another, in order to then seek alternative
possibilities of producing particular effects. From such a perspective

*the object of interest is subjected to direct examination and, so
to speak, to lateral examination ... This perspective is aimed,
in other words, at showing how the object under study
contributes to the solution of a problem and, by the same
token, at pointing out that it proceeds in a form that is
different from other, functionally equivalent forms of
proceeding.[91]*

It is possible to further clarify the abstraction involved in Luhmann's
reconceptualisation of 'function' by examining his re-interpretation of a
functional statement taken from the very context of the origin of
anthropological functionalism. If, for example, as Malinowski notes, the
function of ritual is found in the easing of adaptation to emotionally
difficult situations, this conclusion, from the perspective of functional
analysis, implies the much more penetrating follow-up question of
identifying

*alternative possibilities for resolving this problem. Ritual, then, is
put in relation, in terms of functional equivalence, with other
possibilities, such as ideological frames of explanation or private
reactions like lamentation, annoyance, humour, nail-biting, or
retreat into imaginary worlds. This is precisely the most interesting
aspect of Malinowski's insight. What matters is not the statement of
a law-like or more or less probabilistic relationship between
particular causes and particular effects, but* the conclusion that
several possible causes, from the vantage point of a problematic
effect, are functionally equivalent.[92]

Unmistakeably, in this argument, the concept of 'functional
equivalence' takes a key position, and it does so in a manner which is
twofold. On the one hand, it is raised up as the defining criterion which
makes it possible to differentiate the distinctiveness of functional

reasoning from conventional functionalism (i.e. a functionalism interpretable in causal terms). The reason for this is that in the perspective of functional reasoning, a functional relationship is no longer seen as a special form of causal relationship. On the contrary, a causal relationship is seen as an exception, a "borderline case of entirely reduced equivalence", within a variable range of alternative options that may exist with respect to a particular point of reference.[93] Accordingly, the concept of function, in this view, serves as a "regulative schema" which in the framework of functional systems theory takes the place occupied by the principle of causality in the frame of hypothetico-deductive theorising.[94] The function refers, in other words, to a distinctive observation technique which inquires across particular causal relationships, and which is aimed at establishing relations between problems and problem solutions with a view to "comprehending existing relations as contingent and diverse relations as comparable".[95]

It is thereby indicated, on the other hand, that the concept of 'functional equivalence' also refers to a long-standing career as a concept whose role in comparative reasoning has been pivotal. Its conceptual content is not least the outcome of comparative analyses' experience with the "dreadful variety" of socio-cultural patterns of problem-solving. The concept also serves as a bridging principle that enables the extrapolation of functional reasoning into the reconstruction of comparative methodology. Comparative methodology re-phrased in terms of functional equivalence, in that it is aimed both at (i) ascertaining varying input and output performances, systems strategies, or problem solutions relative to a reference problem of interest and at (ii) relating these performances, strategies, or solutions to one another from the vantage point of their interchangeability, maintains the elaborated form of establishing relations between relationships that has been characteristic of the social scientific method of comparison. In so doing, however, this methodology is no longer based on the method of concomitant variation (given special prominence since Durkheim's time), but follows the heuristics implied by the very idea of equivalence. Comparative analysis, correspondingly, undergoes a far-reaching change. It is transformed from *a quasi-experimental procedure of testing hypothetical statements assuming, in universalist terms, some definite consequences following from particular causes or the necessary conditions for producing particular effects* into *the empirical uncovering of a range, structured with reference to a functional vantage point, of alternative possibilities of producing particular effects.*

Section VI: a functional-cum-configurational
model of comparative explanation

Comparative approaches based on the idea of functional equivalence are not completely new. An attempt at specifying in greater detail a comparative methodology based on these grounds should start out, however, not so much from those disciplines – e.g. Comparative Education or Comparative Politics – which deal with subject matters that are easily observable and largely defined in institutionally homologous terms (like schools, organisational structures of educational systems, parliaments or forms of government). Such an attempt should start, rather, from disciplines such as Comparative Law and, in a sense, Comparative Anthropology which, due to the extraordinary multiformity of their object domains, have always been compelled to practice a more abstract approach. The breadth of variation of legal norms stemming from different legal doctrines and traditions explains why it is less useful to compare as such, for example, the clauses stipulating, in various legal systems, a bill of sale (like one can compare different organisational structures of institutionalised schooling). This breadth of variation, rather, makes it necessary to start from a significant reference-problem – such as the protection of the contracting parties against deception – and then to take into consideration the whole array of varying legal devices and even, if necessary, non-legal practices of social regulation that achieve functionally equivalent performances with respect to the regulation problem in question.[96]

On the basis of such experience with their respective object domains, both Comparative Law and cross-cultural research in Anthropology have developed a largely analogous line of reasoning – a line of reasoning, moreover, which to a great extent corresponds to the functional type of argument specified above. Its underlying quasi-ontological assumptions imply that the historically distinct regulation and organisation patterns encountered in different legal systems or socio-cultural settings can be understood and analysed as varying solutions for ubiquitous problems of structuration as following from a number of "objective and homogeneous" tasks linked with regulating life in society. Resulting from these assumptions are two heuristic principles which have been defined, in methodological consideration proper to Comparative Law, as the "law of the *functional equivalence* of legal principles and norms considered *across* different legal systems" and as the "law of the *interdependency* of institutionalised norms *within* a particular system".[97] Comparative approaches structured by this line of reasoning typically develop, then, an analytical perspective that is both *functional* and *genetic* in orientation. Such approaches do relate, in other words, culturally varying institutions – understood as discrete problem solutions – to general problems and necessities of legal regulation, on the one hand, and to particular structural conditions or resources for problem-solving as given in historically distinct social systems on the other. They seek to explain, furthermore, the institutions under observation in terms of this twofold relation: both as instrumental with regard to objective regulation problems determined at a trans-cultural level and as shaped out of the socio-cultural conditions of a distinct historical setting.

> *Historical conditions do not represent the reason but only the modality for the development of a particular legal institution. The latter remains linked, rather, well beyond its national traditions, with the universal problems implied by its very task of regulating social order. We cannot, however, explain such an institution, and compare it with other solutions, by emphasising this universal task alone; we have to also consider it as a component part of its overall historical configuration, in which it fulfills the same function as analogous institutions do in the system configurations that are being compared.[98]*

In essence, the type of comparative analysis developed in Comparative Law has turned out to be capable of methical elaboration and of wider application. Comparative investigations into, for example, the role of education in processes of state formation and nation-building or of successful management of the challenges resulting from rapid socio-economic change have indeed revealed its analytical advantages.[99] Above all, such studies have offered evidence that a non-reductionist flexibility in dealing with the "dreadful variety" of socio-cultural phenomena is possible – a flexibility that springs from the line of comparative reasoning which they have in common, characterised above as combining both a functional and a genetic perspective. By the same token, however, these studies also underline a prerequisite which, although its urgency has often been stressed in Comparative Law's methodological debate, has been realised in practice in a highly uneven and controversial way. This prerequisite concerns the conceptualisation of significant reference problems of analysis, a step which is indispensable for a comparative approach aimed precisely at ascertaining functional alternatives with respect to a particular angle of reference. A comparative approach based on the idea of functional equivalence is closely dependent, in other words, on the prior conceptualisation of its subject-area of study in terms of a relevant social theory. The main task of such a theory would be to avoid mere randomness in the necessary problem conceptualisations and to base the specification of significant problems of analysis on systematic theorising. It is, moreover, an advantage of a theoretically explicit problem conceptualisation that it sharpens one's view for the differences between varying problem solutions and the socio-cultural (national, societal, etc.) circumstances that helped to shape them. A more encompassing theory, finally, sharpens an awareness of the fact that problems take on the character of 'problems' not as such, not in splendid isolation, but as elements of interrelated sets, systems, or hierarchies of problems.

It is exactly with regard to such criteria that the theory of self-referential social systems offers a promising option – an option, to be sure, that represents just one possibility among others. Comparative analyses informed by this theory resume the line of reasoning found in Comparative Law, consisting of equally relating discrete problem-solutions (from a functional perspective) to a significant point of reference identified at the general level of theory and (from a genetic perspective) to distinct socio-cultural settings. On the other hand, functional systems theory makes it possible to further elaborate and conceptually specify this line of reasoning. Comparative analyses take the form, then, of a combination of opposite intellectual operations, of *generalisation* and *re-specification*, or of the act of "establishing (in general terms) and [that of] eliminating (in concrete settings) functional alternatives".[100] Accordingly, the comparative explanation of culture-specific solution patterns can only result from the process of analytically working off the tension, opened by these operations, between theoretically expanding and historically limiting the range of that which is possible.

In this combined approach, the *generalising* operation denotes the theoretical conceptualisation of a particular subject-area of study. In so doing, it is aimed at achieving two objectives. First, making use of the conceptual means offered by the theory of self-referential social systems, the *generalising* operation is intended to determine the problematique which is to inform the particular analysis and, at the same time, to identify this problematique's status in a more encompassing set of problems specific to the field of socio-cultural activity under investigation. Secondly, and complementary to this, it is intended to mark out a range of equivalent – hence comparable – options, the realisation of which is thought to be possible with respect to the problematique previously defined. This twofold operation ensures that, on the one hand, the range of alternative possibilities does not present itself at random but is organised by a distinctive reference problem and that, on the other hand, the functional perspective is aimed precisely at opening the relation between problem and problem-solution for substitutable forms of producing particular effects. This kind of problem conceptualisation, which may be further extended and differentiated, if necessary, into a successive ordering of different (alternative) problem-solving strategies and corresponding follow-up problems, constitutes the essential benefit to be derived from theory for the structuring of subsequent comparative analyses. This prerequisite has to be stated as such, even though it cannot be fulfilled but in relation to a particular theme and, thus, in terms of a specific subject-area.

The *specificative* operation, in contrast, means "assigning restrictive conditions for the realisation of (alternative) possibilities".[101] Possible problem-solutions supposed to be equivalent from the perspective of the preceding problem conceptualisation will be examined, in other words, under conditions of historical realisation. A conditional analysis of this kind may in turn embrace two perspectives. It can emphasise, firstly, the decisions taken in favour of particular – and, by the same token, against other – problem solutions. It can also focus, then, on the consequences and follow-up problems resulting from such decisions. The former perspective is aimed, in other words, at genetically reconstructing the initial conditions that have had a decisive impact on a particular decision-taking process; thus, following conceptual developments in sociology and anthropology, it is described by the term *configuration*. The latter perspective addresses processes both of structural elaboration and attendant system formation that follow from such decisions; in accordance with the self-organisation paradigm, it is described, then, by the term *morphogenesis*. Finally, this twofold emphasis underscores the weight claimed by socio-historical specification, as opposed to the functional perspective of the theoretician, in the construction of comparative explanations.

A *functional-cum-configurational* explanation constructed after such premises takes on the shape, then, of a series of stepwise operations of elimination. Starting from systematic structuration problems of, e.g. institutionalised schooling, its purpose is to trace the (positively given) necessary resources and ascertain the (restrictively conditioned) degree of liberty for decision-taking available in different societal (national, cultural, etc.) settings. The *configuration* concept emphasises the fact that in historically distinct socio-cultural settings such initial conditions are not distributed at random, but are to a considerable extent predetermined through problem solutions in other social fields or sub-systems.[102] Therefore, inquiries into pertinent initial conditions for effective problem-solving as given in different settings need not proceed *ad hoc,* groping for new grounds from case to case. Such inquiries may gain from being informed, rather, by historically based typologies – pertaining to, e.g,, the different historical developmental paths, varying processes of state-formation or the basic socio-political cleavage lines of different countries, societies, or civilisations [103] – which may in turn complement the theoretical conceptualisation of the subject-area of study. The process of "eliminating (in concrete settings) functional alternatives" called for by a functional-*cum*-configurational explanation finds empirical support in this recourse to the non-random structuredness of historical situations. Different problem solutions, regarded as contingent from a functional perspective, are, in configurational analysis, traced back to the point of identifying their actual realisation as non-haphasard, as historically probable or even, in some cases, as the only possible solution. In that it is able to pursue alternative problem-solutions simultaneously and at the same time to show that they are actualisable only selectively, only in a particular socio-historical setting but not in others, comparative analysis underscores the elimination process implied by this line of reasoning; and it gains evidential value to just the extent that these eliminative procedures, following the same conceptualisation, stand the test of different cases. In other words, comparative analysis turns into an explanatory argument insofar as it succeeds in identifying, by way of conceptually informed re-constructions, historically realised problem solutions as particular realisations of that which in differing socio-cultural settings – or configurations – is structurally possible.[104]

Structural decisions, once made, channel subsequent decisions and give rise to attendant problems. One decision which entails structural consequences meshes, then, with another impact-laden decision, and emergent patterns grow together which neither permit random options nor can be altered at random:

> *The initial structure conditions the options of later actors; subsequent generations pay for the freedoms of earlier ones* en grande série.[105]

The *morphogenesis* concept denotes such processes of structural elaboration and attendant system formation, towards which the second of the above specification perspectives is directed. Significant examples of this type of investigation are found in the works of Margaret Archer, both at the level of conceptual development and of comparative-historical evidence.[106] These works meticulously reconstruct the intricate interweaving of socio-cultural interaction and structural conditioning; the conflict-laden relations, the negotiation patterns, and the transaction processes between individual actors and corporate actors; as well as the "complex sequences of structure–interaction–structural elaboration" reiteratively resulting from such interplay. The structural properties of an educational system and their successive transformations in time are equally important in this framework, then, as the result of past structural elaboration and as restrictive conditions for ongoing elaboration processes.

However close to empirical reality Archer's morphogenetic approach may be, on the other hand, the fact that it primarily focuses on the interactive nature of such systemic elaboration processes causes it to remain too unspecific to fully grasp the substantive nature characteristic of particular sub-systems of society (in general) or of system-like areas of institutionalised education (in particular). In this respect, the concepts developed in the frame of the theory of self-referential social systems – such as (on a general level) 'a system's differentiation from the rest of society' and 'its internal differentiation', 'orientation towards function' and 'input/output performances', 'self-reference' and 'self-reflection' or (on a more concrete level) 'communication media' and 'system-specific symbolic structures', 'systemic codes' and 'systemic programs', 'area of overlap' and 'functional symbiosis', 'discipline' and 'career' – promise more penetrating insight. If Archer follows, for example, the self-assertive strategies and self-interests of the teaching profession, the Luhmannian categories turn one's attention to the educational system's particular code – i.e. performance-based discrimination in terms of assessments, marking schemes, or organisational differentiation – which is disliked by the teaching profession, to be sure, but structurally inevitable, as well as to the dovetailing of educational and social selection following from this structural feature. If Archer focuses on reconstructing systemic growth in terms of the ultimately unintended consequences resulting from the interaction and transaction processes of primary and corporate actors, the concepts of functional systems theory, moreover, invite an explanation of the structural elaboration processes of a particular subsystem of society in terms of its distinctive meaning orientation and functional logic as well as in terms of its relations of interdependency with its social environment. By means of the intertwining of both (different but complementary) theoretical models, then – to sum up – the comparative process-analyses here discussed can be structured so as to make possible both the detailed description of culturally specific system-formation processes *and* their interpretation in the framework of general theory.

A comparative-historical social science which takes up the theoretical-*cum*-methodological options outlined thus far will no longer be located in the dichotomy of either 'nomothetic' or 'idiographic' approaches. Neither will analyses carried out along the lines of such options reduce the comparative approach to a mere procedure of macro-social hypothesis testing, nor will they let it wither into a dry accounting of socio-historical particularities. Investigations that take up these theoretical-*cum*-methodological options achieve, rather, specifically comparative knowledge in that they explore their object domain with a view to uncovering varying patterns of relationships between trans-cultural models of systemic organisation and socio-historically structured configurations.[107] They display, in other words, in the shape of discrete historical realisations, the variety of structural organisation possible in the socio-cultural world of humankind and, by the same token, show that these realisations follow the logic of system-like structural elaboration. They enrich, thus, our systematic knowledge and, at the same time, underscore the idea of evolutionary openness of social praxis.

Notes

[1] Emile Durkheim, *Les règles de la méthode sociologique*. Bibliothèque de philosophie contemporaine (Paris: Alcan, 1895); 22nd edition (Paris: Presses Universitaires de France, 1986); English edition translated by W.D. Halls as *The Rules of Sociological Method* (New York: Free Press, 1982).

[2] Durkheim, *Rules*, p. 157. A good example of the continuation of such fundamental positions is, *inter alia*, Joseph Farrell, The necessity of comparisons in the study of education, in P.G. Altbach & G.P. Kelly (Eds) *New Approaches to Comparative Education* (Chicago: University of Chicago Press, 1986), p. 208: "*There can be no generalizing scientific study of education which is not the comparative study of education*" (author's emphasis).

[3] Of considerable influence were, among others, Morris R. Cohen & Ernest Nagel, *An Introduction to Logic and Scientific Method* (London: Routledge & Sons, 1934) as well as Ernest Nagel, *The Structure of Science: problems in the logic of scientific explanation* (London: Routledge & Kegan Paul, 1961). The particular commitment of the comparative approach "to certain assumptions of the orthodox philosophy of science" is underlined by Klaus von Beyme in *Die politischen Theorien der Gegenwart* (Munich: Piper, 3rd edn, 1976), p. 126.

[4] In this sense, Adam Przeworski & Henry Teune, *The Logic of Comparative Social Inquiry* (New York: Wiley-Interscience, 1970), p. 12, state that "general theory consisting of nomothetic statements can be formulated and tested in the social sciences if proper names of social systems are replaced by variables in the course of comparative research".

[5] Compare, among others, Stein Rokkan (Ed.) *Comparative Research across Cultures and Nations* (Paris & Den Haag: Mouton, 1968); Arend Lijphart (1971) Comparative politics and the comparative method, *American Political Science Review*, 65, pp. 682-693; Stein Rokkan, *Vergleichende Sozialwissenschaft* (Frankfurt am Main: Ullstein, 1972); Donald P. Warwick & Samuel Osherson (Eds) *Comparative Research Methods* (Englewood Cliffs: Prentice Hall, 1973); Neil J. Smelser, *Comparative Methods in the Social Sciences* (Englewood Cliffs: Prentice Hall, 1976); Lawrence C. Mayer, *Redefining Comparative Politics. Promise versus Performance* (Newbury Park: Sage, 1989).

[6] See, e.g. Lutz Eckensberger, *Methodenprobleme der kulturvergleichenden Psychologie* (Saarbrücken: Sozialwissenschaftlicher Studienkreis für Internationale Probleme, 1970); S. Bochner, R.W. Brislin & W.J. Lonner (Eds) *Cross-Cultural Perspectives on Learning* (New York: Wiley, 1975); Rolf Wirsing (1975) Probleme des interkulturellen Vergleichs in der Ethnologie, *Sociologus*, 25, pp. 7-126; and Thomas Schweizer, *Methodenprobleme des interkulturellen Vergleichs* (Cologne: Böhlau, 1978).

[7] Harold J. Noah & Max A. Eckstein, *Toward a Science of Comparative Education* (London: Macmillan, 1969), which is along these lines, was the most widely read textbook in the field throughout the 1970s. See also Dieter Berstecher, *Zur Theorie und Technik des internationalen Vergleichs* (Stuttgart: Klett, 1970), as well as Manfred Niessen & Jules Peschar (Eds)

International Comparative Research. Problems of Theory, Methodology, and Organisation in Eastern and Western Europe (Oxford: Pergamon, 1982).

[8] In this same sense, see Smelser, *Comparative Methods in the Social Sciences*, p. 5, "Despite this diversity in substance, strategy, and technique, the methodological principles governing comparative investigation ... turn out to be very few in number".

[9] Adam Przeworski, Methods of cross-national research, 1970-83: an overview, in M. Dierkes, H.N. Weiler & A.B. Antal (Eds) *Comparative Policy Research* (Aldershot: Gower, 1987), p. 35.

[10] Mayer, *Redefining Comparative Politics*, Chapter 2, is exemplary: "The central theme of this chapter is that comparative analysis should be considered as a method that plays a central role in the explanatory mission of political science itself". Likewise, according to Fritz K. Ringer, *Education and Society in Modern Europe* (Bloomington: Indiana University Press, 1979), pp. 1-2, while historical study is necessary in order to grasp the very systemic character of institutionalised schooling and the "kind of inertia" involved in "the underlying reality of an educational system", there is an obvious need for the comparative approach, since "there is simply no other means of arriving at explanations, and not just descriptions, of change in education". The connections between comparative analysis, theory-building, and explanation are discussed in Farrell, 'The necessity of comparisons in the study of education', pp. 204ff.

[11] According to Przeworski & Teune, *The Logic of Comparative Social Inquiry*, *passim*.

[12] Charles C. Ragin, *The Comparative Method. Moving Beyond Qualitative and Quantitative Strategies* (Berkeley: University of California Press, 1989), p. 5. Likewise, according to Mayer, *Redefining Comparative Politics*, p. 15: "We no longer seek to understand a place or nation as such but to use nations as settings or groups of contextual variables in seeking to explain processes and generic patterns of behavior" .

[13] According to Alfred Brunswig, *Das Vergleichen und die Relationserkenntnis* (Leipzig & Berlin: Teubner, 1910).

[14] Presuppositions and consequences of this distinction are specified in Jürgen Schriewer, The method of comparison and the need for externalization: methodological criteria and sociological concepts, in Jürgen Schriewer in cooperation with Brian Holmes (Eds) *Theories and Methods in Comparative Education*, 3rd edn (Frankfurt am Main: Peter Lang, 1992), pp. 31 ff.

[15] John Stuart Mill, *A System of Logic, Ratiocinative and Inductive* (London: Longman, 1843).

[16] Claude Bernard, *Introduction à l'étude de la médecine expérimentale* (Paris: Baillière, 1865), and *Rapport sur les progrès et la marche de la Physiologie générale en France* (Paris: Imprimerie Impériale, 1867).

[17] Cf., in this sense, Fred L. Strodtbeck (1964) Considerations of meta-method in cross-cultural studies, *American Anthropologist*, 66, pp. 223-29, and similarly Bochner et al (Eds) *Cross-Cultural Perspectives on Learning*, p. 4.

[18] Cf., e.g. Berstecher, *Theorie and Technik des internationalen Vergleichs*, pp. 29ff.

[19] This is the concept used in René König (Ed.) *Handbuch der empirischen Sozialforschung*, 3rd enlarged edition, vol. 4, Komplexe Forschungsansätze (Munich & Stuttgart: dtv & Enke, 1974), and in Lijphart, 'Comparative politics and the comparative method', p. 683, respectively.

[20] "Physiologie sociale" is the term coined by Emile Durkheim, La sociologie et son domaine scientifique, in Victor Karady (Ed.) *Emile Durkheim. Textes. Tome 1: Eléments d'une théorie sociale* (Paris: Minuit, 1975), p. 24.

[21] Durkheim, *Rules*, p. 150.

[22] The characterisation of the 'principle of causality', as the "metaphysical hypostatisation" of a nomological research programme can be found, *inter alia*, in Karl R. Popper, *The Logic of Scientific Discovery* (London: Hutchinson, revised edn 1968), pp. 61 and 246 ff. Accordingly, it is almost ontological explanations of the constitution of the world that underlie the considerations of comparative methodology by Farrell, 'The necessity of comparisons in the study of education', p. 203: "It is assumed that there exists a certain degree of order and uniformity in the world, that events are not random but are connected in a regular and constant way. As Einstein's famous aphorism put it, 'the Lord is subtle, but he isn't simply mean'. In the specific field of human behavior it is assumed that there is regularity in the activities of human beings, and that some at least of these regularities hold across cultures."

[23] Marc Bloch, Pour une histoire comparée des sociétés européennes, *Mélanges historiques*, vol. 1 (Paris: SEVPEN, 1963), pp. 24-26.

[24] Ringer, *Education and Society*, p. 1.

[25] According to Niklas Luhmann, Die Weltgesellschaft, in *Soziologische Aufklärung* 2 (Opladen: Westdeutscher Verlag, 1975), p. 57.

[26] In the following, I refer back to some strands of argumentation which have been developed more fully in Jürgen Schriewer, Comparación y explicación en el análisis de los sistemas educativos, in Miguel A. Pereyra (Ed.*) Los Usos de la Comparación en Ciencias Sociales y en Educación* (Madrid: Centro de Publicaciones del MEC, 1990), pp. 77-127, and World-system and interrelationship-networks, in Thomas S. Popkewitz (Ed.) *Educational Knowledge: changing relationships between the state, civil society, and the educational community* (Albany: State University of New York Press, 1999).

[27] The state of research is discussed, with respect to the theoretical models implied, by *inter alia*, Marc Maurice (1980) Le déterminisme technologique dans la sociologie du travail (1955-1980). Un changement de paradigme? *Sociologie du travail,* 22, pp. 22-37, as well as in the papers assembled in Martin Heidenreich & Gert Schmidt (Eds) *International vergleichende Organisationsforschung. Fragestellungen, Methoden und Ergebnisse ausgewählter Untersuchungen* (Opladen: Westdeutscher Verlag, 1991).

[28] Cf. Ringer, *Education and Society*.

[29] Cf., for example, Peter W. Musgrave, *Technical Change, the Labour Force, and Education* (Oxford: Pergamon, 1967), as well as Burkart Lutz's essay on Bildungssystem und Beschäftigungsstruktur in Deutschland und Frankreich, in Institut für sozialwissenschaftliche Forschung, *Betrieb – Arbeitsmarkt – Qualifikation I* (Frankfurt: Aspekte, 1976), pp. 83-151; and his 1981 article, Education and employment: contrasting evidence from France and the Federal Republic of Germany, *European Journal of Education* 16, pp. 73-86.

[30] Cf., for example, Ronald Dore, *British Factory-Japanese Factor: the origins of national diversity in industrial relations* (Berkeley: University of California Press, 1973); Philippe d'Iribarne, *La logique de l'honneur. Gestion des entreprises et traditions nationales* (Paris: Seuil, 1989); as well as the recent volume *From School to Work: a comparative study of educational qualifications and occupational destinations*, Yossi Shavit & Walter Muller (Eds) (Oxford: Clarendon Press, 1998).

[31] As has been shown, for example, by Thomas P. Hughes, *Networks of Power. Electrification in Western Society, 1880-1930* (Baltimore: Johns Hopkins University Press, 1983), even the implementation of technological innovations in large-scale technical systems took shape, in different industrial societies that were competing with each other, in such diverse forms that these systemic processes' complexity can be grasped only by resorting to concepts like 'technological styles', 'sociotechnical systems', 'internal dynamics', and 'momentum'.

[32] Ingemar Fägerlind & Lawrence J. Saha, *Education and National Development: a comparative perspective* (Oxford: Pergamon, 1985); Gérard Grellet (1992) Pourquoi les pays en voie de développement ont-ils des rythmes de croissance aussi différents, *Revue Tiers Monde*, Vol. XXXIII, 129, pp. 31-66.

[33] Alex Inkeles & David H. Smith, *Becoming Modern* (London: Heinemann, 1974).

[34] Fägerlind & Saha, *Education and National Development*, pp. 88 & 195.

[35] See, for example, Lester M. Salamon (1970-71) Comparative history and the theory of modernization, *World Politics*, 23, pp. 83-103, as well as Shmuel N. Eisenstadt, *Tradition, Change, and Modernity* (New York: Wiley-Interscience, 1973), p. 362.

[36] Heidenreich & Schmidt (Eds) *International vergleichende Organisationsforschung*.

[37] Ulrich Menzel (1991) Das Ende der 'Dritten Welt' und das Scheitern der grossen Theorien, *Politische Vierteljahresschrift*, 32, pp. 4-33.

[38] For modernisation theory this has been shown by, among others, Theodor Hanf, Karl Ammann, Patrick Dias, Michael Fremerey & Heribert Weiland (1975) Education: an obstacle to development? *Comparative Education Review*, 19, pp. 68-87; and Eisenstadt, *Tradition, Change, and Modernity*. Likewise, dependency theory has been found wanting, when confronted with comparative evidence, by Theodor Hanf, Astochastische Dependenz als Entwicklungshindernis, in F.-M Schmölz (Ed.) *Christlicher Friedensbegrif und europäische Friedensordnung* (Mainz: Grünewald, 1977), pp. 151-164, and Harold J. Noah & Max A. Eckstein, Dependency theory in comparative education: twelve lessons from the literature, in Schriewer & Holmes (Eds) *Theories and Methods in Comparative Education*, pp. 165-192. Incisive critiques are similarly levelled, on the basis of comparative analysis, against other social and organisation theories expressed in universalist terms by, respectively, Manfred G. Schmidt, Politische Konjunkturzyklen und Wahlen, in M. Kaase & H.-D. Klingemann (Eds) *Wahlen und politisches System* (Opladen: Westdeutscher Verlag, 1983), pp. 174-197, and Marc Maurice, Theoretical and ideological aspects of universalism in the study of work organizations, in M.R. Haug & J. Dofny (Eds) *Work and Technology* (London: Sage, 1977), pp. 27-34.

[39] Such are the conclusions to be drawn from overviews of the state of comparative research in education and the social sciences presented by, among others, Francisco O. Ramirez & John W. Meyer, Comparative education: synthesis and agenda, in J.F. Short (Ed.) *The State of Sociology. Problems and Prospects* (Beverly Hills: Sage, 1981), pp. 215-238; Margaret S. Archer, Theorizing about the expansion of educational systems, in M.S. Archer (Ed.) *The Sociology of Educational Expansion* (Beverly Hills: Sage, 1982), pp. 3-64; Erwin Epstein (1983) Currents Left and Right: ideology in comparative education, *Comparative Education Review*, 27, pp. 3-29; Burton

R. Clark (Ed.*) Perspectives on Higher Education. Eight Disciplinary and Comparative Views* (Berkeley: University of California Press, 1984); or Przeworski, 'Methods of cross-national research'. These conclusions are also in line, however, with the insight produced by detailed comparative-historical investigation such as Mary Jo Maynes, *Schooling for the People: comparative local studies of schooling history in France and Germany, 1750-1850* (New York: Holmes & Meier, 1985), p. 194: "The findings presented here challenge both traditional interpretations of schooling history and some aspects of the recent revision of that history".

[40] Bertrand Badie & Guy Hermet, *Politique Comparée* (Paris: P.U.F., 1990), pp. 10 and 19-44.

[41] Menzel, 'Das Ende der "Dritten Welt" und das Scheitern der grossen Theorien', and, similarly, Raymond Boudon (1992) Grandeur et décadence des sciences du développement: une étude de sociologie de la connaissance, in *L'Année sociologique*, 3rd series, Vol. 42, pp. 253-274.

[42] Przeworski, 'Methods of cross-national research', p. 40.

[43] Compare Popper, *The Logic of Scientific Discovery*, as well as the methodologies which, in line with Popper, emphasise the potentials of comparative research for theory-testing and critique, such as Farrell, 'The necessity of comparisons in the study of education', or Ariane B. Antal, Meinolf Dierkes & Hans N. Weiler, Cross-national policy research: traditions, achievements and challenges, in Dierkes et al (Eds) (1987) *Comparative Policy Research*, p. 14.

[44] Erich Rothacker, *Logik und Systematik der Geisteswissenschaften* (Munich: Oldenbourg, 1965), p. 97.

[45] According to the graphic expression coined by American historian James J. Sheehan in a conference presentation on the astonishing breadth of variation of European liberalism, compare the report in *Frankfurter Allgemeine Zeitung* (3 November 1987), p. 31, as well as Dieter Langewiesche (Ed.) *Liberalismus im 19. Jahrhundert. Deutschland im europäischen Vergleich*, (Göttingen: Vandenhoeck & Ruprecht, 1988).

[46] See the parallel critique of Archer, 'Theorizing about the expansion of educational systems', p. 3, on the "*general* explanations which pinpoint some *particular variable or process* as universally responsible [for expansion]".

[47] The differentiation between 'exogenous' and 'endogenous' models lies, as Mohamed Cherkaoui, *Les changements du système éducatif en France, 1950-1980* (Paris: P.U.F., 1982), pp. 16-21, rightly asserts, crossways to the often stressed difference between structural functionalism and conflict theory.

[48] Alasdair C. MacIntyre, *Against the Self-Image of the Age: essays on ideology and philosophy* (New York: Schocken Books, 1971), pp. 260ff.

[49] Niklas Luhmann (1995) Kausalität im Süden, *Soziale Systeme. Zeitschrift für soziologische Theorie*, 1, pp. 7-28, here p. 12.

[50] See e.g. Immanuel Wallerstein, *Unthinking Social Science. The Limits of Nineteenth-Century Paradigms* (Cambridge: Polity Press, 1991); and Philip McMichael (1990) Incorporating comparison within a world-historical perspective: an alternative comparative method, *American Sociological Review*, 55, pp. 385-397.

[51] Friedrich H. Tenbruck (1981) Emile Durkheim oder die Geburt der Gesellschaft aus dem Geist der Soziologie, *Zeitschrift für Soziologie*, 10, pp. 333-350.

[52] Tenbruck, 'Emile Durkheim', p. 348.

[53] Albert Bergesen, Preface; and From utilitarianism to globology: the shift from the individual to the world as a whole as the primordial unit of analysis, in A. Bergesen (Ed.) *Studies of the Modern World System* (New York: Academic Press, 1980), pp. xiii-xiv and 1-12.

[54] Bergesen, 'Preface', p. xiii; and 'From utilitarianism to globology', p. 10.

[55] Bergesen, 'From utilitarianism to globology', p. 8.

[56] In the final section of Max Weber (1904) Die 'Objektivität' sozial-wissenschaftlicher und sozialpolitischer Erkenntnis, in Weber, *Gesammelte Aufsätze zur Wissenschaftslehre*, 4th edn (Tübingen: Mohr, 1973), pp. 146-214.

[57] As described, e.g. by Philip Altbach (1991) Patterns in higher education development, *Prospects*, XXI, pp. 189-203; and Rudolf Stichweh, From the *Peregrinatio Academica* to contemporary international student flows – national culture and functional differentiation as emergent causes, in C. Charle, J. Schriewer & P. Wagner (Eds) *The Emergence of Transnational Intellectual Networks. Forms of Academic Knowledge and the Search for Cultural Identities* (Oxford: Berghahn, forthcoming 1999).

[58] According to, *inter alia*, Dietrich Goldschmidt, *Die gesellschaftliche Herausforderung der Universität. Historische Analysen, internationale Vergleiche, globale Perspektiven* (Weinheim: Deutscher Studienverlag, 1991); Clark Kerr (1991) International learning and national purposes in higher education, *American Behavioral Scientist*, 35, pp. 17-42; and Ulrich Teichler, *Convergence or Growing Variety: the changing organization of studies* (Strasbourg: Council of Europe, 1988), and *Europäische Hochschulsysteme: Die Beharrlichkeit vielfältiger Modelle* (Frankfurt am Main: Campus, 1990).

[59] Compare Fritz Ringer, *Fields of Knowledge. French Academic Culture in Comparative Perspective, 1890-1920* (Cambridge: Cambridge University Press, 1992); as well as Jonathan Harwood, *Styles of Scientific Thought. A Study of the German Genetics Community, 1900-1933* (Chicago: University of Chicago Press, 1992), and 'Mandarine' oder 'Aussenseiter'? Selbstverständnis deutscher Naturwissenschaftler (1900-1933), in J. Schriewer, E. Keiner & C. Charle (Eds.) *Sozialer Raum und akademische Kulturen. A la recherche de l'espace universitaire européen* (Frankfurt am Main: Lang, 1993), pp. 183-212.

[60] See, e.g. in the field of educational studies, Jürgen Schriewer & Edwin Keiner (1992) Communication patterns and intellectual traditions in educational sciences: France and Germany, *Comparative Education Review*, 36, pp. 25-51, as well as Jürgen Schriewer, Etudes pluridisciplinaires et réflexions philosophico-herméneutiques: la structuration du discours pédagogique en France et en Allemagne, in P. Drewek, C. Lüth et al (Eds) *History of Educational Studies – Geschichte der Erziehungswissenschaft – Histoire des sciences de l'éducation, Paedagogica Historica*, Supplementary Vol. III, (Gent, 1998), pp. 57-84. Similar continuities are described for the field of history by Winfried Schulze, *Deutsche Geschichtswissenschaft nach 1945* (Munich: Oldenbourg, 1989).

[61] Compare, among others, Dan A. Chekki, *American Sociological Hegemony. Transnational Explorations* (Lanham: University Press of America, 1987); Nikolai Genov (Ed.) *National Traditions in Sociology* (London: Sage, 1989),

pp. 1-17; as well as M. Albrow & E. King (Eds) *Globalization, Knowledge and Society* (London: Sage, 1990).

[62] Anthony G. McGrew, Paul G. Lewis et al, *Global Politics. Globalization and the Nation State* (Cambridge & Oxford: Polity Press & Blackwell, 1992).

[63] See, e.g. Alan S. Milward with the assistance of George Brennan & Federico Romero, *The European Rescue of the Nation-State* (London: Routledge, 1992).

[64] Compare Jean Charpentier & Christian Engel (Eds) *Les régions de l'espace communautaire* (Nancy: Presses Universitaires de Nancy, 1992); Victor Scardigli (Ed.) *L'Europe de la diversité: la dynamique des identités régionales* (Paris: Editions du CNRS, 1993); Barry Jones & Michael Keating (Eds) *The European Union and the Regions* (Oxford: Oxford University Press. 1995).

[65] Anthony G. McGrew, Conceptualizing global politics, in McGrew et al, *Global Politics*, p. 23; compare also Neil J. Smelser (1991) Internationalization of social science knowledge, *American Behavioral Scientist*, 35, pp. 65-91.

[66] As shown by Robert Cowen, The importation of higher education into Brazil and Japan, in P. Cunningham & C. Brook (Eds) *International Currents in Educational Ideas and Practices*. Proceedings of the 1987 Annual Conference of the History of Education Society, held jointly with BCIES (Evington: History of Education Society, 1988), pp. 41-49.

[67] Michel Espagne & Michael Werner (1988) Présentation, *Revue de synthèse*, 4th series, no. 2, April-June, pp. 187-194; M. Espagne & M. Werner (Eds) *Philologiques I. Contribution à l'histoire des disciplines littéraires en France et en Allemagne au XIXe siècle* (Paris: Editions de la Maison des Sciences de l'Homme, 1990).

[68] Detlef Kantowsky (1982) Die Rezeption der Hinduismus/ Buddhismus-Studie Max Webers in Südasien. Ein Missverständnis, *Archives Européennes de Sociologie*, 23, pp. 317-355; Michael Pollak (1986) Die Rezeption Max Webers in Frankreich. Fallstudie eines Theorietransfers in den Sozialwissenschaften, *Kölner Zeitschrift für Soziologie und Sozialpsychologie*, 38, pp. 670-684.

[69] Masao Terasaki, *Oyatoi Kyoshi Emil Hausknecht no Keukyu* (Tokyo: University of Tokyo Press, 1989). Equally informative are, e.g. the essays addressing the theoretical and political adoption of Jean Piaget during different periods of time in France, Argentina, and Brasil, which are assembled in Barbara Freitag (Ed.) *Piaget: 100 anos* (São Paulo: Cortez Editora, 1997).

[70] See, e.g. Bertrand Badie, *L'Etat importé. Essai sur l'occidentalisation de l'ordre politique* (Paris: Fayard, 1992).

[71] Karel van Wolferen, *The Enigma of Japanese Power: people and politics in a stateless nation* (New York: Alfred A. Knopf, 1989).

[72] Bertrand Badie (1992) Analyse comparative et sociologie historique, *Revue Internationale des Sciences sociales*, 133, pp. 366-367. Likewise, intricate mixtures of convergent and divergent patterns of adaptation to processes of social change are also identified in advanced industrial societies by Simon Langlois with Theodore Caplow, Henri Mendras, Wolfgang Glatzer, *Convergence or Divergence? Comparing Recent Social Trends in Industrial Societies* (Frankfurt am Main: Campus; Montréal: McGill-Queen's University Press, 1994). Currently, the economic and social transformation processes going on in the formerly socialist countries of Central and Eastern Europe

provide ample evidence for the adaptation and appropriation mechanisms stressed by Badie. See e.g. Gernot Grabher & David Stark (Eds) *Restructuring Networks in Post-Socialism. Legacies, Linkages and Localities* (Oxford: Oxford University Press, 1997).

[73] Exemplary of such research and modelling is *inter alia* George M. Thomas, John W. Meyer, Francisco O. Ramirez & John Boli, *Institutional Structure. Constituting State, Society, and the Individual* (Beverly Hills: Sage, 1987).

[74] See, taking up a Parsonsian concept, Christel Adick (1988) Schule im modernen Weltsystem, *Zeitschrift für Kulturaustausch*, 38, pp. 343-355, and El enfoque de sistemas mundiales en educación comparada, in J. Schriewer & F. Pedró (Eds) *Manual de Educación Comparada. Vol. II, Teorías, Investigaciones, Perspectivas* (Barcelona: Promociones y Publicaciones Universitarias, 1993), pp. 387-421.

[75] See, e.g. Arnold J. Heidenheimer, *Disparate Ladders. Why School and University Policies Differ in Germany, Japan, and Switzerland* (New Brunswick: Transaction Publishers, 1997), on the "striking variation among the political characteristics [of] highly developed democratic countries" and their expression in the form of considerable differences in structure and growth of these countries' educational systems. Cf also the detailed case studies contrasting German and Russian school education by Detlef Glowka, *Schulen und Unterricht im Vergleich – Russland/ Deutschland* (Münster: Waxmann, 1995).

[76] Compare McMichael, 'Incorporating comparison within a world-historical perspective' (note 50). The concept of socio-historical modernisation is not used here in the sense of a Westernisation inherent in a purportedly inevitable logic of world-history; rather, it serves, according to McGrew, 'Conceptualizing global politics', pp. 25-26, as an "umbrella label", as a "functional expression of those interlinked processes of secular social, political, economic and cultural change (such as industrialization, democratization, bureaucratization and urbanization) whose effects are experienced world-wide, albeit in a highly uneven way. ... Accordingly, modernization does not imply the emergence of some kind of world society in which cultural homogeneity or cosmopolitanism prevail. Rather, because its effects are unevenly experienced throughout the globe and because it promotes resistance wherever it permeates, it is more accurate to conclude that modernization reinforces the tendencies towards both integration and disintegration in the contemporary global system."

[77] Rothacker, *Logik und Systematik der Geisteswissenschaften*, (note 44), p. 97.

[78] Badie,'Analyse comparative et sociologie historique', p. 364; cf. also Immanuel Wallerstein, Historical systems as complex systems, in Wallerstein, *Unthinking Social Science* (note 50), pp. 229-236.

[79] As discussed in Jürgen Schriewer (1984) Vergleichend-historische Bildungsforschung: Gesamttableau oder Forschungsansatz?, *Zeitschrift für Pädagogik*, 30, pp. 323-342.

[80] See, *inter alia*, Wolfgang Krohn & Günther Küppers, *Selbstorganisation. Aspekte einer wissenschaftlichen Revolution* (Braunschweig: Vieweg, 1990); Françoise Fogelmann Soulié (Ed.) *Les théories de la complexité* (Paris: Editions du Seuil, 1991); R.K. Mishra, D. Maass & E. Zwierlein (Eds) *On Self-Organization. An Interdisciplinary Search for a Unifying Principle* (Berlin: Springer, 1994); Esther Thelen & Linda B. Smith (Eds) *A Dynamic Systems Approach to the Development of Cognition and Action* (Cambridge: MIT Press, 1994).

[81] Major works by Margaret S. Archer include: Theorizing about the expansion of educational systems, in M.S. Archer (Ed.) *The Sociology of Educational Expansion. Take-off, Growth and Inflation in Educational Systems* (Beverley Hills: Sage, 1982), pp. 3-64; Structuration versus morphogenesis, in S.N. Eisenstadt & H.J. Helle (Eds) *Macro-Sociological Theory. Vol. I. Perspectives on Sociological Theory* (Beverly Hills: Sage. 1985), pp. 58-88; and *Realist Social Theory: the morphogenetic approach* (Cambridge: Cambridge University Press, 1995).

[82] Edgar Morin, *La Méthode* (Paris: Seuil): *Vol. 1, La Nature de la Nature,* (new edn 1981), *Vol. 2, La Vie de la Vie,* (new edn 1985), *Vol. 3, La Connaissance de la Connaissance* (1986), *Vol. 4, Les idées* (1991).

[83] English translations of Luhmann's works include *The Differentiation of Society* (New York: Columbia University Press, 1982); *Essays on Self-Reference* (New York: Columbia University Press, 1990); and *Social Systems* (Cambridge: Cambridge University Press, 1996).

[84] Wolfgang Lipp (1987) Autopoiesis biologisch, Autopoiesis soziologisch, *Kölner Zeitschriff für Soziologie und Sozialpsychologie*, 39, pp. 452-470.

[85] *Open the Social Sciences. Report of the Gulbenkian Commission on the Restructuring of the Social Sciences* (Stanford: Stanford University Press, 1996), quotations pp. 61, 64 and 78.

[86] See Wolfgang Schluchter, *Die Entwicklung des okzidentalen Rationalismus* (Tübingen: Mohr, 1979). The emergence of a global 'world society' out of the intensification of highly specialised communication processes specific to societal sub-systems – transcending, therefore, geographical barriers and nation-state frontiers – is conceptualised in terms of both communication and differentiation theory by Luhmann, *Die Gesellschaft der Gesellschaft* (Frankfurt am Main: Suhrkamp, 1997), especially Vol. I, pp. 145ff. on 'Weltgesellschaft'.

[87] The increasing differentiation of traditional concepts of causation is discussed, e.g. in Magoroh Maruyama (1974) Paradigmatology and its application to cross-disciplinary, cross-professional and cross-cultural communication, *Cybernetica*, 17(2), pp. 136-156, & 17(4), pp. 237-281; Michel de Coster, *L'Analogie en sciences humaines* (Paris: P.U.F., 1978), pp. 54ff.; Shuhei Aida, Peter M. Allen, Henri Atlan, et al (Eds) *Science et pratique de la complexité* (Paris: La Documentation Française, 1986); Ernest Sosa & Michael Tooley (Eds) *Causation* (New York: Oxford University Press, 1993).

[88] Morin, *La Méthode*, Vol. 1, pp. 257ff.

[89] De Coster, *L'Analogie*, pp. 62ff., and Maruyama, 'Paradigmatology', pp. 149ff.

[90] Morin, *La Méthode*, Vol. 1, pp. 269-70.

[91] Niklas Luhmann, *Funktion der Religion* (Frankfurt am Main: Suhrkamp, 1982), pp. 9ff.

[92] Niklas Luhmann, Funktion und Kausalität, *Soziologische Aufklärung*, Vol. 1 (Opladen: Westdeutscher Verlag, 1970), pp. 13ff. (emphasis in original).

[93] Luhmann, 'Funktion und Kausalität', pp.16ff.

[94] Luhmann, 'Funktion und Kausalität', p. 14. Compare note 22.

[95] Niklas Luhmann, *Soziale Systeme. Grundriss einer allgemeinen Theorie* (Frankfurt am Main: Suhrkamp, 1984), pp. 83ff.

[96] This example is discussed, in the framework of more general considerations, by Konrad Zweigert (1966) Des solutions identiques par des voies différentes, *Revue Internationale de Droit Comparé*, 18, pp. 6-18.

[97] *"Jus unum"* – *"lex multiplex,"* reads, therefore, the motto of the vignette printed on the front cover of the *Revue Internationale de Droit Comparé*. The quotations are taken from Josef Esser, *Grundsatz und Norm in der richterlichen Fortbildung des Privatrechts. Rechtsvergleichende Beiträge zur Rechtsquellen- und Interpretationslehre* (Tübingen: Mohr, 2nd edn, 1964), pp. 346ff.; compare also Zweigert, 'Des solutions identiques', and Max Rheinstein, *Einführung in die Rechtsvergleichung* (Munich: Beck, 1974).

[98] Esser, *Grundsatz und Norm*, p. 349. Also compare the analyses in, for example, Frank Rotter (1970) Dogmatische und soziologische Rechtsvergleichung. Eine methodologische Analyse für die Ostrechtsforschung, *Osteuroparecht*, 16(2), pp. 81-97, or in Filippo Ranieri (1985) Stilus Curiae. Zum historischen Hintergrund der Relationstechnik, *Rechtshistorisches Journal*, 4, pp. 75-88.

[99] Cf. Peter Flora, Die Bildungsentwicklung im Prozess der Staaten- und Nationenbildung, in P.C. Ludz (Ed.) *Soziologie und Sozialgeschichte* (Opladen: Westdeutscher Verlag, 1972), pp. 294-319; Wolfram Fischer & Peter Lundgreen, The recruitment and training of administrative and technical personnel, in C. Tilly (Ed.) *The Formation of National States in Western Europe* (Princeton: Princeton University Press, 1975), pp. 456-561; Stein Rokkan, Dimensions of state formation and nation building: a possible paradigm for research on variations within Europe, in the same volume, pp. 562-600, and by the same author, *Citizens, Elections, Parties. Approaches to the Comparative Study of the Processes of Development* (Oslo: Universitetsforlaget. 1970). For the second line of research cf. also Fritz W. Scharpf, Economic and institutional constraints of full-employment strategies: Sweden, Austria. and Western Germany, in John H. Goldthorpe (Ed.) *Order and Conflict in Contemporary Capitalism* (Oxford: Clarendon, 1984), pp. 257-290, as well as Charles F. Sabel, Gary B. Herrigel, Richard Deeg & Richard Kazis, *Regional Prosperities Compared: Massachusetts and Baden-Württemberg in the 1980s* (Berlin: Wissenschaftszentrum Berlin, 1987).

[100] Luhmann, *Soziale Systeme*, p. 85ff. *et passim.*

[101] Luhmann, *Soziale Systeme*, p. 84.

[102] In this sense, Eisenstadt, *Tradition, Change, and Modernity* (note 35), p. 361, rightfully contends that "it is this multiplicity of levels of social organization and cultural forces that provides some structure to historical situations and points to the possibilities and limitations of 'choices' within them".

[103] See e.g. the typology of European developmental paths constructed on the basis of geographical, historical and political parameters by Stein Rokkan. Out of his numerous publications, one might refer to Rokkan, 'Dimensions of state formation and nation-building: a possible paradigm for research on variations within Europe' (note 99), as well as to the analytical overview by Peter Flora, Stein Rokkan's macro-model of Europe, in Peter Flora et al, *State, Economy, and Society in Western Europe 1815-1975, vol. 1: The Growth of Mass Democracies and Welfare States* (Frankfurt am Main: Campus; London: Macmillan; Chicago: St. James, 1983), pp. 11-26.

[104] See, in this sense, the phrasing coined by Karl-Georg Faber, *Theorie der Geschichtswissenschaft* (Munich: Beck, 1974), pp. 86ff., stating that "historical reality corresponds to the realization of the possible". Compare also, in a more pragmatic tone, Maynes, *Schooling for the People* (note 39), p.

10 "It is instructive to find out how the constraints on people's actions were indeed constraining, whatever their ideas".

[105] Archer, 'Theorizing about the expansion of educational systems' (note 39), p. 6.

[106] Margaret S. Archer, *Social Origins of Educational Systems* (London: Sage, 1979).

[107] In so doing, they would only correspond to the insight produced by interdisciplinary research on self-organising systems, according to which even minimal deviations in the initial conditions may lead to largely divergent structural elaboration processes. Compare also Eisenstadt, *Tradition, Change, and Modernity* (note 35), p. 362: "instead of assuming the existence of general sequences of patterns of social mobilization ..., we must investigate the possibility of different variations in such patterns and their influence on the development of different modes of response to the challenges of modernization and on the consequent emergence of different types of post-traditional social, political, and cultural orders".

Late Modernity and the Rules of Chaos: an initial note on transitologies and rims

ROBERT COWEN

Introduction

Comparative education, at the time of writing, is going through a dangerous moment. Comparative education (of a certain sort) is too popular. The use of examples of educational practices from other countries has been absorbed into the advocacy discourse of politics. Advocacy comparative education is being offered in television and print media, in the public pronouncements of politicians and political parties, and in the recommendations of numerous policy advisory groups constituted, in the American term, as 'think-tanks'.

It is now widely believed by the major political parties in the United Kingdom (UK) that our schools are in crisis, standards are low, and an important minority of teachers are incompetent. On the public measuring scales currently used, some of our university departments have been classified as not reaching 'national standards'. It has also been demonstrated, on international tests of achievement, that the scores of English and Scottish children in mathematics place them on international league tables in a relatively low position.

It is now publicly known, mainly by reiteration and the directions of UK governmental policy, that solutions to these problems should include competency and school-based teacher education (combining some of the themes of American teacher education reforms of the 1970s with the return of much teacher preparation to the schools, as in an earlier period of English educational history). New certification systems in the UK combine the retention of some of the rigidities of the European tradition of school leaving examinations (A level, the *Abitur*, or their equivalents) with the aspiration to have a Learning Society; though whether on the model recommended by the OECD is not completely clear. Higher education policies, in England in particular, have embraced the febrile immediacy and financial instabilities of the American graduate school and research university in combination with bureaucratisation, modularisation and routinisation of doctoral programmes (Cowen, 1997). This sudden fashionability of the foreign in the UK has been framed by combining some of the characteristics of French and Soviet education – strong standardisation of curriculum content and evaluation practices (and potentially, pedagogy) with some of the odder characteristics of American education: a fixation with quantifiable measures of educational process and a conviction that the more schools and universities approximate in their comportment and management styles to those of business, the better (Callahan, 1962).

In these circumstances, there is considerable pressure on comparative education specialists to be 'relevant': that is, to devote such skills as they have to resolving problems of inefficiency and ineffectiveness in the school, post-school, or university systems by specifying solutions. Much of our tradition has after all stressed the importance of learning things of practical value from foreign educational systems or educational problem solving. The aspiration to provide policy advice to governments has been common enough for long enough (Cowen, 1973). At the very least, both as specialised academics and as responsible citizens, should we not join wholeheartedly in this new celebration of the foreign, and get on and 'do' comparative education?

Probably not, and this is not merely because of professional impatience with the crudity and cultural crassness with which the solution of 'whole-class teaching' in Taiwan or even in East Asia is assumed to be (a) whole-class teaching, (b) transferable to the UK (or the USA), and (c) the guarantor of any or all of the following: economic growth, social discipline, social mobilisation, lower teenage pregnancy rates and high mathematics scores on international tests. Cargo-cult comparative education (magnet schools; European vocational-technical training systems; the American research university; the DfEE as *Monbusho*) has begun to produce some expensive tears; most of them so far brilliantly mopped up by Sir Ron Dearing. Cargo cult comparative education in Africa (vocational schools, UPE, the unadapted university) and in East Asia (the Soviet influence in the People's Republic of China (PRC) and the Meiji and American educational reforms in Japan) has produced not only tears but human tragedy.

We should probably not get on and 'do' comparative education until we have refreshed our memories about some of our major historical assumptions and noted their deficiencies. And we should probably not advocate 'solutions to problems' until we have reflected on some of the epistemic challenges of late modernity. Here I believe that those of us privileged to work in comparative education from a university base face theoretical challenges that are complex. Until we see these challenges more clearly we are, by proposing 'solutions', merely likely to magnify the errors of those more cavalier than ourselves. Advocacy comparative education has increased, is increasing and ought to be diminished until we have first re-read *kosmos*. University studies in comparative education may still be useful – by insisting on the complexity of problems and by occasionally using a Cassandra voice. The correct social usage of Cassandra herself would have been remarkably cost-effective.

In a recent paper 'Last past the post: comparative education, late modernity and perhaps post-modernity' (Cowen, 1996a). I drew a distinction between our *episteme*, the intellectual traditions through which we have traditionally done our work and the ways we have read, and should read, the world: our view of *kosmos*. Today's paper pushes that distinction a bit further.

Episteme

There are, I think, three groupings of apparently dissimilar ideas in our traditional professional epistemology which share a characteristic. That characteristic is linearity – and thus implicitly – predictability. It is the linearity and the predictability inherent in that canon which makes reading of the current *kosmos* so difficult and probably erroneous. The three examples of linearity I am suggesting are (i) equilibrium theory, (ii) theories of social development, and (iii) positivist expectations of the social sciences.

Equilibrium Theory

By the 1960s the world which was inspected by comparative educationists who were also theoreticians had become somewhat limited. Much attention was given to Europe. Sometimes this attention stretched to include substantive work on, or at least substantive description of, the USSR and even East Europe. And as much comparative education was done in the Anglo-Saxon world, the USA, Canada, Australia and New Zealand came within the circle of inclusion and visibility. Of course, other descriptive work was done, some of it comparative, on Africa or India or Latin America; but those who combined descriptive writing with theoretical, often methodological, redefinitions of the field (Bereday, 1966; Eckstein & Noah, 1969; Holmes, 1965; King, 1968; King, 1973; Lauwerys, 1965; Noah & Eckstein, 1969) were most alert to the problems of education in countries of relative political stability: Australia, Canada, East Europe, Japan, New Zealand, North-west and South Europe, the USA and the USSR.

The consequence – with two clear exceptions – was that it was possible for Anglo-Saxon comparative education to solidify its methodological propositions around a variety of equilibrium theories. The two obvious exceptions are Hans, whose factors (unlike his value system) were predisposed to the analysis of immanent disequilibrium, and King, at the heart of whose later methodological position is the concept of 'uncertainty' (and 'newness') which is always – whether in the form of Sputnik, the female contraceptive pill or the computer chip – creating dissonance and disequilibrium.

The other comparativists used some version of an equilibrium theory – with varying degrees of self-awareness. Bereday (1966), for example, always begins with a (metaphorical) photograph of pedagogic description. Regardless of what subsequently happens in later stages of his methodology – and his range of illustrations is astonishingly eclectic – the original pedagogic photograph is the equilibrium point of the analysis. Noah & Eckstein's methodological work (1969) specifies or leads to the specification of an equilibrium of correlations. These are interestingly unstable, of course, and the specification of their causes will likely lead to the identification of disequilibriurn conditions. But at the core of the Noah & Eckstein's methodology is the identification of a stable moment, whose index is a correlational statement.

Rather than correlations, both Mallinson (1975) and Lauwerys (1965) chose culture. For Mallinson, the more or less permanent (and none too flexible) equilibrium around which comparative education should be constructed was the concept of national character. This caused, framed, and was reinforced by the educational patternings with which it was linked. For Lauwerys, the cultural framing was smaller, neater and in some ways therefore sharper: the philosophical models of man (or the concepts of 'general education') which provided the rules of each national game, defining in their concepts of good knowledge the national specificities of what it was to be (well) educated.

The most sophisticated version of equilibrium theory in comparative education was, in my opinion, the work of Brian Holmes (1965; 1986). Paradoxically taking much of his sociology from Popper and much of his philosophy from Dewey – and with his overall epistemic position deducible from both – he constructed a detailed definition of his problem approach; with 'problems' needing to be defined as disturbances to an equilibrium. 'Solutions' established a new equilibrium; attached to which was a specification of anticipated consequences.

Within the context of my argument the key point about Holmes (1986) is not his concern for taxonomies or his astonishing flirtation with sociological laws, initially perceived as 'determinants', nor even his use of Pareto as a sociologist. The key point is his technical specification of what counts as 'a problem'. For Holmes a 'problem' was not produced by multiple changes. Only one change was permitted to be specified.

Thus, within his taxonomy of the social, philosophic and environmental universe – his three circles – only one change could be specified as problem-producing. This change might be normative (e.g. taking The Koran as the new national guide to educational practice; or deciding that an educational system must be market-framed and market driven, as in England in the 1980s). Against this normative change, other patterns of institutional or environmental circumstance were to be identified as not changed at all, or as having changed more slowly. The point also applies to, and is in no way disturbed by, his subsequent addition of the concept of 'Mental States' to his methodological apparatus. A Holmesian problem can be specified through only one change, within an equilibrium model of other non-change areas.

In fact it is here that Holmes's sociological assumptions become relevant. Normative assumptions are, in his view, relatively easy to change. Sociological laws and Mental States are assumed to be less tractable, less easily able to be altered by reforming élites. Thus his equilibrium model contains within it an implicit prioritisation of the probable sources of change: alterations in the normative. The ideational rather than the material is stressed – a little like Hans. On the basis of this initial specification of a 'problem' in the technical sense, 'solutions' can be specified hypothetically and their probable consequences deduced. In principle, a new equilibrium with consequent and predictable effects emerges.

Of course, there are complex characteristics of context (other norms, other institutional patterns, Mental States and environmental circumstances) which need to be taken into account. In a phrase reminiscent of Hans, these aspects must be 'weighed' – an issue which remains even more methodologically nebulous in Holmes's work than in that of Hans. Holmes largely deals with that issue by asserting its existence; at least Hans is forced by the intellectual organisation of his text to illustrate the issue. But amid all the muddle and amid the accumulation of models for particular investigations (models of a profession; of a university; of élite formation) the framing metaphor of Holmes's analysis (1965; 1986) is (problem) equilibrium and disequilibrium; and (problem) solutions and the hypothetical stability of the new equilibrium. Despite Holmes's protestations about drawing from Popper's views of post-relativity science, I believe that a central theme in his work is Newtonian: a predictable social, almost mechanical, universe strongly framed by sociological laws and open to the social physicist or social engineer to fine-tune back to an equilibrium position.

Thus, overall, I suggest that many of the classic methodological positions of comparative educationists in the period from 1946 to 1966 were varieties of equilibrium theory. Within these positions, culture and its constraints was the 'grand narrative' (in the work of Hans, Lauwerys and Mallinson) until Holmes: for whom equilibrium itself, wrapped within a discourse of Popperian post-relativity science, becomes the grand narrative in a 'problem-solving approach'.

Within these grand narratives, the national framing of culture, or the national framing of a problem and its solution, was the central concern. There was a paradoxical element in this comparative education: it looked outwards to other nations and cultures and to foreign educational practice. But the lessons were to be brought home. The melioristic intent was to improve a domestic system of education. Perhaps because of the tension between Marxist and structural-functionalist sociologies in the 1960s, there is little hint in the Anglo-Saxon comparative education of the 1960s of the possibility of a world-system. Piecemeal social engineering was primarily a domestic activity. The apparent exception to this proposition was the modernity literature.

Linearities of Social Development

The classic literature on development is very large, but it overlaps with 'comparative education' both in its departmental structures, especially in Australia, Canada and the USA and in some of its epistemological assumptions. The classic literature ranges across economic, sociological and psychological approaches in the work of scholars such as Anderson & Bowman (1966), Carnoy (1974), Altbach & Kelly, (1978), McLelland (1967) and Inkeles & Smith (1974). The point I want to draw out here is not the manifest differences between the 'modernisation' and 'dependency' literature, nor the obvious differences between Anderson & Bowman, and Altbach & Kelly for example, but some similarities.

All the literature specifies a preferred condition (modernity; non-dependency) which is contrasted with a position of disadvantage (traditionality; dependency). The structural, political, sociological, economic and psychological point of the analysis is how to get from the position of disadvantage to the preferred condition. In both schools, the world is in disequilibrium and strategies can be developed to redress the disequilibrium.

In the modernity school, those 'solutions' for the creation of a new equilibrium are relatively clear. The classical factors of production in the 'Third World' can be improved. Land can be fertilised and technical agricultural knowledge diffused. Capital, through agencies such as Development Banks, can be made available. And labour will be improved through the removal of ineffectiveness in educational systems, the improvement of teacher education systems, advanced training of local experts in foreign universities, and the creation of vocational-technical schools (of an appropriate type).

There is a sort of a system-in-the-world, but it is benign and it is the source of solutions which promise the delivery of a new equilibrium of (i) 'development' and (ii) linear social progress.

The dependency school assumed a less benign world. The world was inherently unequal – there was a 'world system' which was exploitative and the First World exploited even itself (through the domestic patterns of its metropoles and peripheries). The social universe was more complicated than the First, Second and Third World distinctions of the international agencies and much modernisation theory. There was a very complex pattern of multiple metropoles (São Paulo and its hinterland; but also São Paulo as a periphery to the Inter-American Development Bank or Japanese, British and American capital). However, the world was in disequilibrium: structured on a world scale, and characterised by cultural and political – and not merely economic penetration – of local élites. The tentative solutions were not more aid, but more struggle: initially the creation of perceptions of the sources of the disequilibrium in those who were structurally disadvantaged in Brasil or Chile or Uganda or Vietnam.

Overall then, linear social development was possible – we can all become metropoles, like Japan, Taiwan, Singapore and South Korea, or at worst, self-conscious semi-peripheries like Greece, Italy, Portugal and Spain, and Canada. What was required was internal revolution – Chile, Cuba. Nicaragua, Tanzania – and policies consciously framed in the knowledge of the existence of the world economic system itself (Camoy & Sarnoff et al, 1990). Progress would be hard, but progress could be made.

Revolution and independent development were the grand narrative; and the dependency school at least offered a shift from Habermas's technical knowledge to Habermas's emancipatory knowledge. It is this tension between technical and emancipatory knowledge which takes me to my third and last theme of this group of arguments: the theme of positivism.

The Simpler Aspirations of Positivism

It is Jullien of Paris who sets the tone and much of the epistemological stance of classic comparative education. His wish to remove comparative education from 'the whims' of administrators represents an important assertion of the possibilities implicit in the *idea* of science – and a science of comparative education. The trouble with that proposition is that you have to have scientists – experts who know. It is no mark of disrespect to the work of a distinguished generation of scholars to point out that by the 1960s the search for a 'science' of comparative education had become frenetic and pathological. Of course, the search was driven by issues of disciplinary space and real resources in university systems that had embraced the concept of ever more exact sciences, including exact social sciences (Cowen, 1982a). But what the search for a science obscured was that 'science' itself with its promise of exactness and control over the social and material world had become an ideology. As an ideology it obscured legitimate questions about the social role of knowledge, and the social role of the scientist as expert. It muddled the technical questions with the ethical and political questions. It assumed that questions of value were resolved; all that was required was the technical skills of the expert (Burns & Welch, 1992).

Thus the promise of a science of comparative education, offering predictability, steady linearities of social and economic melioration, or even improvements in the human condition, obscured the questions of whether state educational projects are invariably benign, how the role of the scientific expert as consultant or policy adviser to governments is legitimated, the top-down model implicit in the advisor's role, and the issue of to whom 'scientific' knowledge should be distributed. For example, we are on the edge of having a substantial corpus of technical knowledge about how to construct 'effective schools'. There are prior questions: should we be constructing 'effective schools' or 'good schools'; and who should be constructing them? What are the correct distinctions to be drawn between technical and emancipatory knowledge and what should be the social role of the expert scientist? Friedman and Freire give rather different answers.

What about us today? Do we still hold to predictive social science as an appropriate, powerful, ethically correct meta-narrative – as an answer worth striving for? Is a meta-narrative currently possible in the social sciences, or in the current *kosmos*? There are a number of pessimistic answers, which are embraced with optimism on the grounds that all grand narratives are bad. I personally do not hold this position. I read the literature on postmodernism as being useful in that it raises powerful questions about ethnocentric or Eurocentric elements in the thinking of Descartes, Kant, Hegel and Marx and by extension as asking important questions about the epistemologies of science. But I read the literature on postmodernity as inviting a re-reading of the world; rather than an acceptable invitation to escape from it into the ludic or the nihilistic, the interstitial or the despairing. But certainly the literature on postmodernism and postmodernity reminds us forcibly of the possibilities of tragedy and chaos and invites us to step away from our earlier confidence about the possibilities of knowing, with certainty.

In my final theme for this paper, I would like to illustrate some of the new difficulties, imposed by *kosmos*, in constructing a comparative education, or even moments of comparative understanding. The world has changed, and perhaps our first responsibility – as we are not politicians – is to understand some of the ways in which it has changed before we suggest professionally how to act upon those changes.

Kosmos

Permit me to illustrate my general argument by concentrating on two contemporary events. The first of these is the new salience of 'rims'; the second of these is what I wish to call 'transitologies'.

Rims

Newly made visible is the idea of the Pacific Rim. Here, it is suggested, the new balance of world economic power is under contestation (Porter, 1990; Reich, 1992). China itself, but also the states of Japan, South Korea, the Republic of China (Taiwan) and what was once Hong Kong are, it is being argued, likely to rebalance the long domination by the United States of the world economy. Very practical questions follow. In what ways, for example, should France, Germany, Spain, Portugal or the UK restructure their educational systems'? How is the United States to achieve excellence in education? Is the Japanese (Taiwanese, Singaporean, South Korean) system of education creating enough 'creative' persons?

But before we, as comparative educationists, can begin to think about such issues it should be noted that comparative education is very loosely located in a theory of international relations. At the moment we seem to be making do with vapid propositions about interdependence. We lack an appropriate theory, of the nature of international relations, including educational relations, across rims – whether the Mediterranean. Baltic, Atlantic or Pacific Rim. Our epistemic tradition means that the problem has never been central to our concerns. Our frame, our deeply embedded agenda of equilibrium, of the linearities of social development. and our anxiety to build technically useful knowledge, leaves us in some difficulty in specifying what is problematic about rims.

'Rims' are nominally a geographic proposition; but, for our purposes as comparative educationists, they are a political one. Rims in this latter sense highlight the question of patterns of political, economic and cultural relations across, literally, bits of water. Our former theorising has trivialised international educational relations as piecemeal social engineering or as 'cultural borrowing'. Thinking about rims means that we cannot start from the domestic, and we cannot start from domestic disequilibria in education. With the exception of the modernisation and dependency paradigms we have no way to think about and to pull international political, and cultural relations into our frame of reference.

We need to specify,, theoretically, an inter-national context: the context of relations around a rim (and even relations between rims, as between the Atlantic and Pacific Rims). This relocates dramatically much of our classical canon of work. The Hans's factors of race, language, religions and political philosophies, or Lauwerys's 'philosophic models of man' or McLean's (1996) 'national traditions' now become subsumed within a broader conceptualisation: the inter-State and inter-national relations of the rim. But we have no way to approach those relations currently.

It is argued here that thinking about these relations takes us immediately into new categories of analysis. Central to such a new perspective in comparative education become the concepts of border, diaspora, immunology and permeology as well as the now routine theme of 'globalisation'. Permit me to illustrate.

The concept of border as it has sharpened in the 20th century takes one of its main meanings from a relation between territorial States. The idea of 'border' is often a legal statement of boundary sanctified by international law and of course breakable by invasion, or revolution and self-determination. But 'border', as it might be treated within comparative education, is a rather more interesting and flexible concept. It has both legal and cultural dimensions: legal in the sense that laws about school attendance will be in force, but cultural in that, for example, a secular or religious philosophy will establish cultural boundaries. The tension between, say, Mao's and Chiang Kai-Shek's definitions of their respective national and political agendas is an illustration. 'Border' in this sense may be marked by a deliberate effort at economic openness, but cultural closure (Law 1996). Thus from the Deng period, Taiwanese inward investment in South China is acceptable, but not Taiwan's political messages. The message of cultural closure is enforced right down to refusing direct flights for travellers between the two countries. Similarly concepts of cultural border around the Pacific Rim are marked by strenuous disagreement – based in long traditions of political thought – about definitions of human rights. The mutual incomprehensibility of such inter-national and inter-cultural disagreements potentially affects economic, and certainly ideational, relations around the rim (Cowen, 1997). It is unlikely, for example, that the Western concept of academic freedom will continue to inform university culture in Hong Kong. After all, it survived only in modified form in Singapore (Cowen, 1996b).

The concept of border also cross-relates strongly with the diaspora of peoples around rims. Diaspora around the Pacific Rim is already historically marked and contemporaneously urgent. The history of Japanese immigration produced significant minorities in, for example, São Paulo, Brasil and on the West Coast of America before the Second World War. Reverse diaspora (for example, of persons of Japanese descent in Brasil returning to Japan) has compounded the relatively recent problem of 'returnees' in Japan and has created, along with older minorities and new immigrants from other Asian countries, something like a 'multicultural problem' in Japan.

This is not the same problem as the classical problem of the absorption of immigrants through the educational system so visible in American educational history. The issue has changed from one of assimilation of permanent immigrants to one of ever-shifting diasporas, as barriers to the freer movement of capital *and* labour alter. The experience of families of 'returnees' of high socio-economic status in Japan is different from the absorption and Americanisation of the "huddled masses" of the 19th century.

It is a different problem for both education policy and comparative theory. Thus a theory of rims (or, for that matter, regions) is forced to address the new complexities of contemporary diasporas. Contemporary migrants, the people who construct diaspora are – in a completely non-pejorative sense – 'pollutants' and 'translators'. That is, they introduce into their new societies their transported visions of a good society, appropriate knowledge and their own versions of what it is to be well educated. They also can interpret at least two societies in their daily lives – in this sense they are very important as social translators. However, in crossing borders and in being part of a diaspora, they raise a new theoretical problem for comparative education, to which their existential experience is only a small part of a solution.

The theoretical problem which participants in a diaspora raise takes magnification in structural and cultural *immunologies* and *perineologies*. What will be filtered in; and what will be filtered out? We have no theory of this, despite a professional canon which includes 'cultural borrowing'. We have examples of extreme immunology: Taiwan and the PRC, Greece and Turkey around the Mediterranean Rim, the 'Iron Curtain' itself.

But we have no understanding which is more delicate than these extreme examples of immunologies, based on explicit political conflict.

Yet we are acting, at the level of educational policy, as if immunologies and permeologies were epiphenomenal. The Australian effort, for example, at marketing higher education to Asian students is running into the immunological obstacles of curriculum content, pedagogic practice and evaluation styles which differ in school and university systems. These problems, in Australia and in the UK, are now attraching emergency remedial discussion - which is having difficulty in getting above the practical issues of accommodation, languages, and rapidly created statements about institutional ethics and finance (OECD, 1996).

Comparative educationists did little to anticipate the generic problem. I am suggesting, of course, that we could not. Our comparative education was organised around equilibrium thinking, piecemeal adjustments to educational practice in democratic societies and positivist assumptions about the possibility of having a 'science' of comparative education in a stable economic and political universe. Our comparative education was domestic, oriented to nations treated as cultural boxes and not to understanding an unstable international universe of rim relations, diaspora, collapsing economic and cultural borders and the complex international relations involved therein. For those issues dependency theory – our best approximation – is of surprisingly little use.

More briefly, I would like to sketch a second illustration of the instabilities we are, as a professional group, not quite ready to address. For these instabilities I use the term 'transitologies'.

Transitologies

Transitologies will be treated more briefly than rims: the exemplars are clearer, the concept was discussed in the paper 'Last past the post' (Cowen, 1996a) and I am currently developing the concept for the *World Yearbook of Education* for the year 2000, though no doubt the concept will go through considerable revisions, not least with and by my editorial colleagues David Coulby and Crispin Jones.

The exemplars are straightforward, the former Czechoslovakia, Hungary, Poland, Latvia, the Ukraine, Russia itself now; and contemporary South Africa and Iran. There is the merging of East and West Germany. At the time of writing Algeria and North Korea may well be transitologies about to happen.

Conceptually 'transitologies' can be defined as the more or less simultaneous collapse and reconstruction of (i) state apparatuses (ii) economic and social stratification systems and (iii) the central value system, especially the political value system to offer a new definition of the future. Crucially, I define transitologies as occurring in a short time span; operationally say 10 years. Thus Cuba was a transitology (and a revolution). China was a revolution but not a transitology. as it took from 1911 to 1949 to work out its future. Transitologies may thus be revolutions; but not all revolutions are transitologies. Transitologies do not always involve the violent overthrow of the State, nor are they based on movements of mass mobilisation especially on a class basis as in the French, Russian and Chinese revolutions. (Skocpol, 1979).

Transitologies are, however, major social turbulences. My simplest question is what are their rules – that is, what are the rules of their chaos, what are the patternings of educational variation that we may expect? I suggest that we do not know – and more importantly there is little in our previous canon of work, except that on socialist revolutions, which permits us to create approaches of any subtlety. We can, of course describe: we can describe aims, school structures, curriculum, finance and administration patterns, vocational technical provision and so on. In other words, we can use taxonomies of the sort useful to the International Bureau of Education (IBE) (Cowen 1982b). But this does not get us much further forward. For example, what are the immunologics and permeologies of the new Hungary? Hungary manifestly has changed its international 'filters'. Curriculum theory now owes as much to the thinking of Dewey as to Krupskaya. Language as a cultural marker has altered, in the preferences of both the State and 'consumers', from Russian to English and German (Ministry of Culture and Education, 1996). These are new permeologies and are to be understood not merely through the domestic educational politics of Hungary but by its absorption into a late modern world which has mobile capital, increasingly mobile labour, weaker principles of political immunology in Central and Eastern Europe, and new educational expressions of purity and pollution. But we lack the conceptual apparatus – even of categories of educational description – to compare the South African and the Hungarian transitology in the same academic paper. except at the mundane level of the IBE taxonomy.

Until we can, we are hardly ready to give policy advice – except perhaps as advocates, e.g. of a peaceful world or a United Europe. But that is to escape, not to embrace, our professional responsibilities.

Conclusion

The classical professional problem of an interpretative comparative education has always been, at least since Sadler, how to understand educational patterns through forces and factors outside the educational system. All the major comparative educationists have addressed this problematique. A partial statement of such relationships was attempted and illustrated by Hans, for example. Comparative education begins, not with the description of foreign educational systems, but with a tentative theory and illustrations of the dynamic between, the patterns of societies and the patterns of educational systems. Inserting a foreign educational practice (e.g. Taiwanese whole-class teaching) into these patterns is a recipe for an expensive disaster, without a clear theory of the immunologies and permeologies of social and educational patterns. However, our own equilibrium theories, our professional assumptions about the linearity of social development and the more simplistic versions of our positivism have left us singularly unprepared to tackle the new turbulences of the late modern world of which, I have suggested, transitologies and rims are illustrative.

The point is of importance for two reasons. We clearly need to address what I think of as the theoretically challenging educational themes of late modernity – positional knowledges, performativity, diaspora and border, cultural identity, immunologics and permeologies – from a fresh set of assumptions about the significance of international political and economic relations. From time to time, we shall experience moments of chaos – in both *episteme* and *kosmos*. Can we do better than merely take photographs – or write *haiku* – of these moments of metamorphosis?

The second reason is equally pressing. The positivist project of comparative education is now seriously trivialised. We now know (as countries) where we stand on international tests of educational achievement. Policy makers wish to climb up that international ladder. Is the contemporary comparative project – positivistically construed – merely reduced to working out how to do that'? To create schools of greater and greater effectiveness and universities of greater and greater 'performativity' (Cowen, 1996b)?

I hope not. Such a project takes the world of the policy makers and governments too much for granted. Such a project may indeed address the formal Sadlerian question: how far can we learn anything of practical value from the study of foreign educational systems? But such a project leaves Sadler's other question about the forces outside of education systems seriously under-explored and leaves us with the current fashionability of educational 'solutions' tom from cultural context. Cargo cult solutions to educational problems are a violation of a long epistemological tradition of comparative scholarship. However, rather urgently, that tradition needs revitalisation under the conditions of late modernity, to include a theory of chaos, and a more sophisticated treatment of' the 'impalpable' forces and factors outside of school which affect educational patterns. Above all this means more theorisation, not less, aimed at thinking through and thinking afresh about the international and domestic relationships of late modernity and educational processes.

The alternative is the snake-oil salesman. Let us change that to 'snake-oil salesperson'. The change is more correct, politically, but the change remains cosmetic and slick: rather like advocacy comparative education.

References

Altbach, P.G. & Kelly, G.P. (Eds) (1978) *Education and Colonialism.* London: Longman.

Anderson, A. & Bowman, M.J. (Eds) (1966) *Education and Economic Development.* London: Frank Cass.

Bereday, G.Z.F. (1966) *Comparative Method in Education.* New York: Holt, Rinehart & Winston.

Burns, R.J. & Welch, A.R. (1992) Introduction, in R.J. Burns & A.R. Welch (Eds) *Contemporary Perspectives in Comparative Education.* New York: Garland Publishing.

Callaghan, R.E. (1962) *Education and the Cult of Efficiency: a study of the social forces that have shaped the administration of the public schools.* Chicago: University of Chicago Press.

Carnoy, M. (1974) *Education as Cultural Imperialism: a critical appraisal.* New York: David McKay.

Carnoy, M. & Samoff, J. with Burns, M.A., Johnstone, A. & Torres, C.A. (1990) *Education and Social Transition in the Third World.* Princeton: Princeton University Press.

Cowen, R. (1973) A query concerning developments within and the responsibilities of comparative education, *Canadian and International Education*, 1(2), pp. 15-29.

Cowen, R. (1982a) The place of comparative education in the educational sciences, in L. Cavicchi-Brouquet & P. Furter (Eds) *Les Sciences de l'Education. perspectives et Bilans Européens.* Geneva: CESE.

Cowen, R. (1982b) *International Yearbook of Education*, Vol. XXXIV. Paris: Unesco.

Cowen, R. (1996a) Last past the post: comparative education, modernity and perhaps post-modernity, *Comparative Education*, 32, pp. 151-170.

Cowen, R. (1996b) Performativity: postmodernity and the university, *Comparative Education*, 32, pp. 245-258.

Cowen, R. (1997) Intercultural education and the Pacific Rim, in D. Coulby, J. Gundera & C. Jones (Eds) *Intercultural Education: world yearbook of education, 1997.* London: Kogan Page.

Cowen, R. (1997) Comparative perspectives on the British PhD, in N. Graves & V. Varma (Eds) *Working for a Doctorate: a guide for the humanities and social sciences.* London: Routledge.

Eckstein, T. & Noah, H. (Eds) (1969) *Scientific Investigations in Comparative Education.* London: Collier-Macmillan.

Hans, N. (1958) *Comparative Education: a study of educational factors and traditions.* London: Routledge & Kegan Paul.

Holmes, B. (1965) *Problems in Education: a comparative approach.* London: Routledge & Kegan Paul.

Holmes, B. (1986) Paradigm shifts in comparative education, in P.G. Altbach & G.P. Kelly (Eds) *New Approaches to Comparative Education.* Chicago: University of Chicago Press.

Inkeles, A. & Smith, D.H. (1974) *Becoming Modern.* London: Heinemann Education Books.

King, E.J. (1968) *Comparative Studies and Educational Decision.* London: Methuen.

King, E.J. (1979) *Other Schools and Ours: comparative studies for today,* 4th edn. London: Holt, Rinehart & Winston.

Lauwerys, J. (1965) Opening Address, in *General Education in a Changing World. Proceedings of the Comparative Education Society in Europe.* Berlin: CESE.

Law, W. (1996) Fortress state, cultural continuities and economic change: higher education in mainland China and Taiwan, *Comparative Education*, 32, pp. 377-393.

Mallinson, V. (1975) *An Introduction to the Study of Comparative Education.* London: Heinemann.

McClelland, D.C. (1961) *The Achieving Society.* New York: The Free Press.

McLean, M. (1996) *Educational Traditions Compared: content, teaching and learning in industrialised countries.* London: David Fulton.

Ministry of Culture & Education Hungary (1996) *National Core Curriculum.* Ministry of Culture and Education.

OECD Documents (CERI) (1996) *Internationalisation of Higher Education.* Paris: OECD.

Porter, M. (1990) *The Competitive Advantage of Nations.* London: Macmillan.

Noah, H. & Eckstein, H. (1969) *Toward a Science of Comparative Education.* New York: Macmillan.

Reich, R.B. (1992) *The Work of Nations: preparing ourselves for 21st century capitalism.* New York: Vintage Books.

Skocpol, T. (1979) *States and Social Revolutions: a comparative analysis of France, Russia and China.* Cambridge: Cambridge University Press.

Resilience, Resistance and Responsiveness: comparative and international education at United Kingdom universities

MICHELE SCHWEISFURTH

Introduction and Perspectives

Being Canadian gives one a natural affinity for comparative and international [1] education. Like Canada, the field of comparative and international education is pluralistic, with a multiplicity of viewpoints and approaches within it. As in Canada, this diversity is essential to identity; yet the marriage of academic cultures, like the union of national cultures, is not always as tolerant, supportive and harmonious as the idealists would have us believe. In fact, it sometimes feels as though only the slimmest of majorities keeps dissolution and chaos at bay. Visitors to Canada are often surprised by the amount of media coverage and general attention paid to the question of what it means to be Canadian; similarly, conference 'state of the field' speeches, and a long history of articles in comparative education journals, signal comparativists' preoccupation with the nature of their own subject. In the cross-referenced subject index for the *Comparative Education Review*, there are far more articles listed as being on the very theme of comparative and international education than on any other topic. As Canadians, we tend to define ourselves by what we are not: in our case, of course, we are not American. Comparativists seem on the defensive in the same way: we are not ethnocentric, not parochial, not naive borrowers. There is also a touch of the same self-effacing pride that manifests itself as patriotism among Canadians and as academic camp-guarding by comparativists. The reticent and apologetic Canadian backpacker with an enormous red-and-white Maple Leaf conspicuously displayed has some essential commonality with the doom-saying academic who laments the inevitability of the decline of comparative and international education as a discipline and our lack of influence in the wider debate on education while flying the flag of globalism in a Comparative and International Education Society conference t-shirt.

In the tradition of state of the field addresses and articles, the aim of the study at hand has been to conduct an initial survey into the institutional base of comparative and international education at universities in the United Kingdom (UK). The project was based at the Centre for Comparative Studies in Education, University of Oxford, and funded by the Standing Conference for Studies in Education. The initial stages of the survey involved procuring prospectuses from all institutions offering courses in education, and trawling through this information to determine wide trends in comparative and/or international education courses. A summary of the results of this review is contained in the next section. From this exercise, four institutions which appeared to be loci of comparative endeavour of varying representative kinds were chosen as examples of how institutions are responding to the current academic, political and financial climate. The information was obtained by examining course documents and interviewing key members of the departments in question. Note that the choice of these particular universities (Bristol, London, Oxford, and Warwick) is not meant to imply their pre-eminence in the field; it was felt, however, that in their varying responses to the question of how best to meet the demand for comparative and international education at an academic institution they represented a range of possibilities. In the light of the findings concerning the field as a whole in the UK and the more in-depth look at four institutions, combined with interviews with other leading figures in the field, an attempt will be made to explicate current trends. The most glaring of these is seemingly a paradox: on the one hand, taught courses in comparative and international education are believed to be on the decline; on the other hand, there definitely appears to be an increase in interest and activity in the international dimension of educational studies, and this is evidently a buoyant trend. How might this anomaly be explained?

General Developments: an overview from the prospectuses

In striving to gain a 'snapshot' perspective on current academic activity in the field of comparative and international education, information was solicited from institutions throughout the UK. The data gained are, of course, limited to the particular year of the prospectuses (1995-1996), and cannot reveal changes over time, or the degree of commitment to comparison and internationalism in education. Also not apparent is the level of activity in other departments, which may be bases for research within the field.

Ninety-one universities or colleges of higher education in the UK [2] sent prospectuses or further information about course offerings; most of these had little or no discernible international or comparative study or activity. Several trends emerged from an examination of the remaining prospectuses. While comparative and international education as a purely academic course is becoming almost non-existent, fragments of the content and methodology of the field continue to permeate other education department programmes at several institutions. These relevant courses or course components may be categorised into three types, which often overlap: those which are modular in nature, with some comparative or international content; those which have an education in developing countries focus; and those courses which have a more narrow, often professionally-oriented approach.

In some cases, there are compulsory or optional modules in comparative education, international education, or a combination of the two, as part of a varied 'menu' of components which may be put together to create an individualised programme of study leading to a qualification. This modular format has become popular in many fields because of the flexibility it offers students to combine their own interests and professional aspirations in a less rigidly structured course. The University of Wolverhampton and the Roehampton Institute, London, for example, include optional modules in Comparative Education in their undergraduate Education Studies courses, and the University of East Anglia has a module in World Issues in Education as part of their International Bachelor of Education degree. Examples of modules from Advanced or Masters level programmes include: Comparative Education at Queen's University, Belfast, and the Universities of Dundee and Leeds; The European Dimension in Education Management at Sheffield Hallam; Education in an International Context and Issues in International Primary Education at Bath, and Systematic Studies in Comparative Education at Hull. This modular approach obscures somewhat the extent of a given programme's international focus; only a small portion of participants may choose the module, or if there are insufficient numbers, it may not be offered at all.

Many degree-bearing courses in the field of international education focus on some aspect of education in developing countries. This has long been an important branch of study, but with the decline of comparative and international education as a "self-conscious academic specialisation" (Altbach & Kelly, 1986), it has gained in relative importance. The graduate courses appear under a variety of titles, for example: MEds in Education and Development at Bristol, and MAs at the London Institute; and Education, Curriculum Evaluation, Planning and Management in the Context of National Development, and Teacher

Education in the Context of National Development at the University of Sussex. Several institutions also offer modules focusing on education and development issues, such as Education for Developing Countries at the University of Reading, Education in Developing Countries at Hull, Training and Development and Adult Education and Literacy for Rural Development at Manchester, and Post-Compulsory Education and Developing Societies at Surrey.

At other institutions, more specialised courses are offered within the general field of comparative and international education; many of these courses lead to a practical qualification, often for students from overseas, or home students hoping to work abroad. Bolton Institute's MEd in Comparative Technical and Vocational Education, Sunderland's MA in International Vocational Education and Training, Reading's Diploma of Literacy in Development, Exeter's BPhil and MEd in International Teacher Education, Oxford Brookes's MA in Education for International School Teachers, and Warwick's MA in International and Comparative Studies in Continuing Education stand as examples of these narrower and more professionally-oriented programmes.

Another apparent trend in International Education has been the establishment of centres within universities. Several institutions have centres which cater to the needs of education students from overseas, or which conduct research into international education, whether or not the subject is taught. There are many examples: the International Centre for Education in Development at the University of Warwick; the Centre for International Studies in Education at Newcastle; the International Unit in the School of Education at Birmingham; the Centre for International Studies in Education, Management and Training at Reading; the Centre for Comparative Studies in Education at Oxford; the International Centre for Research on Assessment (and a number of other centres) at the University of London Institute of Education; the Centre for International Studies at the University of Bristol, and the Centre for International Education at Moray House of Heriot-Watt University.

Finally, many of the prospectuses do not indicate particular comparative or international programmes or components, but the descriptions of the courses are suffused with references to European or international ideals, and to the important place of the perspectives of foreign students. Other courses are described as being specifically for Education students from overseas, but it is not made clear in what ways they differ from the version catering to home students. To what extent this 'rhetoric of internationalism' is reflected in course delivery and content, and to what extent it is a public relations measure, is difficult to say.

Trends in Institution-based Comparative and International Education: patterns from Bristol, London, Oxford and Warwick

Four institutions were chosen as cases to be examined in terms of their provision of courses in comparative and international education and in terms of activities in the comparative sphere. At each university, interviews were conducted with the main people involved, and documentary evidence was examined. The approaches to comparativism in the institutions varied widely on a number of fronts, such as the extent to which the subject was offered as a traditional academic course or as a quasi-vocational professional option, and the degree to which the facets of comparative and international education were integrated into a wider programme of educational studies. The structure of the courses varied, as well as the content, with modularisation being the format in most cases. Beyond the courses offered, the nature of interests and operations in the field was manifested in a number of different ways in the different institutions: the establishment of centres, the undertaking of comparative research and international consultancies, and collaboration with European and other partners. Here these patterns will be demonstrated, and possible explanations for their existence will be posited.

The first noticeable trend has been the decline in discrete academic courses of study, and the virtual disappearance of comparative education as a component of pre-service teacher education or undergraduate offering. None of the four institutions include comparative or international education as part of the regular teacher-training programme, while it used to be an option at some. There are two full courses (exceptional, based on the prospectuses), and only a handful of unit components of other courses, which are devoted to comparative and international education. Among the case studies explored here, lecturers at Bristol pointed to a decline in the quantity of explicitly comparative units on offer as part of the Education and Development course. However, the remaining module, Comparative and International Research in Education, has two lives: one as a core module for the MEd programme in Education and Development, and one as an option among the units in Research Methods. Interestingly, external assessors have advocated the inclusion of a comparative education module for all overseas students at the School at Bristol. At London, the number of course participants on the Comparative Education MA declined about a decade ago, but has been stable since, yet there are ongoing fears for the chances of maintaining the general academic focus of the course in the face of pressures from within the institution. What Angela Little calls the "*implicitly* comparative" MA courses in Education and Development continue to be popular. At Warwick, the comparative course in Adult and Continuing Education is a growth area, but in terms of other course offerings, there is a general decline. However, a comparative unit focusing on development issues will be compulsory for a group of Malaysian students starting in 1998. The successful establishment of an academic course in Comparative and International Education at Oxford is anomalous, but not difficult to explain; the nature of the institution gives it a "natural advantage" in terms of attracting students from all over the world seeking an academic course and a prestigious degree. Demand is ever increasing.

To what might this general – but apparently not as dramatic as some have reported – decline be attributed? I would suggest three possible explanations, linked to wider patterns in higher education and its context. First, there is the decline in academic discipline courses generally within education faculties, made acute by the current government's attitude to the nature of teaching, as evidenced by recent moves to create a national curriculum for the training of teachers. As teachers are viewed less and less as professionals, their training is viewed more and more as an apprenticeship of sorts, and encouraging active academic engagement with the larger questions of the nature of teaching and learning becomes superfluous (if not dangerous). Secondly, the recession has created an employment market where job-searching is a difficult task for which one needs to be armed with as many advantages as possible, and on the whole employers see courses with a direct bearing on the job to be done as being of greater relevance than more general, academic courses (although there are naturally exceptions to this generalisation). The market for purely academic qualifications is therefore reduced. Market is a key word, leading to the third contributing factor: the growth of managerialism within educational institutions, combined with the constraints dictated by funding cutbacks, means that courses not likely to be easily marketed and filled will not be maintained through meagre times.

The second trend which is apparent is linked to the one above: faculties of education and course tutors are being highly responsive to the demands of students and sponsors, and the result has produced two important changes to the majority of courses in comparative and international education. The first is structural: many courses (not only those in comparative and international education) are now modular, and integrated with a wider scope of related units, allowing students greater freedom of choice and flexibility, and more ready transferability to other institutions. The courses at London and Bristol are typical of this pattern. The second is in the general nature of the course and its content: there is a trend towards vocationalisation and specialisation. Many of the comparative courses, such as the International and Comparative Studies in Continuing Education at Warwick, and most of the international education courses focusing on developing countries, such as the MA degrees on offer at London and the MEds at Bristol, are quasi-professional in nature, or are virtually a professional qualification. This is certainly not to say that they are not intellectually challenging, nor that they lack theoretical foundations; however, some of the organisers have found themselves under pressure to sacrifice these to greater instrumentality, and striking the right balance is an ongoing concern.

These phenomena parallel the decline of the academic courses, and have related root causes. Here too, the beliefs held by the government and employers, and, importantly, sponsors of overseas students, that a tailored professional course will be the best job preparation, have a large impact on what is on offer. In times of austerity, it seems that the more obviously related a qualification is to the niche it is targeting, the more likely it is to be subscribed, as it is perceived to offer a measure of security in its more concrete outcomes. The financially-driven need to attract large numbers of overseas students makes meeting their requests and especially those of their sponsors a vital part of the decision-making process in designing, marketing, and delivering courses.

A problem arises, of course, when more than one niche needs to be filled by the provision of a course, and the needs of participants may conflict. Courses are typically filled with mainly overseas full-time and UK part-time students, who have different needs in terms of course content and structure. It is a challenge to balance these needs, but on the whole the needs of full-time overseas students may be put foremost, with the demands of their sponsors rightly given high priority, and, at the risk of sounding cynical, the higher fees they pay are a likely motivating factor.

What are the repercussions of these structural changes, and of this shift away from an academic focus towards a greater emphasis on the professional? Modularisation has its advantages to students, which have already been stated: it allows students to tailor-make a programme based on their own interests. On the other hand, it reduces the organised focus of the programme as a whole, and reduces the common identity of the course members: factors which may contribute to a dilution of an individual's holistic feeling for and commitment to a field. Regarding the decline of the academic focus: on the positive side, it may have helped to end the 'baronial approach'; what Edmund King refers to as 'the treachery of the cleric': "... we have been too 'priestly' and other-worldly by far" (King, 1989, p. 375). While the approaches of 'the great comparativists' still figure on most comparative education courses, they are of less importance on the whole than issue-driven topics, and with the decline of the focus on these key figures, perhaps there will be a coinciding decline in the methodological (and at times personal) in-fighting that has plagued the field, and greater tolerance (but hopefully not at the expense of rigour) will prevail. There are potential pitfalls to this shift in emphasis, however. Several interviewees expressed concern at the potential for superficiality that arises from the loss of theoretical underpinnings that may accompany a steering away from a purer academic approach. As Patricia Broadfoot noted, the field needs to continue to be, or to become to a greater extent, grounded in social science theory if it is to be taken seriously, and to develop its own theoretical foundations. An emphasis on current issues also poses the danger of embedding the course participants' thinking too firmly in the present and too explicitly in a given context, reducing their flexibility to adapt to the rapid changes which have become an inevitable part of our world. Among others, Robert Cowen expressed his concern at the tendency to dwell on prescriptive and superficial solutions to complex problems:

> *Those ways in which you can form views on how to think*
> *about education are being replaced with issues of how to: how*
> *to create effective schools, how to manage schools effectively,*
> *how to run evaluation and assessment schemes ... We're going*
> *to get ... technicians emerging who will run 'effective' schools*
> *and run 'good' assessment programmes but they will be*
> *'flimsy' effective schools and 'flimsy' assessment programmes*
> *because they are uninformed by sociological and*
> *philosophical and cross-cultural principles.*

The solution seems to lie in a carefully thought-out and monitored balance that allows the benefits of both the academic and instrumental approaches to be experienced by the participants, or in stating clearly (as in the case of the Oxford course, which the course outline states explicitly to be academic) exactly what the focus will be so that only students seeking and understanding the chosen emphasis will participate.

A third, and universally acknowledged trend is the general growth in activity in the comparative and international education domain both within and outside of higher education institutions, despite the decline in taught courses. This growth is manifested on a number of fronts: within universities, the growing numbers of centres established; the increasing numbers of educational researchers pursuing comparative studies, many of them from outside of the field of comparative education; and subject growth areas in policy studies, school effectiveness, and cross-national studies of standards of achievement. Outside universities, government and media interest in the latter two areas especially has led to the commissioning of a number of important studies not necessarily based at academic institutions.

All four of the universities investigated for this study have centres which provide a unified focus for the international endeavours of the members: endeavours which, in addition to teaching, include consultancies, funded research projects, seminars, publications, visiting fellowships, collaborative research with overseas partners, links with overseas institutions, and a 'home base' for international students. London, in fact, has several internationally-focused centres, each specialising in a specific aspect of education (such as the International School Effectiveness Centre) or a particular geographical area (such as the Research on Education in South Africa Programme). At Warwick, there are the International Centre for Education in Development at the Adult and Continuing Education department, and, at the Institute of Education, the new (since 1996) Centre for Research in Elementary and Primary Education, which "from its inception ... has given high priority to international collaboration and to remedying the relative neglect of primary education as a field for comparative research" (Alexander, 1996). Oxford has the University of Oxford Centre for Comparative Studies in Education, and Bristol's School of Education houses the Centre for International Studies in Education; both are well-established. The significance of such centres to the field has been noted elsewhere:

> *... the subject (comparative and international education) has been developing in a new, and often practical, way by scholars from different academic backgrounds who have an interest in international education, usually related to education in developing countries and whose institutions have developed 'International Centres' or 'Overseas Education Units', partly to capitalise on income generation from overseas students and partly to attract project funding and consultancies ... The development of such 'centres' is one of the most interesting features of institutional development in the UK during the 1980s. (Watson & King, 1991, p. 12)*

Existing centres, not necessarily devoted exclusively to international activities, are very likely to have an international dimension to their repertoire and to be open to the possibility of research overseas; this openness is often reflected in the literature on the centre or in the centre's name (as in the case of the Centre for Research in Elementary and Primary Education at Warwick, which additionally employs the term 'elementary' to avoid the exclusivity of the more UK-based 'primary'). In any case, in addition to the work being done and the images fostered, as Professor Alexander points out: "initiatives apart, it's a state of mind".

Centres from different universities are also seeking to link up in order to strengthen the field and their own interests in it. A significant, and potentially very influential, example of this is the Economic and Social Research Council (ESRC) sponsored seminar series entitled Learning from Comparing: the uses and abuses of comparative education research, whose outcomes form the basis of this book, which is being run collaboratively by comparativists at centres at the Universities of Bristol, Oxford and Warwick. The series aims to provide a forum for discussion among academics and user groups involved in comparative education, attempting to bridge some of the gaps between them, and to open up new areas for exploration as well as revisiting traditional ones.

The increasing numbers of researchers involved in cross-national studies, especially in applied research, can be attributed in part to economics. The growing importance of regional bodies (especially the EU) has led to increased opportunities for receiving funding for research beyond national boundaries, and when research grants are hard to come by, as they currently are, academics are quick to put their hands to whatever possibilities arise, regardless of whether or not they have previous international experience or training in comparative methodology. But significantly, there are other, less purely pragmatic, reasons for expanding into the international and comparative domain from a home-country focus. The growth of comparative education "beyond the traditional boundaries", the "growing globalisation of education discourse" and the limitations of "coming up time and time again against the brick wall of parochialism" have inspired Robin Alexander, perhaps best known up to now for his involvement in primary education in this country, to undertake a five-country comparative study of pedagogy.

The government and media interest in the educational practices of other countries has led to strong growth areas in policy studies, school effectiveness, and the analysis of educational standards. Unfortunately, the government's own agenda for reform, the media's oversimplification of the comparisons, and the hegemony of a new set of 'clerics', the school effectiveness researchers who use quantitative input/output models, has led to a mood of impotence among academic comparativists, whose independent voices are not heard in the throng demanding Japanese or Taiwanese teaching styles in English classrooms.

This could prove to be the greatest challenge to those who call themselves comparative and international education academics at UK institutions. In their recent OFSTED review outlining the rationale for cross-national school effectiveness studies, David Reynolds and Shaun Farrell were vehemently critical of the contribution of the field; in a surprisingly harsh (and largely unfair) attack, they lament:

> ... *the presence of a large body of theories, without any apparent empirical backing ... a large range of descriptive case studies of individual schools which it is impossible to synchronise together because there are no common measures of outcomes or processes utilised ... descriptions of the range of educational, political, economic and cultural phenomena within different countries, with no attempt ever made to*

*assess the contribution of the educational system as against
that of other factors. (Reynolds & Farrell, 1996)*

If comparativists want to participate fully in this important national debate, in order to contribute a necessary voice of caution, subtlety and contextualisation, means will need to be found to raise the profile of the field and to enter into serious dialogue with this 'new wave' of comparative researchers. This might perhaps be accomplished at the institutional level and could be facilitated through cross-institutional co-operation, and there is evidence of the beginnings of such initiatives.

But this would hopefully not be at the expense of other domains of enquiry. As Robert Cowen recently put it:

... it is of major importance that academic comparative education re-reads the kosmos *and broadens its research agenda and recaptures its concern with culturalist analyses, with the historical dimensions in its tradition, and with an emancipatory critique of policy (Burns and Welch, 1992) and not merely with policy advice. The state, even the Western liberal state, is part of the problem, and not necessarily part of its 'solution'. (Cowen, 1996, p. 166)*

Finally, it would be misleading to extricate the above patterns from the variety of courses, activities and approaches to comparative and international education at UK universities without pointing out the diversity that remains. As Erwin Epstein has pointed out, and as has been confirmed by every person interviewed for this study: "Comparative education has not evolved as a unitary field but as a loose unity of separate though thriving currents" (Epstein, 1983, p. 28). In addition to the wide range of differing emphases and methods that have always been part of the field, new avenues are being pursued. Some examples include Michael Crossley and Graham Vulliamy's work on qualitative methodology in comparative education, Mark Bray and R. Murray Thomas's examination of the units of comparison and questioning of the focus on national boundaries, and Robin Alexander's mixing of diverse methodology in investigating the frequently overlooked micro-level of classrooms across cultures. The begged question is whether this diversity is healthy or destructive, and opinions vary widely on this issue. Edmund King has always believed it to be a positive attribute of the field, and feels that comparative education is today in its heyday. Less convinced commentators have lamented the 'electric fence' that some groups within the field, especially the more traditional comparativists, have erected around their own academic camp. The factionalism that was a powerful force within comparative and international education in the UK a generation ago is not dead enough, despite the new forces that are creating current patterns in the field. At its worst it could stand in the way of opportunities for extending influence.

Conclusions

The changes to the institutional base of comparative and international education in the UK as uncovered by this study largely back up previous findings regarding the state of the field. There has been a general decline in academic taught courses (with a couple of notable exceptions) and those courses which remain, almost exclusively at the MA degree level, are on the whole adopting a more professionally-oriented approach and are more likely to be modular in structure and integrated with a wider selection of education course offerings. These adjustments are in response to the demands of students, sponsors, employers and institutional management, which are in turn fuelled by the current economic crisis and the growing importance of managerial approaches and generally negative attitudes to the traditional academic disciplines within educational studies. It is important to note again, though, that this decline is not universally perceived to the same degree, and in any case is not true elsewhere in the world. There is also some evidence – such as the ESRC seminar series, revivals at institutions such as Oxford, and hopes of establishing courses at Warwick and elsewhere – that a more optimistic mood may be slowly surfacing in this country as well.

This general decline in the supply of academic taught courses is contemporaneous with an increase in activities in the international sphere, both within and outside of institutions. This interest may be explained in a number of ways: on the one hand, the force of globalisation makes it an imperative, and the increasing importance of regional and multi-national bodies provides more opportunities for more people to participate. At the same time, the government's interest in the educational policies and practices of other nations (however sincere and well-founded such interest may or may not be) has vitalised work in cross national policy studies, school effectiveness and comparisons of standards. Unfortunately, the bulk of people who would consider themselves serious comparativists, including most institution-based academics, remain effectively alienated from this much-publicised debate, and much of it remains shallow and lopsided, if not naive, without the balancing effect of independent voices of experience.

It is a bit like being Canadian, really. To stretch an analogy, and at the risk of propagating national stereotypes, people tend to think that Canadians are generally fairly liberal and global-thinking in a vague kind of way, and pretty nice too. However, with the exception of a few Spanish and Cornish fishermen and other special-interest groups, no-one really pays very much attention to us and we are given little credit for speaking independently of the louder and more influential voices around us, and we are best known for fighting among ourselves. The potential exists for comparative and international educationists at UK institutions to avoid this pitfall, and create a renaissance in the field, by making ourselves heard at this critical juncture when interest is at an all-time high and the need for the collective expertise of the field is so glaringly apparent.

Acknowledgements

This project was funded by the Standing Conference for Studies in Education through the University of Oxford Centre for Comparative Studies in Education. Thanks to David Phillips for guiding the research and this report. Thanks also to all those who were interviewed at their institutions or at the Comparative and International Education Society (CIES) conference, and who commented on early drafts: Robin Alexander, Mark Bray, Patricia Broadfoot, Robert Cowen, Michael Crossley, Edmund King, Angela Little, Martin McLean, David Phillips, Rosemary Preston, and Margaret Sutherland.

Notes

[1] The lower case has been used throughout for comparative and international education, except in reference to titles, in order to avoid awkward distinctions between officially and nominally comparative or international studies.

[2] It is important to bear in mind that the trends outlined in this section, and throughout the report, reflect only the status of the field in UK institutions. The situation is believed to be similar in much of North America and Europe, but there are other growth areas, notably in the Asian nations of the Pacific Rim. In addition, the information in this section may be out of date by the time of publication, and it is intended to illustrate the range of activities rather than to provide accurate course details about the institutions involved.

References

Alexander, R.J. (1996) *Other Primary Schools and Ours: hazards of international comparison.* Warwick: University of Warwick, Centre for Research in Elementary and Primary Education.

Altbach, Philip G. & Kelly, Gail P. (Eds) (1986) *New Approaches to Comparative Education.* Chicago: University of Chicago Press.

Altbach, Philip G. (1991) Trends in comparative education, *Comparative Education Review*, 135, pp. 491-507.

Altbach, Philip G. & Tan, Eng Thye Jason (1995) *Programs and Centers in Comparative and International Education: a global inventory.* Buffalo: State University of New York.

Bray, Mark & Thomas, R. Murray (1995) Levels of comparison in educational studies: different insights from different literatures and the value of multilevel analyses, *Harvard Educational Review*, 65, pp. 472-489.

Cowen, Robert (1996) Comparative education, modernity and perhaps post-modernity, *Comparative Education*, 32, pp. 151-170.

Crossley, Michael & Broadfoot, Patricia (1992) Comparative and international research in education: scope, problems and potential, *British Educational Research Journal*, 18, pp. 99-112.

Crossley, Michael & Vulliamy, Graham (1984) Case-study research methods and comparative education, *Comparative Education*, 20, pp. 193-207,

Dyer, Caroline & King, Kenneth (1993) *The British Resource in International Training and Education: an inventory.* Edinburgh: University of Edinburgh.

Epstein, Erwin H. (1983) Currents Left and Right: ideology in comparative education, *Comparative Education Review*, 127, pp. 3-29.

Halls, W.D. (Ed.) (1990) *Comparative Education: contemporary issues and trends.* London: UNESCO/Jessica Kingsley Publishers.

King, Edmund (1989) Comparative investigation of education: an evolutionary process, *Prospects*, 19, pp. 369-379.

Reynolds, David & Farrell, Shaun (1996) *Worlds Apart? A Review of International Surveys of Educational Achievement Involving England.* London: OFSTED.

Schweisfurth, Michele (1996) *International Research into Primary Schooling: sources, approaches and cautions.* Warwick: University of Warwick, Centre for Research in Elementary and Primary Education.

Sutherland, Margaret (1996) Rising and falling: comparative Education teaching and research in Scotland, *Proccedings of the Scottish Educational Research Association [SERA] Annual Conference*, pp. 193-197. Edinburgh: SERA.

Watson, Keith & King, Kenneth (1990) Comparative and international education studies in the United Kingdom: an analysis, *Comparative and International Education Society Newsletter*, pp. 12-13.

Postscript

JULIA BETTS & STEPHANIE WILDE

This postscript summarises the comments made by respondents to the original conference papers, which form the basis of this part of the book, and highlights some of the issues raised in the ensuing open-floor debate. It serves as a reminder of the complex task facing modern researchers as we strive to draw conceptual and theoretical boundaries around the discipline we define as 'comparative education', and which was reflected in the diverse and wide-ranging nature of the discussion. Research into comparative theory, method and content, it seems, often concludes by posing more questions than it answers. Yet by taking the opportunity to pool ideas in a conference arena such as this, academics and theorists can both distinguish existing common conceptual ground, and locate areas where further research is needed in the years to come. By doing so, we can not only reflect on Comparative Education's 'place' within the 1990s, but also identify its future directions and paths for the next century.

Professor Edmund King's response to Patricia Broadfoot's paper ('Not so much a context, more a way of life?') reflected an almost total concurrence with her argument. He emphasised the extreme difficulty of attempting to provide definitions of comparative education and cited his own careful avoidance of the term. He made reference to the call made by Nicholas Hans that comparative education should be 'essentially reformative' and emphasised his support for this motivation for purposeful investigation. He concurred with Broadfoot's insistence on the significance of context, and echoed her contention that young people learn more outside the school than within it, through media such as television and computers.

Professor King advocated that the discipline should question the Establishment, as the satirical 1960s television programme which had inspired Broadfoot's title had done. He also contended that it should not be content with its inheritance, but should be 'carried forward'. He himself now perceived the discipline of comparative education as an area, rather than an arena, of complementary investigation, since in the context of a future of increasing uncertainty there was a need to provide pointers. He cited the complementary input of other disciplines as a vital part of the process of investigating educational practice, and as part of a conscious endeavour to find out more.

Rosemary Preston commented on the problems of "jockeying to create market niches", and indicated the negative impact of this process in the history of the discipline of comparative education. She pointed to the current renaissance of interest in the subject and called for renewed interest in both the micro- and the supra-national levels. She agreed with Broadfoot's emphasis on non-school education, asserting that a good deal of so-called formal education takes place outside the school, and also contended that all research is explicitly or implicitly comparative in nature.

Professor Denzil Saldanha discussed the impossibility of contextualising information fully and asserted that a researcher would need several incarnations to provide a comprehensive internal. view. He advocated using a process of elimination with regard to other disciplines in order to gain an understanding of what constitutes comparative education. He held that the comparative approach should focus on the 'in-between', on understanding the relationships between different contexts, rather than concentrating on the contexts themselves.

Responding to Jürgen Schriewer's paper ('Coping with complexity in comparative methodology'), Michel Lemosse argued that the main aims of comparative education must be to improve education and to raise levels of understanding. He asserted that the 'meanings' of systems should be investigated, and emphasised the higher levels of causality implicit in increasing interdependence and 'globology'. David Johnson raised the issue of global connectedness and the transfer of global narrative in cultural and emblematic terms. He referred to the dichotomy between diffusion and local diversity, with particular regard to inequality, and suggested that individual identity seems to become lost in theorisation. Professor Schriewer added that awareness of global interdependence seemed to be less developed in Europe than elsewhere.

Colin Brock, responding to Robert Cowen's paper ('Late modernity and the rules of chaos'), reiterated his critical emphasis on linearity and positivism, which have constrained the capacity of comparative education to investigate problems, and he discussed assumptions of equilibrium in the context of the enormous changes in Europe during the late 19th and early 20th centuries. He stressed the nature of constantly changing politicial parameters, with particular reference to rims and transitologies. He went on to analyse the nature of the conflicts between spheres of influence at the core and at the periphery and the difficulty of identifying appropriate geographical, spatial and temporal scales. He contended that the choice of an appropriate scale of investigation was vital within this comparative study.

Professor Joseph Tobin referred to the power of migrant workers, the power inherent in being at the core of a periphery and the intellectual richness which can thrive when "things are rotten at the core". David Johnson added that there seemed to be no recognition that people create their own political space, as in Namibia, which has rejected World Bank influence.

Harry Judge identified the growing disequilibrium in the modern world, and argued that comparative education is expanding in ambition while contracting in capacity, particularly with regard to the widening gap between theorists and researchers. In his view, comparative education was an alliance between history arid utility, and should have reformative aims.

Professor Saldanha described rims as 'meeting points of social processes' and asserted that a location on a rim provides certain strengths. He reiterated the importance of the relationship between two entities in the context of comparative education, and warned that an overemphasis on specificity would damage the subject – in his view it should develop the notion of relations.

Professor King introduced the closing session by discussing the importance of the wide range of actors involved in the process of implementation of educational decisions, as well as that of school systems and institutions. He made a plea for broader contextual identification and referred to the persistence of local diversity amid the current trends of globalisation; he considered too the dichotomy between the content of education inside and outside school systems.

The need for a 'living context' for comparative education was addressed, as well as the need to approach aspects of education thematically, and the usefulness of Karl Popper's 'falsification' theory. Professor King noted that researchers should accommodate the 'inside view' of the subjects under investigation, and stressed the need for partnership in conducting educational research. He advocated increased attention to global, as well as educational, realities.

Patricia Broadfoot contended that comparative education as a discipline is currently very exposed, and she referred to the need to find intellectually defensible ways to link the various levels of comparative research. Nicholas Beattie asserted that the mode of discourse chosen can be inappropriate for the 'consumers' of the discipline, and stressed the importance of identifying with the 'audience'. Michel Lemosse echoed this view with a plea for accessibility and increased universalisation of the language employed. Detlef Glowka drew attention to the need for discussion of methods of teaching comparative education, in an era of increasing complexity.

Finally, Professor William Boyd reiterated the powerful force of globalisation and the growing influence of the media and large multi-national corporations. He advocated the production of a 'buyer's guide' for educational policy makers to facilitate the detection of raw empiricism untempered by contextual analysis of the cultural matrices involved.

PART TWO

Comparing Classrooms and Schools

Comparing Classrooms and Schools

ROBIN ALEXANDER

From the start of the seminar programme which gave rise to this book and its companion volume, it was clear that we would need to give particular prominence to teaching, learning and the classroom transactions which are at the heart of education. It was not just that comparativists have tended to concentrate on national systems and policies rather than school and classroom processes and that this imbalance of attention needed to be rectified. There was also the increasingly powerful pragmatic argument that comparativists could no longer ignore what was going on elsewhere: the growing prominence being given to 'process' variables in input-output studies of the kind conducted for OECD (OECD 1994; 1995; 1998); the rise of school effectiveness research and the extension of its focus from the levels of the system and the school down to that of the classroom; the attempts of educational statisticians, in their turn, to encompass the totality of the educational enterprise, including teaching, in multi-level modelling; the belated discovery by policy-makers caught up in the international league table game that what happens in classrooms is actually rather important; and the equally belated development of pedagogy as a central focus for educational research.

The neglect of pedagogy by comparative researchers is fairly easy to explain. It is not, by and large, the intellectual field from which comparativists have traditionally emerged. It encapsulates all that is most difficult and problematic about cross-cultural and cross-national investigation, being time-consuming, labour intensive, methodologically fraught and acutely vulnerable to charges of cultural naivete and ethnocentrism. And of course we need to reiterate – lest comparativists, wrongly, be deemed uniquely culpable on this score – the fact that pedagogy, internationally as well as in the United Kingdom (UK) (indeed more so in some other countries than in the UK) is a relatively new and exploratory branch of educational research.

This section of the book confronts many of the problems in comparative classroom research, and exposes some of the paradigm wars which are the hallmark of any academic field worth pursuing.

Joseph Tobin draws on his influential study of preschooling in Japan, China and the United States to address a sequence of questions about anthropological perspectives and ethnographic procedures in classroom research. Through his 'polyvocal ethnography' he offers not just a way of avoiding the risks of cultural colonialism but also a powerful tool for enabling comparative educational analysis to fulfil its most significant promise: by 'making the strange familiar' to 'make the familiar strange', and to command a fresh look at what in our own educational systems and institutions we take for granted. By using video as its primary tool, Tobin's method captures classroom life in the raw and then subjects it to an essentially dialectical process of analysis in which the researcher's (and the reader's) assumptions are constantly challenged by those who are being researched.

David Reynolds, while riding on the tide of political interest in school effectiveness research, is yet properly cautious about some of its uses and abuses. He draws on his nine-nation International School Effectiveness Research Project (ISERP) to show how school effectiveness methodology – which in its arms-length measuring and model-building could hardly be more different from Tobin's direct and informal engagement with teachers, parents, administrators and children – is responding to some of the criticisms levelled against it. Most notable among these are the charges that school effectiveness research neglects culture and oversimplifies pedagogy. Reynolds's study also offers an intriguing example of research which is cross-cultural not just in its focus but in its personnel: its team from different countries had to resolve basic differences in perception and understanding before they could claim to operate a shared methodology.

Robin Alexander uses his five-country qualitative study of primary teaching to explore the relationship between pedagogy and culture. He exposes some of the dilemmas of comparative classroom research, sets down a series of challenges or requirements which it should meet, and uses his project data to illustrate ways that this can be done. Thus, he advances and demonstrates the idea of 'cross-cultural' continua to represent the range in key dimensions of pedagogy both within and across cultures, to provide an antidote to national pedagogical stereotypes, and to begin to separate what is universal in teaching from what is culture-specific; and he presses for a more open use of models, metaphors and analogies to penetrate beyond the behaviours of the classroom to their meaning. He ends by being sharply critical of the direction of the UK debate about educational 'standards' and 'effectiveness'.

This section of the book ends with two brief additional papers. Maurice Galton's is in the nature of a critical commentary on what he sees as the misdirection of attention and effort in some recent cross-national pedagogical research, and its misuse in the policy arena. Michele Schweisfurth's postscript provides a round-up of the discussion from the seminar at which the papers by Tobin, Reynolds and Alexander were first presented.

All five papers attend not just to research issues per se but also to the application of research in the context of policy. Their treatment of this matter is generally critical. Policy 'users' argue, reasonably, that educational research should address their concerns, and in fact all the papers in Part 2 do just that. But a research report is a total package: it offers critique and warning as well as encouragement and legitimation; it provides not just findings but also caveats about their application; it examines options but is not invariably able to give unqualified support for any one of them.

There has always been a tendency for policy-makers to use research to justify rather than to inform or guide their prior decisions, and therefore to do so selectively. However, in education perhaps more than in other aspects of social policy recent UK governments have shown a growing resistance to the critical, restraining function of research. Where pedagogy was concerned this tendency did not matter too much, for decisions about teaching in the UK have traditionally been left to teachers. That, since 1997, is no longer the case. The inexorable process of centralisation has now broken through the final barrier: curriculum in 1988, pedagogy a decade later. Classroom research faces its toughest test yet.

References

Organisation for Economic Co-operation and Development (1994) *Quality in Teaching*. Paris: OECD.

Organisation for Economic Co-operation and Development (1995) *Measuring the Quality of Schools*. Paris: OECD.

Organisation for Economic Co-operation and Development (1998) *Education at a Glance*. Paris: OECD.

Method and Meaning in Comparative Classroom Ethnography

JOSEPH TOBIN

Preschool in Three Cultures: Japan, China, and the United States by Joseph Tobin, David Wu & D.H. Davidson was published in 1989. The book was based on a research project my co-authors and I conducted in the mid-1980s. With the passage of time since the book's publication, I have reached greater clarity about what worked and did not work in our study's method, and more generally about methodological, ethical, and epistemological issues in comparative classroom ethnography. In this paper I will review the 'Preschool in Three Cultures method' and then reflect on a series of issues raised by the study, concluding with a question anthropologists rarely ask about their work: 'What effects (if any) has our comparative study of classrooms in three cultures had on educational practice or policy?' Or to put this question more generally: 'How can comparative classroom ethnography change what goes on in schools?'

The *Preschool in Three Cultures* Method

It has been more than a decade since we came up with our method, and we still have not found a good name for it. We have tried names such as 'reflexive comparative ethnography' and 'visually cued polyvocal ethnography,' but for obvious reasons these names haven't caught on. So by default, I am left calling it the 'Preschool in Three Cultures method'.

The Preschool in Three Cultures project began in 1984. I had just moved to Hawaii from Japan, where my older son had been a student in a Japanese preschool. I was offered a postdoctoral fellowship by David Wu, a researcher at the East West Center (EWC) in Honolulu. David was just back from studying the first generation of single children in China. As we talked about our interests in childrearing and preschool education in these two East Asian countries, we found that comparing the Japanese and Chinese approaches raised interesting issues. Eventually, our discussions led to the decision to embark on an ambitious comparative study of preschool education in Japan and China.

We approached this study as anthropologists, rather than as educational researchers – our training and previous work were in anthropology rather than education, and we conceptualised our study primarily as one of culture rather than of preschools. We reasoned that preschools are ideal sites for anthropological study because in modern societies they are cultural institutions that stand at the interface between parenting and education and thus which can reveal core cultural values and concerns. As the project developed, our focus shifted. By the time we wrote the book, we were as interested in using cultural knowledge to understand each nation's preschools as in using preschools to explicate features of each culture.

As the focus of the study shifted from ethnography to comparative educational research, I found myself changing professionally. I went into this study an anthropologist and came out an educational researcher. This is a version of an occupational hazard of anthropology ethnographers call 'going native.' My ethnographic study of preschools in three cultures transformed me into an expert on early childhood education. Or at least having published a book on early childhood education in three cultures made me look enough like an early childhood educator for me to be invited to join a faculty of teacher education. Now, after eight years of working in a college of education, I am starting to feel like I belong. I have decided I prefer being an ethnographer in a college of education than a school ethnographer in a anthropology department.

But back to the start of our project: as ethnographers our primary interest was in meaning. We needed a research method which would give us access not just to what goes on in each cultures' preschools, but more importantly to the meanings behind the practices. We chose not to rely on the traditional ethnographic approach of participation observation and thick description because we were uncomfortable with the dynamics of anthropology which puts the power to interpret, to decide what things mean, in the hands of the anthropologist rather than the informant. This, remember, was 1984, the beginning of anthropology's post-structural, reflexive turn.

We were searching for a method which would allow our informants to be able to speak for themselves in our study when we had the good fortune to attend a presentation by Linda Conner, a fellow anthropologist at the EWC. Conner and her colleagues, the ethnographic film makers Patsy and Timothy Asch, were studying Balinese shamans (Conner et al, 1986). In their study, they filmed a Balinese medium go into a trance state to help a client. Some months later they made another film in which they showed the original footage to the shaman and asked her to explain the meanings of her actions and to recall what was going through her mind during each stage of the seance.

The use that Conner and the Aschs made of ethnographic film to stimulate reflection gave us the idea of using videotape to stimulate a comparative discussion on preschool education. Conner and her collaborators used video to get one key informant talking; we went much further. We began by videotaping typical days in preschools in Japan, China, and the United States (we added the United States as a third culture for reasons I will explain later). Before leaving for the field (I to Japan and David to China), we agreed that in each country we would choose a typical (or at least not obviously atypical) good urban preschool and we would videotape a day that included shots of arrival (drop off by parents), morning opening, free play, lessons, lunch, toileting, and departure. We also agreed to record segments of teachers dealing with children's disputes and misbehaviour. Back in Honolulu, we reduced the six hours or more of footage from each site to a 20-minute stimulus tape. The result, once we added an American site to our study, was a one-hour long videotape, showing typical days at preschools in three cultures.

A key point to keep in mind is that in our study the tapes are not the data. One way to think of our tapes is as projective devices, such as TAT cards or Rohrshach images, intentionally ambiguous cues which draw people out and get them to reveal something of how they make sense of the world. Following the projective test analogy, we can assume that if Japanese and Chinese viewers of our videotape of St Timothy's, the American preschool, tell different stories about what they see, these differences reflect their differing perspectives and concerns. Another way to conceptualise the videotapes in our study is to think of them as non-verbal interview questions. Just as in a conventional educational study a researcher might develop an interview schedule that includes questions on classroom management, lesson structures, and so forth, we selected videotape segments to achieve the same purpose. We believed that for the kinds of things we wanted to learn from our informants, video cues would work better than verbal questions. For example: if we were to ask an informant, 'How do you deal with a misbehaving child?' we would require our informant to imagine what we mean by misbehaviour. One teacher might picture a child not sitting straight at her desk, another teacher might picture a child being sassy with a caretaker, and a third might picture a physical altercation between two children. When you show your informants situations on tape instead of describing situations verbally, your questions become less abstract and more compelling.

The creation of an effective stimulus tape is not as easy or as straightforward as it may seem. In this paper I will not go into the specifics of the process that guided our taping and editing other than to say that these tapes must have compelling characters, interesting dilemmas, and a clear narrative line. It may be that a video-cued method works better for preschools than for studies of higher levels of education, because much of what we want to know about preschools can be captured on videotape, while our questions about primary and secondary education tend to concern things that occur mostly on pieces of paper and in people's heads.

Once we had prepared the 20-minute stimulus tapes, we showed them to various stakeholders in early childhood education in each culture to elicit what we came to call a polyvocal conversation, a conversation composed of a series of voices each commenting on the same incidents. We were influenced by the Kurosawa film, *Rashomon*, in which a chance meeting between three people in a woods is described very differently by each of the participants. The first and most important voice in our study is that of the classroom teacher. We asked the classroom teachers, 'Was this a typical day? How did our presence effect you?' We handed the remote control to the teachers in each culture so they could pause the tape when they came to something they thought needed explanation. We also asked the teachers to stop the tape when we had questions. Working in this way, it took about ninety minutes to get through a twenty-minute segment. We videotaped these sessions, and then transcribed the discussions.

The second voice in our polyvocal study came when we showed the 20-minute tapes of typical days in each preschool to other stakeholders at the school – teachers, administrators, parents and, sometimes, children. The third voice came in when we took the tapes to other sites in the country to learn about regional, ideological, and class differences. For example, we showed the staff of an upper-middle class nursery school in Tokyo the tape we had made at the more blue-collar Komatsudani daycare centre in Kyoto, and we asked these middle-class Tokyo informants to explain to us in what way practices in their preschool are the same and different. Finally, we showed audiences in each country not just the tapes of the preschool from their own country but also from the other two countries in the study. We used questionnaires and video-taped focus-group interview sessions to record their responses.

I have presented our method often enough that I know that inevitably there are questions about typicality and generalisability. I assume, for instance, that some readers are wondering how we can argue that a day in one preschool is typical. I can best address this concern by stressing that the videotapes are not the data in our study. The data are the comments our various informants made about the videotapes. In each of the three countries in our study, we showed the tapes to approximately 300 people, in six or more separate sites. Our study of three preschools is based on the comments of 900 informants.[1]

I have stressed that the videotapes are not the data in our study. At least we did not intend for the tapes to function as data. One thing we have come to realise about this study only in retrospect is that despite our protestations, the tapes we made to function as visual cues also function as data because once we distributed copies of the tape, there was little we could do to prevent viewers from using our tapes in this way. Many viewers treat our videotape as if it were a documentary. We sometimes joke that we should put a warning on the video, like the one on cigarettes: 'Warning: watching this tape may give you an exaggerated or misguided sense of how much you know about these cultures' preschools'.

Three scenes from *A Day at Komatsudani*

To illustrate how our video-cued approach works, I will present brief discussions of the three issues in the Komatsudani videotape which have produced the most interest and controversy: the older children playing with babies; high (by Western standards) student-teacher ratios; and teacher non-intervention in children's fights.

Playing with Babies

Children who arrive at Komatsudani before 9 a.m., when the formal school day begins, choose among various activities. Some play with toys in their classroom, others run and climb on the playground with their friends. And some stop by the nursery to play with and feed the infants and to take the older babies out on the playground for a walk. Our Komatsudani videotape includes a shot of two four-year-old girls carrying an eight-month-old baby and a 14-month-old toddler down some short steps and out to the playground.

Americans who watch our tapes are inevitably surprised, if not horrified by this scene. They express concern that the four-year-olds might drop or otherwise injure a baby. They are also surprised that this practice isn't precluded by liability concerns, as it would be in the United States. Our awareness of these American concerns informed our interviews with the teachers and administrators at Komatsudani. In response to our questions, Vice-principal Higashino explained that the baby-carrying we captured on tape is a common occurrence at the school. She told us that the older children often 'adopt' one of the infants or toddlers as their special charge and visit the nursery several times a day to participate in the feeding and changing and to see if they can take 'their baby' out for a walk on the playground. Thinking of studies of the negative effects of institutional childcare on infant development, we suggested to Higashino that all of this attention is desirable for the nursery-reared infants, Higashino, replied:

> *Not just for the infant. We believe it is good for the infants, of*
> *course, but we also believe it is just as important for the older*
> *children because it gives them a chance to experience what it*
> *feels like to take care of another person. These days most of*
> *our children do not have younger siblings, and we feel this*
> *contact with babies and toddlers gives them a chance they*
> *might not otherwise have to develop empathy [omoiyari]...*
> *(Tobin et al, 1989, p. 35)*

From our discussions with educators at other preschools in Japan, we learned that Komatsudani is unusual among Japanese preschools in the amount of contact allowed and encouraged between older and younger children. But although the practice we captured on videotape turned out to be unusual, the reasoning behind the practice reflects a widely shared Japanese cultural belief. In all the Japanese preschools where we showed our videotapes, teachers, administrators, and parents stressed the importance of helping children develop compassion and empathy. In these discussions, educators and parents described the social world of young children as having grown dangerously narrow (*"kodomo no sekkai semaku natta"*) as a result of social changes including a dramatic decline in the birth rate and the decline of urban neighborhood communities. Strategies for compensating for this narrowness varied from school to school – again, Komatsudani was unique among the schools we visited in encouraging mixed-age play with infants – but no one we talked to in Japan found the reasoning behind this practice to be unfamiliar or strange. Thus our method works better to clarify cultural beliefs than cultural practices.

Student/Teacher Ratios

At 9 a.m., the children at Komatsudani do group calisthenics, and then come into their classrooms. Fukui-sensei, the teacher of the Peach Class, leads the children in a counting song to see how many children are in school that day. On the tape, we hear the children count up to 28 children present, with two absent. Many of the Chinese and most of the Americans who viewed 'A Day at Komatsudani' were horrified by the size of the class and the 30/1 student/teacher ratio. A teacher in Honolulu said, "No wonder there is so much wildness and fighting. It's a wonder there's not more with that many kids in a class." A day-care administrator wrote on her response form, "The worst thing by far is the ratios. 30/1! That's way, way, too high." A Chinese teacher commented, "I'm surprised their classes are so big. They are a rich country."

When asked why they have such large classes, Japanese teachers' and administrators' first response tends to be, "Because of money. With our low preschool tuition we cannot afford smaller numbers of students per teacher. We are barely getting by as it is." But why, then, do American preschools feel they cannot operate with student/teacher ratios of much more than 15 four-year-olds to one teacher, while Japanese preschools, even in an era of growing wealth and great concern with education, choose to hold the line on tuition and maintain large student/teacher ratios?

When we asked teachers and administrators at Japanese preschools directly, "Would you like to have smaller classes?" they almost always replied affirmatively. Fukui-sensei, for example, answered without hesitation, "Sure, it would be much easier to teach a smaller class." Watching a tape of an American preschool that has a student/teacher ratio of about eight to one, a teacher in Kyoto sighed, "It must be great to teach in America. Such small classes!" Another Kyoto teacher added that she envied the way the American teacher in the film played with the children in her class so happily, in what she called a 'barefoot' (uninhibited) manner. But when we followed up by asking, "So you think it would be better to have a class size of 10 or 12 instead of 25 or 30?" Yano-sensei responded, "No, I wouldn't say better. Well, maybe you could say better for the teacher, but not better for the children. Children need to have the experience of being in a large group in order to learn to relate to lots of kinds of children in lots of kinds of situations." Tanaka-sensei, the teacher who had commented favorably about the uninhibited play style of the American teacher, then explained:

> I envy the way the American teachers, with such small classes and such low student/teacher rations, have time to play so affectionately with each child. That's how I like to play with my nieces and nephews. That's a good way for aunts and parents to play with their children. But I don't think that's necessarily the best way for a teacher to relate to children. Teaching is different from being a patent or aunt or family friend to a child. Sometimes I feel like playing very warmly in a down-on-the-floor, barefoot sort of way with my students, and sometimes I feel like hugging some of my students or having an intimate chat with one of the little girls. And sometimes I do these things, of course. I'm a human being, as well as a teacher, and I'm not suggesting that teachers should be cold or formal by any means. What I am trying to say is that a teacher should relate to the class as a whole rather than to each student, even if this is a little harder or even a little bit sad for the teacher sometimes.

If money were not a consideration, many Japanese teachers and administrators would certainly prefer a smaller students-per-teacher ratio than is currently the rule in most of their schools. And many

Japanese teachers and administrators, influenced either directly or indirectly by Western preschool pedagogy (such as those trained in Montessori centres) or by Western values (Christianity), take positions on class size, teacher/student ratio, and indeed on child rearing and education in general that are virtually indistinguishable from the views of American teachers and administrators. And yet, when asked, "Financial considerations aside, what would you consider an ideal class size and student/teacher ratio for four-year-olds?" few Japanese teachers and administrators say less than 15 or, at the lowest, 12 to a teacher, whereas many Americans say ideally they would prefer to see no more than eight, or six, or even four students to each teacher.

In the eyes of Japanese educators, then, very small classes and low student/teacher ratios produce a classroom atmosphere that emphasises teacher-student over student-student interactions and fails to provide children with adequate opportunities to learn to function as members of a group. A teacher in Tokyo said of our tape of an American preschool, "A class that size seems kind of sad and underpopulated." Another Tokyo teacher wondered, "In a class that size wouldn't a child's world be too narrow?" Yagi-sensei commented:

> *I understand how this kind of small class size can help young children become very self-reliant and independent. But I can't help feeling that there is something kind of sad or lonely about a class that size. Don't American teachers worry that children may become too independent? I wonder how you teach a child to become a member of a group in a class that small?*

Komatsudani's ratios are large, then, not because Japanese are good at functioning in large groups; rather, Japanese get to be good at functioning in large groups in part by attending preschool with large classes. The levels of noise and chaos characteristic of Japanese preschools are not unfortunate side effects of large class size; rather, class size is kept large to ensure that the preschool experience will be optimally noisy and chaotic.

Non-intervention in Fighting

The most memorable character in our book is clearly four-year-old Hiroki, a rascally boy who we captured on tape interrupting a lesson by singing television theme songs, making penis jokes during group work, and poking, bopping, and pinching children around him during free play. Here is how we described his behaviour leading up to the moment when he steps on another boy's hand, making him cry:

> *Finishing his lunch as quickly as he had his workbook, Hiroki joined other fast diners on the balcony, where he roughhoused with some other boys and then disrupted a game by throwing*

> *flash cards over the railing to the ground below. The other*
> *children seemed more amused than annoyed by these antics,*
> *although one girl, Midori, ran inside to tattle to the teacher,*
> *who was by now sweeping up under the tables. Fukui-sensei*
> *sent Midori back to the balcony, looked over the railing, and*
> *said, 'So that's where the cards are going.' Soon several of the*
> *children, with the conspicuous exception of Hiroki, ran down*
> *the steps to retrieve the fallen cards. This proved to be a losing*
> *battle as Hiroki continued to rain cards down upon them. It*
> *was now that Hiroki (purposely) stepped on Satoshi's hand,*
> *which made him cry. Satoshi was quickly ushered away from*
> *the scene by Midori, the girl who had earlier reported the card*
> *throwing. Midori, arm around Satoshi's neck, listened very*
> *empathetically to his tale of woe and then repeated it several*
> *times with gestures to other girls who came by ... The girls*
> *then patted Satoshi on the back, suggesting that in the future*
> *he find someone other than Hiroki to play with. (Tobin et al,*
> *1989, p. 21)*

Americans who have watched and discussed the tape with us do not find Hiroki's naughtiness to be so exceptional, but they are shocked and horrified by what they perceive to be Fukui-sensei's failure to prevent Hiroki from hurting other children. Much of our discussion with the staff at Komatsudani centred on trying to understand what to us appeared to be a radically non-interventionist approach to managing Hiroki:

> *When we returned to Komatsudani to show Fukui-sensei and*
> *her supervisors the edited film we had made in her classroom,*
> *we were most curious to see if Fukui-sensei would be*
> *defensive about the way the film depicted her dealing with –*
> *and seeming not to deal with – Hiroki's acts of aggression.*
> *Both Fukui and her supervisors told us that they were satisfied*
> *with the tape and felt that it captured what they are about.*
> *Indeed, they said, the way Fukui-sensei dealt with Hiroki in*
> *the film, including ignoring his most provocatively aggressive*
> *and exhibitionist actions, reflected not negligence but just the*
> *opposite, a strategy worked out over the course of countless*
> *meetings and much trial and error.*

Japanese preschool teachers and, to a lesser extent, preschool administrators generally are pragmatists rather than ideologues, and thus their discipline and classroom-management techniques tend to be eclectic, focusing on what works. And for most Japanese teachers, for most situations, what seems to work best is a nonconfrontational, energetic, friendly, yet affectively neutral approach. After viewing the tape, we discussed their strategy:

> *Higashino: Dealing with Hiroki is really a problem. We've had*
> *him here two years now, since he was less than three. You*
> *should have seen him before, if you think he's something now.*
> *We've tried just about everything we could think of to deal*
> *with Hiroki. But we've found that especially for a boy like*
> *Hiroki the techniques you saw Fukui-sensei using in the film*
> *work best.*

The staff of Komatsudani believes that children best learn to control their behaviour when the impetus to change comes spontaneously through interactions with their peers rather than from above. Thus Hiroki's best chance to learn self-control lies not in encounters with his teachers but in play with his classmates.

> *Fukui: I told Midori and the other children that if they felt it*
> *was a problem, then they should deal with Hiroki's throwing*
> *the cards. If I tell Hiroki to stop, it doesn't mean much to him,*
> *but if his classmates tell him, it affects him.*

This Japanese approach to dealing with a disruptive child was further clarified for us in Japanese teachers' discussion of our St Timothy's videotape, in which we see an American teacher intervening in a dispute over a sand-box toy by asking the children to "use words to let him know how you feel instead of grabbing ..." and "tell him with words that he's made you feel angry."

Japanese preschool teachers were impressed with this approach, but also tactfully critical:

> *Yagi: Wow, that's amazing! Talking so directly with such*
> *young children about their feelings.*

> *Taniguchi: The teacher really gets right in there and deals*
> *with the problem.*

> *Tanaka: Talking with children about disagreements like that,*
> *it seems a bit heavy, doesn't it? It reminds me of marriage*
> *counseling.*

Reflections on Methodological Issues in Comparative Classroom Ethnography

Having described our method and presented a few of our more provocative findings, I want to shift now away from the substance of our study to some of the implications of our approach for thinking about the problems and promises of comparative classroom ethnography.

Issue One: the meaning of the term 'ethnography' in 'classroom ethnography.'

In the years since we began our study, 'ethnography' has become a commonplace approach in educational research. But is this work actually ethnographic? What are the characteristics of classroom studies that need to be in place for a study to be ethnographic? I find these days that a majority of the doctoral students who come to me to talk about their proposed dissertation topics plan to do an ethnography. When I ask them, "An ethnography of what?" they tell me of their plans to do an ethnography of a classroom in a school in Honolulu, often the school where they work, sometimes a classroom of a teacher they heard is doing exciting teaching. I then ask them how they plan to make this work ethnographic. They tell me they will spend a lot of time in this classroom (ideally, one academic year) and they will do 'thick description'.

Thick description, in the style of Clifford Geertzs' analysis of a Balinese cockfight (Geertz, 1973), has become the defining feature of educational ethnography. I think this is unfortunate. My concern is that if ethnography is defined as thick description, it becomes synonymous with 'case studies' and other qualitative inquiry methods. I do not mean to be crotchety or mean-spirited (although this is how these self-proclaimed ethnographers inevitably experience my responses to their projects), but I object to the loose and confusing way that the terms 'ethnography' and 'thick description' are being used in educational research. When I criticise people for calling their case studies and qualitative work ethnography, they often reply "it might not be the same thing *you* mean by ethnography, but *I* can call it ethnography if I want to. You don't own the term." I tend to reply with a riddle: If you call a dog's tail a leg, how many legs does it have? The answer is four. You can call a tail a leg, but that doesn't make it a leg. Similarly, you can call a case study, with thick description, of a school in your own culture an ethnography, but that does not make it an ethnography.

To be fair, many of these educational ethnographies don't really claim to be ethnographies, but only ethnographies by analogy. In these studies, the educational researcher is like an anthropologist, as he or she goes into a classroom field setting which is like a village to study children who are like natives of a tribe. This is a useful way to proceed – nothing is wrong with thinking analogically, as long as we are aware of what we are doing. The key to using ethnography analogically is to imitate the key features of the method, while discarding the undesirable aspects.

For me, the key feature of ethnography is that an outsider goes to live for a period of time among a group of exotic others who, viewed as expert informants, are asked to provide insiders' explanations. The audience for this work are outsiders, that is, members of the ethnographer's culture. I am going to some pains to be specific about insiders and outsiders because to me the key characteristic of ethnography is the way it builds on the insider/outside dialogic encounter. Ethnography is a study of an insider's culture, privileging insiders' meanings, told by an outsider, for a readership of other outsiders. The outsiderness of the ethnographer and the readers is critical: it is a genuine ignorance/naivete/curiosity of a special sort that leads to characteristic dynamics, tensions, insights in fieldwork. This genuine ignorance/naivete of the ethnographer is essential, as it leads to a characteristic intersubjective encounter, with characteristic dynamics and power relations.

Ethnography's goal is to make the strange familiar. You focus on something in another culture which you find strange, by which I mean odd, counter-intuitive, inexplicable, and you ask the insiders from the culture to explain this exotic practice, to help you understand the reasoning behind what they do. This does not necessarily mean that you come to agree with their reasoning, but at least you understand it, and in this way the once exotic features of a culture become familiar. Why work so hard to make the strange familiar? Because if you succeed in making the strange familiar, you end up making the familiar strange. The effect of ethnography should be to expand readers' sense of the range of ways humans can live and in so doing to defamiliarise some of our taken-for-granted assumptions about what how we live our own lives in our own cultures.

Issue Two: the end of anthropology?

In 1989, I was one of a 1000 or so anthropologists in the audience in Chicago to hear Edward Said address us. He said, in essence, "It's over. Get out of our cultures. Go home. We're not just asking you to do your ethnographies more sensitively. We're telling you to stop and close your imperialistic departments." Anthropology currently is in disrepute and retreat in many quarters, based on such accusations as Said's that it is a colonialist discipline. It is ironic that educational researchers are embracing a method just at the historical moment that it is being called into question in so many quarters. And it's ironic, given that I am among those who think that cultural anthropology is a dying discipline and that the end of anthropology in the near future will be a good thing, that in the section above I took such a conservative view on defining ethnography and I fought to defend against its being watered down. My position is that the one part of anthropology that we should retain is the ethnographic method. Comparative classroom studies like we conducted in Preschool in Three Cultures demonstrate that we can have ethnography without departments of anthropology.

The part of anthropology we should drop from our educational ethnographies (literal or metaphorical) is the traditional power of unilateral ethnographic authority. Our methods need to incorporate checks on the ethnographer's power to classify, name, and otherwise describe and explain another culture. One way to decrease the authority of the ethnographer is to build a reciprocal gaze into the study. We did this in several ways. By including the United States in our study, we subjected our own cultural beliefs and practices to the same ethnographic scrutiny we applied to China and Japan. This turned out, by the way, to be disturbing to the American teachers in our study, who had not anticipated what it would feel like to become an ethnographic subject. As one of the American teachers explained to us after the book was published, "It's weird to have the way I teach presented as an example of what Americans believe. I don't teach the way I do because I'm American. I teach the way I do because I think it's the best way to teach, period." Another way we built reciprocity into our method was by asking Japanese, Chinese, and American early childhood educators to talk about not just their own cultures' preschools, but also about each others'. By allowing the teachers from all three cultures to comment on the whole set of videotapes, we allowed our informants to be ethnographers as well as ethnographic subjects. The Japanese and Chinese educators' analyses and critiques of the American preschool are some of the most memorable and striking points in our study. The Chinese and Japanese voices in our study introduce non-Western issues, concerns, and modes of analysis. Ours thus is a study not just of three cultures' preschools, but also of preschools from three cultural perspectives.

Issue Three: the problematic status of comparative studies in anthropology

Only a small minority of ethnographies are explicitly comparative. Most are of only one culture. Comparative ethnographies, including comparative ethnographies of classrooms, are a distinct genre of anthropologically inquiry, with advantages and problems.

Before going into anthropology's ambivalence about the comparative project, I need first to make an epistemological point: All anthropology is comparative, but only implicitly. What the anthropologist and his or her audience find interesting and compelling in another culture is based on an implicit comparison with their own culture. Even single-culture studies are comparative in that readers read the culture presented in the ethnography against their understanding of their own culture.

Joseph Tobin

Explicitly comparative studies are out of favour in anthropology. Contemporary anthropologists take pains to distance themselves from three versions of comparative anthropology which enjoyed their hay days in earlier eras. It is important to understand the historical (mis)uses of comparative ethnography because these are cautionary tales for comparative education.

The Evolutionary Model

The first version of comparative ethnography was anthropology's 19th century project to locate the cultures of the world on a continuum running from the most primitive (the most animal like) to the most civilised (the most like ours). Anthropology began as the study of primitive cultures. But all cultures are not equally primitive. According to the logic of the evolutionary model, cultures evolve away from primitivism toward civilisation. We first-worlders can find the early history of our cultures in the cultures of our more primitive contemporaries. This evolutionary model colours many comparative educational studies, which contain the implicit if not explicit assumption that some educational systems are more primitive and some more advanced than others. Comparative classroom ethnographers must take pains to distance themselves not just from anthropology's early evolutionary assumptions, but also from the contemporary field of educational development, in which first-world educational experts help third-world nations make their education systems more modern and rational. There is an inherent tension between the cultural relativism of ethnography and the hierarchical assumptions that underlie the work of international educational consultants. Organisations such as the Comparative and International Education Society are struggling to keep the anthropologists from leaving an organisation they (we) believe is dominated by World Bank types.

The Scientific 'Natural Experiment' Model

Another version of comparative study in anthropology is the search for universal cultural laws. Over the years, anthropologists with a social science orientation have pursued the notion that a systematic comparison of diverse cultures could be used as naturally occurring experiments to shed light on basic principles of human life. The most ambitious of these comparative scientific projects is certainly the Human Relations Area Files (HRAF), in which more than 10,000 ethnographies of several thousand cultures are housed in a common micro-fiche or CD-Rom archive and categorised according to several hundred variables. This system of organisation allows, for example, for statistical analyses of how swaddling is correlated with animism or how polygamy is correlated with a barter system of trade. An example of a comparative educational use of the HRAF data-base would be to explore the correlation between infant mortality and the schooling of girls. Many multi-national educational studies are based on a similar logic of using pre-existing data from various cultures to uncover universal principles.

I do not mean to imply that there is nothing to be gained by such systematic comparative approaches. But scientific, statistical uses of ethnographic descriptions are viewed with suspicion by anthropologists for several reasons. One has to do with breaking cultures up into separate characteristics, and losing the sense of the whole. A second problem is re-using ethnographies of varying quality – can good science be done using poor ethnographies? The third problem of scientific comparisons of cultures has to do with the use of 'etic' (universal) categories for 'emic' (culturally specific) data. Most ethnographers strive to describe a culture using the meaning categories of the people they study. These insider meanings are 'emic'. Statistical analyses require the use of etic categories. When an ethnography is broken up and turned into characteristics, factors, and codes, most anthropologists believe that much of the original meaning is lost, as emic meanings are collapsed into etic categories.

An alternative to re-analysing other researchers' ethnographies is to do your own multi-cultural comparative study. For instance, a team of ethnographers could agree to focus on the same issues, ask similar questions, and apply a common mode of analysis to several cultures. This is the approach that reached its zenith in the six-culture study organised by John and Beatrice Whiting in the early 1950s. The Whitings assembled a team of six ethnographers, who left for the field having agreed to employ similar methods and to ask similar (but not identical) questions. These ethnographers were anthropologically trained and experts in the region of the world where they conducted their fieldwork. This study led to many publications, including the book *Child Training and Personality: a cross-cultural study* (Whiting & Whiting, 1953), in which the six cultures are compared. One of the keys of the success of the Whitings's project is the quality of the ethnographies. A comparative ethnographic project is only as good as its weakest piece of fieldwork. The ethnographies in the Whitings's study were all very good. Our Preschool in Three Cultures study is a direct descendant of the Whitings's tradition. One of the original six-culture ethnographers was Robert LeVine, who was my doctoral advisor and mentor.

Anthropology as Cultural Critique

A third version of comparative ethnography is using information about other cultures in order to influence practice within the anthropologist's own culture. The best example would be Margaret Mead's comparative ethnographies, especially her *Sex and Temperament in Three Primitive Societies*. I read this and other books by Mead like I read Swift's *Gulliver's Travels* and first-rate science fiction like that of Ursula Le Guin – as allegorical commentaries and critiques of social relations in our own society. Mead's ethnographic work on sexuality and gender relations in other cultures clearly functions (and, I would argue was meant to function) to leverage domestic debates on these topics. The implicit logic of her argument is that if, in other cultures, relations between the sexes are radically unlike our own, than we must question the taken-for-grantedness of our beliefs about what men and women can do alone and with each other.

This is an example of how I believe ethnography should work – by making the strange familiar, as Mead does with the sex and gender practices of exotic 'primitive' cultures, she succeeds in making our Western sex and gender practices strange. Mead's comparative ethnographic work is a powerful argument against essentialising claims, an argument which alters political and social debate by radically expanding the repertoire of the possible.

In cases where we sympathise with the political agenda of the ethnographer who uses comparisons to other cultures polemically (as I do with Mead's), we tend to feel that the end justifies the means. But clearly there are ethical and epistemological problems in the use of comparative ethnography to leverage domestic debates. This is a particularly acute problem in comparative educational studies, where researchers often study other cultures' educational practices in order to support a position they held before they began their research. I would make a distinction between using comparative studies to question the taken-for-grantedness of our beliefs and practices (which I think is a laudable goal) and using comparisons with other cultures to blast one's opponents in battles over educational policy. The latter approach is characterised by simplistic, decontextualised interpretations and representations of the educational practices of other nations.

The United States went through a flurry of such educational comparisons in the 1980s when national attention was focused on the miracles of the Japanese educational system, which was believed to be the secret of Japan's economic success. As I write this paper, the Japanese economy is falling apart, which means that the Japanese education system suddenly seems less attractive as a model. It is axiomatic that educational practices of economically successful countries will seem more effective than educational practices of countries that are struggling economically. Another axiom of comparative education is that studies of school systems in countries that are 'hot' in the popular imagination seem more interesting than countries we don't care much about. Our Preschool in Three Cultures study was conducted during the era of intense American interest in learning from Japan. The American fascination with Japan of the mid-1980s coupled with the interest in China precipitated by the events at Tiannenmen Square was timely for the success of our book, published in 1989.

Another element in the success of our project was that ours was a three-way rather than a two-way comparison. I find three to be an ideal number of sites for this kind of comparative work. When you get more than three countries or cultures in a study, you cannot say that much about each and readers cannot keep each culture straight in their mind. As a result, there is a tendency to lose the sense of cultural context and reduce the ethnographic findings to codable factors. The problem with two-country or two-culture comparisons is that you inevitably fall into a sing-song of dichotomised difference that makes your study read like a children's book: 'Japanese preschools have *big* classes. American preschools have *small* classes. The Japanese favour *groups*. Americans favour the *individual*.' Three-way comparisons effectively break up this tendency to dichotomise and to emphasise only differences. In our study, there are ways in which American and Japanese schools are like each other and unlike schools in China, ways in which Chinese and Japanese schools are like each other and unlike schools in the United States, and ways in which the three cultures are unique. There are also problems, however, with three-way comparisons. If two-way comparisons tend to produce a sing-song of difference, three way comparisons can easily deteriorate into what I call the Goldilocks effect: 'The Japanese preschools are too wild. The Chinese preschools are too controlling. The American preschools are just right.'

Issue Four: classroom ethnographies' audiences and effects

Can classroom ethnographies have an impact on educational practice or policy? I think, occasionally they can, if they succeed in expanding the repertoire of the possible and/or by making the familiar strange. I will apply these two notions to the three issues from our study that I discussed earlier in this paper: older children playing with babies, large student/teacher ratios, and teacher non-intervention in children's disputes.

Playing with Babies. The idea of preschools allowing for interaction between babies and older children is very attractive. It would give institutionally raised infants more stimulation and older children new opportunities to develop socially and emotionally. It would also make the preschool less institutional and more like a family. Americans who watch our Komatsudani tape invariably sympathise with the goals of mixed-age play. But they also find it to be an unfeasible, even unthinkable practice for the American context. In the discussions that follow the screening of our video, Americans express amazement that the staff at Komatsudani are not concerned that an older child would drop an infant. They are even more amazed that the school's insurer would allow such a risky practice. Fears of litigation dominate many areas of American preschool practice, making it unthinkable that older children could be allowed to carry infants around the grounds of a preschool. This is an example of how our comparative research introduced American readers to some new educational ideas which they found to be attractive, but which nevertheless cannot impact American practice because of insurmountable structural barriers.

Student-Teacher Ratios. Two years before *Preschool in Three Cultures* was published (Tobin et al, 1987), my colleagues and I published an article in the *Comparative Education Review* on class size and student-teacher ratios (Tobin et al, 1987). This article earned us the outstanding research award from the Comparative and International Education Society. But it also got us into trouble with the Hawaii early childhood education community. We concluded our paper with a plea to American educators to rethink our belief that a high student-teacher ratio necessarily causes a low quality of care. We thought (naively) that the introduction of the Japanese case to American readers would work to destabilise taken-for-granted assumptions about quality of care and to expand the repertoire of the possible ways adults can interact with large groups of children in preschool settings. But by introducing this argument, we ended up angering early childhood educators in Hawaii who are engaged in battles with employers and government agencies over student-teacher ratios. The director of the Hawaii Association for the Education of Young Children confronted me at our annual meeting: "Do you know how much damage you do to our cause when you tell people that we can increase student-teacher ratios without harming children? You're giving ammunition to our adversaries! We've been working for years to convince these people that we need to lower ratios and then you come along with this irresponsible research." She was referring not just to my having published the paper, but also to my having given a copy of the paper to Ben Cayetano, who then was the Lieutenant Governor and who now is the Governor of Hawaii. By chance, the Lieutenant Governor and I one day were seated next to each other at a luncheon hosted by the Japan-America Society of Honolulu. As we chatted about Japanese education and my research, Cayetano was intrigued by the Japanese argument that student-teacher ratios that are too low are bad for children. He asked me for a copy of the paper, telling me that he was engaged in collective bargaining with the teacher's union, and that ratios was one of the issues they were negotiating. Apparently, Cayetano cited our research in one of these bargaining sessions, and the word got back to the early childhood education community.

Because, in this situation, the issue of student-teacher ratios was already on the table, our comparative ethnographic work had the potential to influence American educational practice. But this is not necessarily a good thing. In our article and book we explained that Japanese beliefs about large class size and high student-teacher ratios are very nuanced. For instance, we introduced the theory of a Japanese educator who argued that student-teacher ratios between 10- and 20-children per teacher are a sort of danger zone. With fewer than 10 children in her care, a teacher can provide individual attention. When more than 20 children share one teacher, they come to realise she is too busy, and give up on the expectation that she will give them individual attention. But in classes that have one teacher supervising 10 to 20 students, the children will seek her attention, seeing her as a scarce resource they must compete for, which will lead to frustration on both sides.

Needless to say, by the time our research reached the collective bargaining deliberations, such subtleties of the Japanese approach were lost. In our paper we concluded that increasing student-teacher ratios could only work in the American context if we also changed our notions of how we interact with children. Classes with 26 four-year-olds and one teacher can only work well if the teacher uses an approach that is suited to such a large class, which would mean an approach that is not predicated on her having a close dyadic relationship with each child. If an American preschool teacher who is already overwhelmed by the task of giving adequate attention to 16 children in her care were suddenly given another two or three children, her job satisfaction as well as the quality of her teaching probably would decline. We were trying to use the Japanese case not directly as an argument for raising American student-teacher ratios, but rather to raise the level of complexity in the debate about ratios, quality of care, and methods of teaching. Perhaps in the long-run, by questioning the taken-for-granted assumption that high ratios means low quality of care, our work may have some impact on practice. But in the short run, our introduction of this argument into the political arena of collective bargaining had an undesirable effect. If I had the chance to go back 10 years, I would do things differently. For instance, instead of giving my information to the Lieutenant Governor, I first would present it to local early childhood educators, and urge them to rethink their prioritising of low student-teacher ratios and instead to put their efforts into raising teachers' pay. I probably would not have succeeded in impacting practice, but at least I would not have found myself in the position of aiding the more powerful employers against the underpaid and not very powerful community of early childhood educators.

Teacher Intervention in Children's Fights

Here, if anywhere, is where I would argue that our project has had a positive impact on practice. Liability concerns make it unlikely that American teachers could consider letting older children play with babies. The politically charged climate of collective bargaining makes it inflammatory for our comparative research to be inserted into the debate about student-teacher ratios. Unlike these two issues, managing children's fights is largely in teachers' hands. This in an area where teachers have more latitude to change their practice, if they choose to.

I argued above that our videos were just tools we used to stimulate the multivocal conversations that are the core of our book. However, after the project was complete and the book published, we began to receive requests from people who wanted to see the videos. Whenever I gave lectures on the project, I showed segments of the videotape. Audiences were particularly enthralled by the Komatsudani tape, and especially by what they saw of Hiroki. These experiences led us to the decision to produce a narrated version of the videotape. For a while we distributed the tape ourselves, and for a while this task was handled by Yale University Press. About 300 copies of the tape were sold, mostly to university audio-visual centres and faculty members in departments of education. I wonder how the distribution of the videotape has impacted book sales. What I do know is that every year students in several hundred teacher education programmes in the United States see the *Preschool in Three Cultures* videotape. If, as I estimate, the video is shown in a 100 or more teacher education courses each year, it is reaching a very large audience of pre-service teachers at a point in their career when they are most open to new ideas.

It is unlikely that a student in a teacher education program would see the videotape and decide to emulate Fukui-sensei and not intervene in children's' fights. The idea that adults are responsible for keeping children from hurting themselves and each other is too firmly in place in the American consciousness for it to overturned by watching a video. I hope, however, that watching the Komatsudani tape leads pre-service teachers to question some of their assumptions about classroom management. My hunch is that watching the tape affects pre-service teachers the way it affected me as a parent and teacher of young children. My fieldwork at Komatsudani became a voice in my head that I hear whenever I have to deal with a dispute between children. The voice speaks to me as a series of questions: Are you sure the children can't resolve this dispute without your intervention? Are you sure that your intervening in the dispute will be effective? What are the costs of your intervening? By intervening, are you communicating to the children that they can't work this out on their own? I often eventually intervene in children's fights, but the time I spend considering Fuqui's questions works for me like counting to ten. It gives the children time to work things out on their own and me time to consider the implications of intervening.

If we are sincere about wanting our comparative classroom work to impact classroom practice, then we must present our research in ways that are accessible to practitioners. Making research accessible to teachers does not mean dumbing down the arguments, but rather writing in a way that does not preclude teachers as readers. In various ways, most scholarly writing lets teachers know that this work is not intended for them. If our Preschool in Three Cultures project has had an impact on early childhood education, it is because the book and video address pre-service and in-service teachers.

In order to reach practitioners, we attempted to publish an excerpt from the book in *Young Children*, the journal of the National Association for the Education of Young Children, distributed monthly to approximately 50,000 early childhood educators. The paper, which was titled 'A Japanese approach to dealing with misbehavior' told the story of how Fukui-sensei and the other staff at Komatsudani deal with Hiroki by not intervening in his fights. I have had my share of critical readers' reports, but never any as angry as the three reports I received from the journal *Young Children*. One reader wrote: "It would be criminally irresponsible for our journal to publish a paper which condones teachers doing nothing while children experience bodily harm." Another wrote, "I can only hope that the teacher described in this paper is the exception and not the rule in Japan. I cannot believe that a civilized society could allow children to brutalize each other while adults stand passively by." A third wrote: "The argument of this paper makes for provocative reading for scholars, who would appreciate that the importance of cultural context would make it unwise to attempt to copy the Japanese approach in the United States. But this would be a confusing and even dangerous message to present to practitioners, who might imitate the Japanese laissez-faire approach, with disastrous results for the children in their care."

My first reaction to these readers' reports was to feel personally insulted. But upon reflection, I realised that the insult really is to teachers, who are represented in these responses as impressionable, naive, and unable to deal with complexity. Scholars, faculty in education, and policy makers (most of whom, not coincidentally, are men) too often think of comparative educational research as something only intended for them. Only after those at or near the top of the feeding chain have had a chance to digest it, can comparative educational findings be repackaged in simpler, prescriptive form for practitioners. I suggest that if this hierarchy were stood on its head, and the primary audience for comparative studies were teachers, the field would be much more lively and the research much more likely to make a difference.

Note

[1] We recorded these responses by videotaping and then transcribing the discussions we held in each site. We also used Likert-scaled items such as 'did you find that classroom too chaotic, too structured, etc' but we didn't end up including our statistical analyses of these responses in our book.

References

Connor, L., Asch, T., & Asch, P. (1986) *Jero Tapakan: Balinese healer.* Cambridge: Cambridge University Press.

Geertz, C. (1973) *The Interpretation of Culture.* New York: Basic Books.

Tobin, J.J., Wu, D.Y.H. & Davidson, D.H. (1987) Class size and student/teacher ratios in the Japanese preschool, *Comparative Education Review*, 31, pp. 533-549.

Tobin, J.J., Wu, D.Y.H. & Davidson, D.H. (1989) *Preschool in Three Cultures.* New Haven: Yale University Press.

Whiting, J. & Whiting, B. (1953) *Child Training and Personality: a cross-cultural study.* New Haven: Yale University Press.

Creating a New Methodology for Comparative Educational Research: the contribution of the International School Effectiveness Research Project

DAVID REYNOLDS

Introduction

The last 20 years have seen an explosion of research in the field of school effectiveness. From a position of considerable marginality within the educational research communities of most societies, what has been called the school effectiveness 'movement' is now increasingly recognised as an educational sub discipline, with its own professional association (The International Congress for School Effectiveness and Improvement), its own journal and own annual meeting. Also, the findings of the discipline have achieved very ready acceptance and take-up within the political system of the United Kingdom (UK), and also more generally within schools themselves, where the notion of being given 'good practice' on which to build has been enthusiastically supported (see Reynolds et al, 1996 for a survey of these developments).

It would be wrong to portray the school effectiveness discipline as being universally uncritically accepted, however. There have been arguments from many within the sociology of education (Angus, 1993) that school effectiveness research takes 'too much for granted' in its definitions of effectiveness, which are usually argued to be the same as those of governments and more conservative educational philosophers. There have also been arguments (Hamilton, 1996) that it is concerned with simplistic, often managerially-based, policies to improve the inevitably highly complex world of schools and classrooms. There have also been arguments (Elliott, 1996) that it has neglected to concern itself with the long term developmental needs of teachers, and that indeed it neglects to add the 'voice' of the teacher to its many sources of ideas, preferring instead to give primacy and in some cases exclusivity to the voice of the school effectiveness researcher in understanding schools and classrooms.

There is no doubt that, by the early 1990s, many of us in the discipline saw these criticisms as partially justified, and also recognised the quite simplistic nature of much of the research base, and the quite simplistic nature of the educational remedies associated with it (Reynolds & Packer, 1992). It was also the case then, and still is the case now, that the number of reviews of the research base exceeds the number of empirical studies by a factor of perhaps ten to one, and that more empirical research is urgently needed to develop the field. The fact that the school effectiveness research paradigm was by the early 1990s gaining considerable influence upon governments and practitioners was itself another reason for some of us wanting a new, 'second wave' of research to be undertaken that might justify some of this attention. For a group of us, the 'second wave' research was planned to be the International School Effectiveness Research Project (ISERP), a project that was to move school effectiveness research onto the comparative education stage.

The Disciplinary Context in the Early 1990s

Six sets of factors had an influence upon those of us in the discipline who chose to go the 'international route' in school effectiveness. First, the early 1990s had for the first time seen research findings which suggested that the effective schools 'correlates' or 'factors' might have been somewhat different in different geographical contexts, with the Dutch educational research community, particularly, being unable to replicate more than a handful of the 'classic' school or classroom factors from the American 'five factor' theories of educational effectiveness (see Scheerens & Bosker, 1997, for a summary). Particularly interesting and potentially important was the failure of Dutch empirical research to show the importance of the leadership of the head/principal in creating effective schools (van de Grift, 1990), in marked contrast to the importance of this role and of the role occupants shown from American research (Levine & Lezotte, 1990).

The apparent 'context specificity' of school effectiveness factors and the existence of this phenomenon even *within* countries that was shown in the American Louisiana School Effectiveness Study (LSES) findings of *different* school effectiveness factors being associated with effectiveness in different socio economic contexts (Teddlie & Stringfield, 1993), suggested an interesting future direction for research, which would involve varying social context systematically both within and between countries in order to see which factors universally 'travelled' and which factors did not, but required particular cultural and social contexts to be potentiated in their effects. Celebrating contextual difference would, some of us thought, present a more complex picture of effectiveness factors than the early simplistic 'snake oil' that had rightly been the subject of the robust criticism from around the world noted earlier.

Secondly, we wanted to increase the chances of our being able to generate theory, since the variation in 'what worked' if it could be explained and theoretically modelled, would force the field towards the development of more complex and multifaceted accounts than the 'one size fits all' mentality that had hitherto existed in the field. Useful contributions were already being made in the area of theory in the early 1990s (Creemers & Scheerens, 1989; Creemers, 1992) – we wanted to take them further. We wanted to force the discipline to ask the 'why' questions.

Thirdly, a number of us had also increasingly come to realise that the importance of comparative international research is that only these kinds of studies could tap the full range in school and classroom quality, and therefore in potential school and classroom effects. *Within* any country we recognised that the range of school factors in terms of 'quantity' variables (such as size, financial resources, quality of buildings) and in terms of 'quality' factors (such as press for achievement) was likely to be much smaller than the variation in such factors *across* countries. Additionally, we felt that other countries might show educational features that were absent from our 'home countries' that might be of use in reform and revision of the educational policies and practices of those home countries.

Fourthly, we had become concerned about the over simple, not to say simplistic, potential transfer of educational policies that was already going on between countries. The 'importation' of educational policies from one country with one context to another country of different contextual conditions is of course something that has had a long history. However, when ISERP was being planned in the early 1990s, the process had reached its peak in North America with the popularity of the Stevenson (1992) cross cultural comparisons of Taiwan and the United States generating simplistic suggestions that the United States should adopt levels of children's time in school and the like that were characteristic of the Pacific Rim (see further elaboration in Reynolds & Farrell, 1996). Although in retrospect it is clear that the ISERP findings and speculations about Taiwan may well themselves have encouraged equally simplistic discussion in the UK (see Reynolds [1997] for a cautionary tale), it is sobering to remember that the possible explication of the *complexity* of these issues and the *difficulty* of cross cultural transfers was one of the principal reasons behind the intention to conduct ISERP.

Fifthly, we had become concerned about the ability of the existing comparative studies from the International Association for the Evaluation of Educational Achievement (IEA) to deliver the increments in knowledge of comparative education that were needed. These studies were usually cross sectionally based, so that attainment at a point in time was utilised as the dependent variable, yet this design meant that cultural, economic, social *and* educational influences were all possible determinants of any achievement scores. Additionally, there was with the IEA studies the 'smell' of a weakly implemented research design, in which countries lacked fidelity with the original study methodology, which was clearly implicated for example in the widely varying response rates to questionnaires across countries. Indeed, the reliance in all these studies on questionnaires, rather than on the direct observation and collection of data by researchers that would of course have been considerably more expensive, severely limited their usefulness (see Reynolds et al, 1994a, for a further critique of these studies).

It also seemed to us that the entire intellectual enterprise connected with the international achievement surveys had been only dimly aware of the potential importance of 'context' in determining research strategy. In the recent Third International Mathematics and Science Study (TIMSS) of variation in mathematics achievement for example, (Keys et al, 1996), it is clear that the only possible explanation for the low proportion of children from Pacific Rim societies reporting that they were 'very rarely' tested, was that the possibility of a 'test' being seen as separate from the conventional routine of instruction that is a clearly 'Western' or 'Anglo Saxon' practice is simply not part of children's or teachers' mind set in the Pacific Rim. The failure of the IEA study of written composition to be able to compare the performance of students in different countries, because they concluded that what was called written composition needed to be seen in a cultural context and not considered a general cognitive capacity or activity (Purves, 1992), is a sobering reminder of the, unappreciated within the IEA paradigm, importance of cultural context and its associated meanings (see also Alexander, 1996).

From all this, we determined that we would use 'cultural immersion' and other techniques to ensure that the 'context' of different societies educational systems was charted and understood. Such qualitatively based methods would, we believed, also help us to paint educational pictures of classrooms, schools and the wider society to act as *explanations* for any differential in school or country performance, which had not hitherto been systematically attempted within the IEA paradigm.

Sixthly, we were very concerned about the ability of the comparative education research community to enhance understanding of cross national school/society interaction. The discipline evidenced, and still evidences, theoretical analyses without any apparent empirical support, often simple and descriptive empirical data in the rare cases where such data are collected, and evidences the constant assumption that educational policy changes have inevitable effects upon educational system functioning and outcomes. The absence of any dependent variable such as achievement scores in virtually all studies made, and makes, it very difficult indeed to assess the relative contribution of the 'independent variables' of culture, educational system and the like to national educational functioning.

For all the above six reasons, we determined that ISERP would be different.

Setting up ISERP

This, then, was the intellectual background which formed the foundations for the design of ISERP. The initial suggestion of doing some internationally based research had come from the American effectiveness researchers Sam Stringfield and Charles Teddlie, who had directed LSES (Teddlie & Stringfield, 1993). David Reynolds and Bert Creemers were approached to represent the European traditions in the field, a natural request since all four of us had collaborated together and helped to organise the founding of the International Congress for School Effectiveness and Improvement, the professional organisation of the discipline.

Early discussions, snatched at the American Educational Research Association in Boston in 1991, were followed by a planning meeting in The Hague in late 1991, at which it rapidly became clear what both the intellectual and the practical problems of international school effectiveness research were to be. Indeed, after participating in the series of planning meetings that were to follow, it became starkly obvious why comparative education as a discipline, and international school effectiveness as a sub discipline, had made so little intellectual progress in the last 30 years.

The problems were twofold. First, simply understanding the nature of other countries' educational systems was itself a major intellectual task. The variation in starting ages for junior school (age six in the United States, age five in the UK for example) was a simple, descriptive factor that was at the beginning unknown to us. The large variation in *per capita* expenditure characteristic of the United States educational system, because of its reliance on property or sales taxes for over 90% of total expenditure, again was unknown to the non-Americans. The difference in national educational histories, cultures, assessment systems (public examination or continuous assessment based) was also substantial for the three countries (United States, UK, Netherlands) involved in the planning study at that stage.

Secondly, the intellectual variation between the four co-founders of ISERP was also marked: a rather surprising factor given the apparently small amount of intellectual territory covered by school effectiveness. Two of the four were intellectually more centred upon teacher effectiveness than school effectiveness (Creemers & Stringfield), one of the four knew both areas (Teddlie) and one of the four (Reynolds) was primarily a school-level researcher who had very rarely entered into observation or work in classrooms. Superimposed upon the basic intellectual variation within the team was a further variation in the national traditions of school effectiveness research, with the UK representative for example being committed to the use of multiple outcomes in social/affective, as well as academic, areas whilst the representative of the Netherlands school effectiveness community regarded social outcomes of any kind with profound scepticism.

To ensure that all persons in the core team understood the knowledge bases that were only partially understood by individual members of the ISERP team, a large scale literature review of the world's school effectiveness knowledge was undertaken, with sections focusing on the existing literature, the lessons of existing studies in the field and the observation systems of classroom settings and teacher behaviours that were already in existence. This was eventually published for wider circulation (Reynolds et al, 1994b) and did have a very positive effect in ensuring a degree of mutual understanding between members of the core team.

The Methodology of ISERP

ISERP eventually came to comprise nine countries, split across three broad regions: the United States and Canada; Australia, Hong Kong and Taiwan; and the Netherlands, Norway, the UK and Ireland. Each country selected either six or 12 primary or elementary schools, with these schools selected to be of high, average or low effectiveness, based upon either prior data on their schools' intakes and outcomes or on the nomination of those with close knowledge of the schools such as inspectors, advisers and the like. Half of the schools were selected from low socio-economic status communities and half from those of middle socio-economic status.

The basic methodology of the study was to follow a cohort of children aged seven through their schools for two years, the age being chosen to maximise the chance of ensuring that school effects did not masquerade as intake effects and because children in many societies of the world, such as Norway, did not begin their education until age seven. Mathematics was to be the dependent variable on which the relative progress of children and societies was to be measured, selected because it was more 'culture free' than any other measure, given its similarity as a body of knowledge across cultures. It goes without saying that the most intellectually interesting outcomes to have studied, such as national differences in achievement in 'history', 'civics' or 'social studies', would have been the most difficult to ensure the comparability of cross-culturally.

The ISERP study did, however, break new ground in the area of outcomes by utilising measures of children's social outcomes in the different countries, such as measures of attitudes to education, self perceived ability in school and attitudes to teachers. Most innovative of all, the research was to include direct observation of teachers in different contexts in different countries, with the use of an adapted version of Robert Slavin's QAIT classroom observation system designed to measure quality (Q) of teaching, appropriateness (A) of teaching, the teacher's use of incentives (I) and the teacher's time use (T) (Schaffer, 1994).

Lastly, the research design was based upon, as might have been expected from our conclusions about the deficiencies in existing quantitative methods, the use of 'mixed' methods, both quantitative and qualitative. Immersion in the schools and cultures of different countries was to be undertaken by the 'core' research team, to understand the cultural 'taken for granted' that might be the explanation for certain effectiveness factors 'travelling' or not. Full appreciation of the educational policies of different countries was additionally to be facilitated by a programme of interviews with key personnel at school, district and national levels.

Conducting Comparative Research: the problems

Although ISERP represented an innovative and pioneering approach to the problems involved in international comparative research, there is no doubt that the study did not possess the time or, at the planning stage, the knowledge base to make soundly-based decisions in all areas of study design and implementation. The pressure to generate instrumentation in the areas of school processes, teacher experiential and biographical variables, teacher behaviours, principal or headteacher factors, and pupils' year/year transitions, as well as to find outcome measures in the areas of mathematics, reading, the social attitudes of pupils, the social attitudes to teachers of pupils and the attitudes to self of pupils (self esteem), all meant that there was a tendency to use pre-existing instruments in cases where team members had used them before. Thus, the key outcome measures of mathematics and also reading (for the restricted number of countries that used it as a measure) were the Comprehensive Test of Basic Skills (CTBS) tests from the United States and the measure of teachers' classroom behaviour as we noted above was taken directly from the Special Strategies Observation System (SSOS), itself devised to measure the impact of various American school improvement programmes (Schaffer, 1994). The measures of teachers' 'locus of control' and 'perception of personal power' were also taken from past work in Hong Kong, although children's 'locus of control' was measured by a scale of American design.

Inevitably, there were problems with these procedures. As instruments were translated from their original language to another, there were difficulties when the meaning of the words in the new culture changed too. The mathematics tests measured children's performance in what can be loosely termed 'basic skills', but did not necessarily pick up performance in the 'investigative' areas of maths that have become a feature of the American and British primary school experience. Concepts in the questionnaires concerning pupils' social attitudes were clearly much closer to the educational discourse of some countries than of others, as in the case of the 'democratic social attitudes' that were measured in all countries because of the justifiable insistence of the Norwegian team, who rightly pointed to the key importance of this area of pupil outcomes in their own country.

One particular problem where a concept did not appear to travel at all well cross-culturally was provided by the use of 'locus of control' measures derived from the American literature (Crandall et al, 1965). Anglo Saxon thinking on this issue posited the existence of children who could be scaled as either internally controlled (seeing themselves as responsible for their own success or failure) or externally controlled (seeing themselves as determined by broader forces that were largely out of their control). Children were accordingly given situations in which they might find themselves, and asked to choose either an 'external' or 'internal' response as the reason for the existence of the situation. Such attempts to use oppositional, 'either/or' categories simply generated confusion and mystification amongst the children of the Pacific Rim, whose Confucian traditions included both a stress on the importance of an individual's effort and striving *and* an emphasis upon the influence of religious and mystic forces outside the control of the individual, both operating at the same time.

The last concern that was generated by the contingencies of group membership, the pace of the enterprise and the inevitable difficulties of conducting work spread across multiple continents was that there was insufficient time to train observers in the standardised use of techniques of classroom observation. This observation of teachers' behaviours in their classes and the related observation of pupils' levels of time on task was a key part of the ISERP design, since the intention was to see whether the same teaching behaviours were associated with effectiveness within the different cultural contexts of various countries and whether the behaviours that were effective were the same across countries. The problem was that the observation instrument was partially one of *high* inference measures, and partially one of *low* inference. The measurement of pupils' time on task was an extremely low inference measure in which observers simply looked around a class every eight minutes, or so, and judged what proportion of the class were 'on task', defined as working, listening or in other ways concentrating upon their class task. However, the measurement of such aspects of the classroom as the teachers' behaviour proved more difficult, since it required the gradation of teachers in terms of aspects such as their 'classroom control' techniques, their 'exhibiting of personal enthusiasm', or their 'skill in utilisation of questioning', all areas in which their behaviour had to be judged by 'high inference'. In Taiwan, for example, it is clear that the concepts of 'positive academic feedback' and 'negative academic feedback' caused particular problems given Taiwanese definitions of 'positive' and 'negative'. The scale item had been chosen with an Anglo Saxon or European conception in mind, in which positive feedback would be a statement by the teacher such as 'well done – keep it up!' and negative feedback would be evidenced by a teacher saying something such as 'that's poor work – you need to improve'. In Taiwan, and to an extent in Hong Kong, such judgements proved more difficult, since it would have been possible *within the culture* to see extreme negativity from a teacher as being 'positive', and likewise an attempt to shield the child from criticism by saying something pleasant about their work as 'negative academic feedback' in the culture, given the perceived need for all children to achieve high achievement levels in the Pacific Rim.

ISERP's problems did not just relate to the difficulties of ensuring that concepts 'travelled' cross-culturally. The enterprise that went into the field in the years from 1992 to 1994 (and to 1996 in the case of the UK) was also intellectually deficient in two further ways. First, the conceptualisation of which school effectiveness and teacher effectiveness factors were to be measured within the nine different countries reflected the literature review about 'what matters' in affecting educational achievement that had been conducted by the 'core' team (Reynolds et al, 1994b). However, this review of course reflected the concerns of the countries that had contributed to the school effectiveness literature, namely those Anglo Saxon societies of the United States, the UK and Australia. No attempt was made to include school effectiveness factors that might have been important within the *different* cultural contexts of other societies in which there had not been school effectiveness research. Vulliamy (1987), for example, noted the importance of contextually specific factors in Papua New Guinea in accounting for whether a school was effective or not, in this case 'an absence of corruption in teaching appointments to the school' which turned out to be heavily associated with effectiveness.

Additionally, many of the factors customarily used within the research literatures of 'Anglo Saxon' societies might have had very limited explanatory power within societies like the Pacific Rim for example. The personal and biographical variables that often explain variance within the Anglo Saxon societies reflect the influence of personal factors in determining individual teachers' and headteachers' ability to construct their practice – one would expect such factors to be much less important in Pacific Rim societies where the giving of a 'strong technology' of agreed practice to all teachers and headteachers is explicitly designed to eradicate such personal influences.

The second way in which the ISERP enterprise was deficient intellectually was in its focus, inherited from the behaviourist assumptions of Anglo Saxon school effectiveness research, upon the importance of studying behaviour, as for example in the teacher behaviour observation schedules described above. As Alexander (1996) notes, this focus misses the discourse that is associated with, but partially independent of, the nature of the behaviour – whole class interactive instruction as practised in some European and Pacific Rim societies should not be seen as just a set of teacher behaviours but as an emotionally intense, rich, fast paced discourse that cannot be fully understood unless one appreciates the nature of the educational discourse that is viewed as appropriate in societies such as Switzerland and those of the Pacific Rim. To try to view the behaviour on its own, without appreciation of the discourse associated with it, is to adopt a one dimensional viewpoint of a three dimensional situation.

The Value of Comparative Enquiry

The very large volume of data that we have collected has so far only been partially analysed. We have established that there are differences between countries in their levels of achievement that seem very similar to those reported in other studies (see Reynolds & Farrell, 1996 for a review), with the Pacific Rim societies obtaining higher levels of achievement than 'Anglo Saxon' societies (Creemers et al, 1996). Interestingly, the UK appears to possess a range of pupil achievement larger than other societies, and the UK system level explains more variation in pupil achievement, suggesting a larger variation in school quality. The social class of parents is a factor more important in determining educational outcomes in the UK than in Pacific Rim societies, and we have speculated about the utility of the strong 'technology' of teaching and schooling that exists in those societies in the attempt to ensure equal treatment for all. Further, and final, analysis is ongoing.

More generally, the ISERP study has validated, for those involved in it, the value of comparative study, for two reasons that have been generally well established and reported so far and one reason that we have discovered for ourselves.

First, we have simply seen in other societies a variety of educational practices at classroom and school levels that would not have been seen had the core research team stayed within their own societies. In the Pacific Rim societies for example, the majority of lesson time is filled with what has been called 'whole class interactive' instruction, in which relatively short lessons of 40 minutes are filled with fast, emotionally intense presentations from teachers, with accompanying very high levels of involvement from pupils. This model of teaching, which is also found within a European context in societies such as Switzerland, is now the subject of considerable debate within UK schools. In Norway, as a contrast, there is no formal assessment of children through the entire phase of their elementary/primary education from the age of seven, a marked contrast to the UK practice of formal assessment and associated publication of results. In the Pacific Rim societies again, one can see micro level educational practices such as teachers teaching from a stage at the front of the class some six inches high (to help those at the back of the class to see), pupils marching to assembly through corridors in which loudspeakers play music (to ensure a relaxed attitude) and pupils starting the afternoon session of school with a 'sleeping' lesson (to deal with the fatigue brought about by the frantic pace of the school and the heat/humidity of the climate). Put simply, comparative investigation shows an enhanced range of what appears to be educationally possible.

The benefits to comparative investigation are more than simply a knowledge of educational factors that might of course be utilised in programmes of experimentation in one's own country. They are, secondly, that one is made aware of educational philosophies that are radically different from one's own, or those of the government of one's own country. In Norway, for example, there is a strong commitment to the child as an 'active citizen', and to what are called 'democratic values' that have no British or American equivalents. In Pacific Rim societies like Taiwan, there is a philosophy that the role of the school is to ensure that all children learn, and that a strong 'technology' of practice should be employed to ensure that children are not dependent on their family background. Such societies are very concerned about the use of practices to improve the achievement of their trailing edge of pupils, therefore, and are rather less concerned with the education of the 'gifted and talented' than are the societies of the UK and United States.

There is a third reason for comparative investigation we have discovered that is even more important than the two above, concerning the possibility that within the right kind of comparative framework one can move beyond looking at the practices of other societies and actually so empathise with other societies that one can look back at one's own society with the benefit of their perspective. Such 'acculturation' is what happened to many of us in ISERP when we were confronted with, and may have identified with, Pacific Rim educational systems. Looking back at the British system through their 'lens', one wonders at the utility of the combination of the very complex technology of practice that is evident in British primary practice, for example, with methods of teacher education that are premised on the importance of teachers 'discovering', or at the least playing an active role in learning about, the appropriate methods to use. To a Taiwanese educationist, this celebrates the desires of teachers for their long term developmental needs above the needs of children to receive a reliable, consistent, predictable and competently provided experience as they pass through their schools.

The use of another culture's 'lens' to better understand the limitations and strengths of one's own educational practice also applies at the level of educational philosophy as well as educational practice. As an example, those of us involved in the British ISERP team would have historically viewed our primary education practice as loosely 'progressive' and indeed would have thought that in many senses it was the envy of the world. The encouragement of children to learn on their own rather than simply being instructed, the new sets of social outcomes that the system is widely argued to concentrate upon (Alexander, 1995) and the reduced emphasis upon the testing of knowledge acquisition are widely argued to be the hallmarks of progressive practice in the British system.

Seen from a Pacific Rim perspective, however, the characteristics of the British system would be seen as regressive, not progressive. Transferring the burden of learning to pupils would be argued as maximising both social class influences and variation between pupils within Taiwanese culture, since pupils' learning gains would depend on what they brought to the learning situation in terms of achievement levels and backgrounds. Removing the constant of the teacher would be seen as further maximising individual variation in knowledge gain. Avoiding the testing of basic skills could be seen as maximising the chances of children who have missed acquiring particular knowledge bases being left without them, through the absence of short term feedback loops that alert school authorities.

Conclusions

The ISERP study has begun to generate its material on educational systems, nested within cultures, and to begin its speculations about which factors may travel across contexts, and which are potentiated within contexts, at precisely the time when such issues are generating controversy within comparative education. On the one side are those who think that educational practices are manifestations of broader cultural patterns, values and styles of discourse that exist at societal level. Seen from this perspective, whole class interactive teaching in French classrooms, for example, can be seen as related to the French philosophic love of discourse. Supporting this view is the evidence from studies such as the IEA Classroom Environment study that once other wider cultural and social factors are accounted for, teacher behaviours themselves add little explanatory variance (Anderson et al, 1989).

Another perspective is to argue that the educational policies and processes of different societies are variable *responses* to cultural and structural situations and therefore have a degree of independence and potential transferability across contexts. Seen from this perspective, methods that are regarded as effective such as whole class interactive teaching or the rapid feedback to teachers produced by the short loops of repeated testing may be utilised in different cultural contexts with good chances of effectiveness independent of cultural context.

One suspects that the answer to these disciplinary controversies is unlikely to lie in the conduct of further studies of the ISERP variety, whatever their utility in terms of pioneering new methodologies and in terms of new insights. What may be needed is for experimentation to take place, in which the methods from certain contexts are experimentally 'tried out' within other different contexts. As the 'implanted' methods interact with societal structures and cultures one may see either educational potency or adverse effects, the precise nature of which will depend upon the systemic/cultural interaction. From this process, in turn, one can gain a deeper understanding of the nature of the cultures of different societies, the values of their inhabitants and their styles of discourse as the methods variably interact with them. In comparative education, as maybe in education more generally, the way to understand something as complex as the educational system may be to try to change it.

Note

[1] Parts of this chapter are adapted from D. Reynolds, B.P.M. Creemers, S. Stringfield & C. Teddlie, (1998) Climbing an educational mountain: conducting the International School Effectiveness Research Project (ISERP), in G. Walford (Ed.) *Doing Research about Education*. Lewes: Falmer Press.

References

Alexander, R.J. (1995) *Versions of Primary Education*. London: Routledge.

Alexander, R.J. (1996) *Other Primary Schools and Ours: hazards of international comparison*. Warwick: Centre for Research in Elementary and Primary Education.

Anderson, L.M., Ryan, D.W. & Shapiro, B.J. (1989) *The IEA Classroom Environment Study*. Oxford: Pergamon Press.

Angus, L. (1993) The sociology of school effectiveness, *British Journal of Sociology of Education*, 4, pp. 333-345.

Crandall, V.C., Katkovsky, W. & Crandall, V.J. (1965) Children's beliefs in their own control of reinforcements in intellectual-academic situations, *Child Development*, 36, pp. 91-109.

Creemers, B.P.M. & Scheerens, J. (Eds) (1989) Developments in school effectiveness research, *International Journal of Educational Research*, 13, pp. 685-825.

Creemers, B. (1992) School effectiveness and effective instruction – the need for a further relationship, in J. Bashi & Z. Sass (Eds) *School Effectiveness and Improvement*. Jerusalem: Hebrew University Press.

Creemers, B.P.M., Reynolds, D., Stringfield, S. & Teddlie, C. (1996) World class schools: some further findings. Paper presented at the annual meeting of the American Educational Research Association, New York.

Elliott, J. (1996) School effectiveness research and its critics: alternative visions of schooling, *Cambridge Journal of Education*, 26, pp. 199-208.

Hamilton, D. (1996) Peddling feel good factors, *Forum*, 38(2), pp. 54-56.

Keys, W., Harris, S. & Fernandes, C. (1996) *Third International Mathematics and Science Study [TIMSS], First National Report, Part 1*. Slough: National Foundation for Educational Research.

Levine, D.U. & Lezotte, L.W. (1990) *Unusually Effective Schools: a review and analysis of research and practice*. Madison: National Center for Effective Schools Research and Development.

Purves, A.C. (1992) *The IEA Study of Written Composition II: education and performance in fourteen countries*. Oxford: Pergamon Press.

Reynolds, D. & Packer, A. (1992) School effectiveness and school improvement in the 1990s, in D. Reynolds & P. Cuttance (Eds) *School Effectiveness*. London: Cassell.

Reynolds, D., Creemers, B.P.M., Bird, J., Farrell, S. & Swint, F. (1994a) School effectiveness – the need for an international perspective, in D. Reynolds, B.P.M. Creemers, P.S. Nesselrodt, E.C. Schaffer, S. Stringfield & C. Teddlie (Eds) *Advances in School Effectiveness Research and Practice*, pp. 217-237. London: Pergamon Press.

Reynolds, D., Creemers, B.P.M., Stringfield, S., Teddlie, C., Schaffer, E. & Nesselrodt, P. (1994b) *Advances in School Effectiveness Research and Practice*. Oxford: Pergamon Press.

Reynolds, D., Creemers, B.P.M., Hopkins, D., Stoll, L. & Bollen, R. (1996) *Making Good Schools*. London: Routledge.

Reynolds, D. & Farrell, S. (1996) *Worlds Apart? A Review of International Studies of Educational Achievement Involving England*. London: HMSO for OFSTED.

Reynolds, D. (1997) Good ideas can wither in another culture, *The Times Educational Supplement*, 19 September, p. 2.

Schaffer, E.C. (1994) The contributions of classroom observation to school effectiveness research, in D. Reynolds, B.P.M. Creemers, P. Nesselrodt, E.C. Schaffer, S. Stringfield & C. Teddlie, *Advances in School Effectiveness Research and Practice*. Oxford: Pergamon.

Scheerens, J. & Busker, R. (1997) *The Foundations of School Effectiveness*. Oxford: Pergamon Press.

Stevenson, H. (1992) Learning from Asian schools, *Scientific American*, December, pp. 32-38.

Teddlie, C. & Stringfield, S. (1993) *Schools make a Difference: lessons learned from a 10-year study of school effects*. New York: Teachers College Press.

Van de Grift, W. (1990) Educational leadership and academic achievement in secondary education, *School Effectiveness and School Improvement*, 1, pp. 26-40.

Vulliamy, G. (1987) School effectiveness research in Papua New Guinea, *Comparative Education*, 23, pp. 209-223.

Culture in Pedagogy, Pedagogy across Cultures

ROBIN ALEXANDER

Why Compare?

This chapter's title encapsulates two of its principal arguments. First, extending Sadler's maxim that education 'is an expression of national life and character', I argue that the educational activity which we call pedagogy – the purposive mix of educational values and principles in action, of planning, content, strategy and technique, of learning and assessment, and of relationships both instrumental and affective – is a window on the culture of which it is a part, and on that culture's underlying tensions and contradictions as well as its publicly-declared educational policies and purposes. Second, like many others these days I argue that the comparative perspective is an important and necessary part of the quest to understand and improve the science, art or craft of teaching, and to enable us to distinguish those aspects of teaching which are generic and cross international boundaries from those which are culture-specific.

Some (no doubt) are born comparative educationists, some achieve a comparative perspective, and some have a comparative perspective thrust upon them. My own route into comparative research has been via a quest over 30 years or so to understand primary education in England in order to play some part in attempting to improve it. In saying this, I endorse David Hargreaves's argument (1996; 1997) that in research fields like medicine and education which are contingent on professional practice the amelioration of that practice is an important and necessary aspiration, though I reject as ignorant and mischievous the claim of those who use Hargreaves's work to justify their accusation that educational researchers are uninterested in the quality of educational practice and have little to offer it. I do not see the amelioration principle, incidentally, as a threat to my intellectual autonomy, for it motivates, but does not predetermine, what I do.

In this quest I have ventured different perspectives and methodological stances, and I have ranged over the English system of primary education as a whole from national policy to Local Education Authority (LEA) mediation, school-level provision and the transactions of individual teachers and pupils (Alexander, 1997). I have undertaken conceptual analysis and critique of the ideas and ideologies by which, ostensibly at least, the practices of English primary education are sustained, guided and justified (Alexander, 1984). I have examined the complex and not always predictable relationship between those ideas and how teaching is actually conducted, or between the public language and private practice of primary education, theory espoused and theory in use (Alexander, 1988). Using methodologies as different as survey and case study, systematic non-participant observation and anthropological fieldnotes, computerised analysis of classroom discourse and teacher biography, I have sought to gain a purchase on that practice empirically, and I have sought to use the resulting data to construct explanatory and predictive theories about primary teachers and primary teaching (Alexander, 1995).

As this work has evolved I have found it increasingly important to keep in view the influence of two contexts: first, the context of *time present* – the system as a whole, the complexity of the contemporary web of policy and culture within which classrooms are embedded; and second, the context of *time past* – the powerful continuities of educational history, especially the continuing resonance in late 20th century English primary education of the structures and assumptions of the 19th century elementary system.

Thus, the comparative perspective for me was not my starting point, for I came to it late. Nor did it mean that I was losing my interest in, and concern for, primary education in England. Rather, comparative research has provided an additional and increasingly necessary element in this enterprise: a third, spatial, dimension – time elsewhere, perhaps – to augment those of time present and time past. This is not that far removed, incidentally, from Tobin's argument that comparative ethnographic narrative should be properly situated in the contexts of time, place and social structure (Tobin, 1989) – though it is a destination arrived at by a different route.

Political, Conceptual and Methodological Imperatives

As I proceeded with this research agenda – and matters came to a head in 1991-1992 with the controversy which attended the publication of my Leeds research (Alexander 1995, 1997) and my involvement in the United Kingdom (UK) government's so-called 'three wise men' enquiry

(Alexander et al, 1992) – the arguments for a stronger international perspective on primary teaching revolved round three imperatives: *political, conceptual* and *methodological*. None of them was novel: all had exercised others besides myself for a long time. But their frustrating longevity was precisely the point. Short of violent revolution, going international seemed the most promising way to make progress.

The *political* imperative was to loosen the rhetorical stranglehold of the traditional/progressive polarisation into which the public debate about standards and quality in primary education has been routinely corralled since the 1960s. On this matter the prognosis is no more encouraging now than it was then. The debate may well have gone international but the flurry of educational cherry-picking which attends each newly-published international league table of educational performance has so far been of a kind which supports rather than challenges the quintessentially English traditional vs progressive polarity (consider the current advocacy of homework, textbooks and whole class teaching, for example).

The *conceptual* imperative was successfully to confront the continuing historical dominance of a particular view of the purposes and content of primary education whose hegemony has informed and reinforced the political polarisation to which I have just referred. In this, the sharp divide between what I have called 'Curriculum I' (the so-called 'basics' of literacy and numeracy) and 'Curriculum II' (everything else) is open neither to discussion nor to negotiation (Alexander, 1984). The model, rooted in the 19th-century elementary system (which had its counterparts in many other countries) was reasserted in the core/non-core hierarchy of the National Curriculum, as implemented from 1988 onwards, and has been given a further shot in the arm by the current obsession with literacy and numeracy targets and by the presumption that educational 'standards' and 'effectiveness' are defined at the primary stage by these alone. The dominant values informing this view of primary education – in the 1990s as in the 1870s – are economic instrumentalism, cultural reproduction and social control. As sociologists or historians we can note such continuities as grist to the mill of social theory. As educationists we have to challenge them. We needed then, and we need now, to enlarge both our repertoire of curricular possibilities and our vocabulary for exploring them: this, of course, is a classic argument for comparativism.

The *methodological* imperative was to find ways of addressing seven familiar but stubborn problems of classroom research.

The first is a sense that if the concepts and practices of primary education are historically and politically constrained, so perhaps are the available methods for researching them. Arguably, the educational division between Curriculum I and II has its methodological counterpart in the polarisation of so-called 'hard' and 'soft' educational research methods – quantitative and qualitative, psychometric and ethnographic, pre-ordinate and responsive, which in turn testifies to the pervasive power in Western (and especially English) thought of dualism, positivism, and the 'two cultures' divide between maths and science on the one hand, arts and humanities on the other. (Actually, this makes four cultures, but C.P. Snow was as ensnared by dualism as the rest of us.) It is therefore necessary to ask whether understanding teaching really turns on a choice between so-called 'quantitative' and 'qualitative' techniques; and whether combining these in the somewhat limp compromise of 'mixed methods' – a bit of qualitative data to soften and (Schaffer et al, 1994) 'humanise' the numbers – is a genuine alternative or merely another kind of capitulation to dualism.

Secondly, and relatedly, it seems important to ask whether 'generalisability' – that cardinal criterion for judging the claim of educational research to provide evidence which is usable in the context of policy – should continue to be defined as an exclusively *numerical* construct. By the rules of this canon, any research can claim to offer *insight* in respect of particular schools, classrooms, teachers or children, but if that research fails to meet the statistical criteria of conventional sampling procedures it is deemed to have a limited evidential basis for claims about the wider educational system of which the particular people and phenomena studied are a part. How far are this insistence, and this arithmetical monopoly, justified?

Thirdly, in the particular field of classroom research there is the problem of the parts and the whole. Somehow, we have become adept at dissecting teaching but poor at reconstructing it: good at isolating factors in 'effective' classroom practice such as opportunity to learn, time on task, cognitively-challenging questioning, informative feedback and so on (e.g. Sammons et al, 1995), but less able to demonstrate how these and other elements are reconstituted by teachers and children as coherent and successful learning encounters with a beginning, a middle and an end. Moreover, the factorisation of pedagogy has proved a boon to policymakers and quangos caught up in the rhetoric of 'standards', for such research provides ready legitimation both for shopping lists of teacher training competencies and school inspection criteria and for disembodied nostrums like 'interactive whole class teaching' (Luxton & Last, 1997). The concern here, then, is to find a way of complementing the increasing *atomisation* of teaching with a convincing kind of *holism*, always assuming that we can rid that word of its gently dotty overtones.

Ethnography, of course, offers holistic narratives, but these are of little interest to policy-makers because they fail to meet their criterion of generalisability. Ethnographers in any case tend to be not that interested in the policy applications of their work, and usually steer clear (or at least claim to steer clear) of those unambiguous judgements of quality, success and failure which policy-makers need, heading off in the opposite direction towards supposedly non-judgemental narrative and interpretation. Actually, the educational literature has more than its fair share of tacitly ethnocentric and judgemental, if not outright colonialist, ethnography.

Fourthly and relatedly, I wanted to develop ways of capturing the sights and sounds of the classroom which would take me forwards from deconstructed behaviours derived from coded observation schedules and 'thick description' based on fieldnotes, both of which I had used before. The phrase 'sights and sounds' is used advisedly. In ethnographic terms, the socially-embedded discourse of teachers and pupils is one of the central 'texts' (Watson & Seiler, 1992) of pedagogy. That text has both verbal and – as my colleague Sean Neill (1991) has reminded us – nonverbal aspects; it is words, behaviours, expressions, gestures – and hence meanings. I wanted to develop a methodology for accessing much more of this than I had been able to capture in previous projects. Moreover, experience as a classroom observer in those projects (and for that matter as a teaching practice assessor) had taught me that while it is possible to reach a general conclusion about a lesson's direction, character and impact within that lesson's time-frame, it is rather more difficult within this temporal constraint to apprehend the lesson's deeper layers of meaning. (That – *pace* Christine Agambar, who at the seminar asserted that OFSTED inspections are a duly rigorous form of qualitative research – is what makes researching teaching so very different from inspecting it). It was therefore important to come away from a lesson with as much of it intact as possible, to permit both extended analysis and writing up in a form which those who created the lesson – teachers and children – would recognise.

Fifthly, in the empirical study of teaching we have tended to oppose, rather than to integrate, *structure* and *meaning*. In one of the dominant research traditions meaning – or in symbolic interactionist terms, meanings (plural) – are all-important and the structures which shape and reflect these become almost incidental; in another, meaning tends to be neglected, and teaching methods are divorced from content, content from values, professional action from professional intention, and professional intention from pupil response. Roughly speaking – and there are always exceptions – the latter tendency is evident in much input-process-product quantitative research, notably that undertaken under the banner of school effectiveness.

Sixthly, there was the familiar macro-micro problem of how to unpack that elusive relationship between Sadler's things outside and inside the school – society, culture and policy on the one hand, school and classroom practice on the other. This is partly the policy analyst's concern to track the impact of educational policy on school and classroom practice, noting with Stephen Ball (1992) that policy is not so much uniformly 'implemented' at school level in accordance with managerialist principles as multifariously and sometimes anarchically re-created; and partly the anthropologist's concern to elicit the culturally-embedded values which shape teaching and learning and are manifested in them.

Finally, coming full circle and tying together the methodological and conceptual concerns indicated in this paper's title, I wanted to say something useful about *pedagogy*, about how we conceive of teaching itself. As an extension of the teaching-as-art-or-science debate, I was particularly exercised by the question of whether there is an irreducible core of elements in teaching which are universal in the sense that in some form they are replicated in any and every context and can therefore form the basis for legitimate extrapolation from one context to another. The school effectiveness community believes that there is such a core, and indeed the universality of teaching and the possibility of constructing a universal pedagogic model would seem to be pivotal to the rationale of a project like David Reynolds's ISERP (Reynolds et al, 1994; Creemers, 1996), and to international school effectiveness literature reviews such as the one undertaken by Sammons, Hillmore and Mortimore (1995) for OFSTED, not to mention the 'best buy' reviews commissioned by international agencies like the World Bank (e.g. Lockheed & Verspoor, 1991) and of course the OFSTED *Worlds Apart?* report (Reynolds & Farrell, 1996). There are those, however, who see such aggregations as dangerously ethnocentric (Fuller & Clarke, 1996), and it is obviously important to ask which aspects of teaching are more culture-specific and, being so, tell us as much about the interplay of culture and education as about teaching as such.

Primary Education in Five Cultures: aims and methods

Such musings led to the project Primary Education in Five Cultures. In this I had two aims: first, to build systematically on methods of classroom enquiry and lines of pedagogic analysis developed in the five-year study of education policy and classroom practice in Leeds (Alexander, 1997) and the subsequent ESRC-funded CICADA project on teacher-pupil discourse (Alexander et al, 1996); and second to venture the new ways of studying and interpreting pedagogy which I have just argued for and which I hoped the comparative dimension would facilitate.

The project was initiated in 1992, shortly after the 'three wise men' episode. As an aside on the problems of comparative classroom research it can be noted that working through two of the governments concerned to negotiate access, identify schools and so on took the best part of two years, and that the project did not start until 1994.

The five countries – England, France, Russia, India, USA – were chosen to provide both contrast and comparison. The contrasts – of scale, geography, history and culture – are obvious. Apart from the specific comparisons I discuss below, the most striking promise of comparison lay in discovering how educational policies and practices reflect five rather different versions of democracy. There were five countries rather than the more usual two or one because I wanted to avoid the risk of replacing one kind of dichotomising – the English brand – by another.

The data were gathered at two 'levels' in order to gain purchase on the macro-micro question. Level 2, the school, provides a combination of interview and observational data, the latter including fieldnotes, completed classroom observation schedules, videotapes, lesson transcripts, documents, photographs and end-of-day journals. The classroom data, the core of all this material, relates to two age-groups – six- and nine-year olds – and therefore both permits cross-cultural comparison of the educational experiences of children of these ages (deliberately chosen as being at the mid-point of Key Stages 1 and 2 in the England/Wales system) and gives purchase on development and progression. The other commonality is that about half the lessons observed were language and literacy, thus allowing, again, a cross-cultural commentary on this most universal and basic of basics. The overriding comparative theme, it will by now be clear, was pedagogy.

Two researchers were present at each lesson: one (myself) to interview the teacher, to complete the observation schedule and write fieldnotes, the other to videotape and take photographs. In the Russian and Indian classrooms there was also an interpreter present who gave a *sotto voce* running commentary and translated for me as necessary, enabling me to obtain a basic grasp of the meanings being exchanged during the lesson, which I could then insert in the fieldnotes for matching against the video-recordings and transcripts. Also present in some of the Russian classrooms, it has to be said – and those who have researched in Russian schools will recognise the scenario – were various significant others, watching, checking, commenting and sometimes even intervening.

The Level 1 interviews with policy-makers and officials, both national and local, punctuated the Level 2 work in schools and enabled me to explore what some (e.g. Archer, 1979; Broadfoot, 1996) see as a key variable in national education systems, the extent, form and impact of centralisation/decentralisation and the balance of power and influence as between government, regional or local administration and the school, and within the school between its head and its teachers. They also provided a useful context for a face-validity check on how far the characteristics of the schools and classrooms observed were typical of the region, state or country, and for testing at one level issues and hypotheses arising at the other.

Primary Education in Five Cultures: data

The lesson videotapes and interview audiotapes were later transcribed and (where the medium was French, Hindi or Russian) translated – an essential but expensive and complex process which took the best part of a year. Complete translation of the interviews also allowed me to check the interview questions as posed and the answers as offered against the interpreters' versions and to examine how far the act of interpretation mixes mere translation (if such a notion is admissible) with cultural or political intervention. Using interpreters, securing authentic translations and using them as comparative data are research problems of considerable and vexing importance in their own right.

This range of data-gathering techniques enabled me to address two of the concerns mentioned earlier: the need for classroom data which though at one step removed from the events themselves retain much of their immediacy and permit revisiting (especially important when access to schools has taken two years to negotiate and is unlikely to be repeated); and the search for holistic ways of analysing teaching. Holism is an easily-enunciated and overused word but an extremely complex concept. In teaching it has both spatial and temporal dimensions. That is to say, to capture a 'whole' lesson one needs not just to record the entire sequence from beginning to end (the temporal dimension) but also to capture as much as possible of the depth and diversity of what is happening at any one moment in time (the spatial dimension). Having said that, it is clear that while holism implies a bounded entity, the paradoxical reality is that the whole, at least where teaching is concerned, is infinite. You can no more see, hear, record or analyse everything that happens in classrooms than you can apprehend the universe, for not only are the dynamics of 30 individuals in interaction immensely complex but what is arguably the most important part of the action goes on inside those individuals' heads.

However, for all their necessary selectivity the combination of lesson videotapes, photographs, lesson fieldnotes, documents, lesson transcripts, interview transcripts, and end-of-day journal entries add up to a rich dataset. Each lesson can be revisited by me, and visited by others. I am also using the videotapes, as did Joseph Tobin, to gain an insider perspective from each culture on my outsider descriptions and interpretations before they attain their final, fixed and published status (Tobin & Davidson, 1990, and Tobin's chapter in this volume) – arguably a necessary condition of all comparative research. But the virtue of revisitability also carries penalties, chiefly that the process of analysis becomes increasingly complex and attenuated because every new commentary or gloss on a tape or a transcript is an addition to the data.

It is an enthralling but – in Research Assessment terms – an utterly uneconomic way to conduct research.

Generalisability: statistical or cultural?

When we consider this kind of material, what can be said about another of the problems I mentioned, that of representativeness and generalisability? Agencies like Leverhulme or the Economic and Social Research Council (ESRC) may well feel that if they are to fund a comparative study of aspects of teaching in countries x and y, the outcomes will be findings which, whatever the methodology, will remain sufficiently valid at country level to allow country-country comparison: otherwise, they may argue, why incur the added expense of overseas travel? But how far can what I derive from individual schools – whether (to locate my own data) in Lansing, Holt or Flint, in Moscow, Kursk, Zheleznogorsk or Okhachevskaya, in Delhi, Gurgaon, Faridabad or Sehatpur, in Paris, Nice, Carros-le-Neuf, St Laurent du Var or Cipières, or in Leeds, Wakefield, Calderdale or York – claim to address the condition of primary education anywhere beyond those schools themselves?

It is important to note that this problem is not confined to qualitative research, for when you consider the size and cultural diversity of India, Russia and the USA, and for that matter France and England, it would take a project of considerable size and astronomical cost to satisfy conventional sampling criteria, and almost certainly you would end up with data which sacrificed depth to quantity. The first stage of David Reynolds's ISERP project, which used a very different methodology from my own, had between just five and 10 schools in each country, a scale similar to mine, and he, like myself, was very much in the hands of the host governments or institutions when it came to selecting those schools. Clearly, though I sought range in the selection of schools – especially on the two dimensions of urban/rural and rich/poor – neither typicality nor generalisability, at least as statistical constructs, are plausible claims. To have some sense of the scale of the problem, bear in mind that there are 20,000 primary (in US parlance elementary) schools in England, but 80,000 in the USA and 530,000 in India.

Confronted, as in India and Russia I was, by a strongly positivistic tradition of educational research, this could be difficult. "Interesting" commented academics in Delhi and Moscow, registering scepticism in the face of references to case study, anthropological fieldwork and symbolic interactionism, "but too small a sample: not scientific". The fact that the Level 1 interviews allowed some degree of cross-checking in respect of the typicality of the schools and classrooms visited did not deal with the objection as expressed, for officials' knowledge of the fine detail of the national system was bound to be limited too. Yet there was also a counter-culture. So in Delhi and Moscow, though educational researchers there who operated within the dominant paradigms of psychometry and large-scale survey were unconvinced by the methodology, sociologists and anthropologists whose reference groups lay outside the education research community were not; and they supported my argument, which I want to repeat here, that if we are prepared to detach them from their usual numerical connotations, 'typicality' and 'generalisability' can be entirely legitimate aspirations of qualitative research. The extent to which this claim can be supported, however, rests on two conditions, one conceptual and the other methodological.

The conceptual condition is that one must accept that the culture in which the schools in a country, state or region are located, and which teachers and pupils share, is as powerful a determinant of the character of school and classroom life as are the unique institutional dynamics and local circumstances which make one school different from another. For culture is not extraneous to the school, nor is it merely one of a battery of variables available for correlational analysis in process-product research. Culture both drives and is everywhere manifested in what goes on in classrooms, from what you see on the walls to what you cannot see going on inside children's heads.

Thus, any one school or classroom can tell us a great deal about the country and education system of which it is a part, but only if – and here I come to my second condition – the research methods used are sufficiently searching and sensitive to probe beyond the observable moves and counter-moves of pedagogy to the values these embody. On this basis, a close-grained ethnographic study of one school in Japan can be generalisable culturally if not statistically. Conversely, a national study which sacrifices intensity of analysis to sample size is likely – unless it really is backed by NASA-level resources – neither to be representative in its own terms nor to offer much by way of insight. It is worth remembering that the word 'generalisation' means not only the act of deriving a universal statement from a particular one, but also the construction of a principle or theory which has general application. Classroom research findings which are generalisable in the statistical sense are of little value unless they lead to the formulation of general principles and theories which take our understanding, and our practice, forward. We are all pretty familiar with the 'so what?' problem in educational research – the textbook research design which yields findings without insight.

From Parts to Whole: identifying elements of pedagogy

I turn now to the question of how one makes sense of classroom data of the kind generated at in the Five Cultures project. The basic unit of analysis was the lesson. For each lesson we had verbatim fieldnotes, same-day preliminary accounts and summaries together with approximations of the range and frequency of teachers' and pupils' actions and interactions (using headings derived from the Leeds and CICADA projects), videotapes, transcripts, photographs and interviews. The first stage of analysis was to pilot a procedure for categorising, quantifying and describing the elements in a lesson. We then took 10 lessons, two from each country, five involving six-year-olds, and five involving nine-year-olds, and applied the resulting two-part framework.

The first part of the framework, which was grounded in the full range of data for the lesson, concentrated on the organisational and behavioural aspects of pedagogy: lesson *aims*; learning *tasks*; lesson *structure*; lesson *stages and sequence*; lesson *elements* (teaching group, task focus, pupil generic activities, pupil differentiation, teacher time, pupil time); and start-to-finish *narrative*.

The second part of the framework was grounded in the tapes and transcripts alone and concentrated on the lesson discourse: the *form* of each interaction 'stanza' (participants, length, focus, characteristics and functions); *key words and phrases* (relating to subject-matter, management, behaviour and other values); and *messages and meanings* (again relating to subject-matter, management, behaviour and other values).

In each case there was a conscious attempt from the start to deploy analytical categories which – as argued for earlier – balanced the parts and the whole, the form and the meaning.

This kind of analysis, grounded as it partly was in the two earlier projects, has generated some useful findings and hypotheses relating to themes which have been prominent in my own classroom research and more generally in the several English lines of pedagogic research which include the work of Bennett (1976; 1984), Galton (1980; 1989; 1998), Mortimore (1988), Tizard (1988), Pollard and his colleagues (1985; 1994), Woods (1995; 1996), Edwards & Mercer (1987). In particular, I can now press much further my earlier analysis in two areas: the way *time* is used in primary classrooms, and the anatomisation of *teacher-pupil discourse* (bearing in mind a crucial caveat about the limits of close-grained analysis of discourse when three-fifths of the material is translated into English from other languages).

Mapping Pedagogy across Cultures

The next stage was to find a way to relate the resulting categorisations and accounts within lessons, across lessons, and across countries. What the preliminary analysis allowed was the setting out of a number of *dimensions* of pedagogy, some grounded in the earlier UK research, some arising from this project's international data, whereby we could chart on continua the similarities and differences between lessons and examine the possibilities and limitations of broader country-country comparisons. The idea is informed by the basic anthropological proposition that education, like social structure, law, kinship, technology, communication and so on is a cultural universal or invariant (cf Lawton, 1983), while pedagogy is its core cultural variable.

The development of what I call *cross-cultural pedagogic continua* is still far from complete, but the idea can be illustrated at its simplest level by taking what in English primary schools is called 'display' but – since that word is so evidently charged with peculiarly English meanings – it is more proper to refer to, cumbersomely but neutrally, as 'wall-mounted teaching materials'. Taking the lessons analysed, the relevant continuum for this dimension of pedagogy extends from the use of such materials as 'rules and reminders' through 'work-in-progress' to 'showcase'. Having located each classroom on the continuum, we can then examine within-country and between-country differences by noting the way that the lessons cluster. As it happens, this is one continuum where there were close similarities between all the classrooms observed within each country (Figure 1).

WALL-MOUNTED MATERIALS	Rules and reminders	Work-in-progress	Showcase
England		————————————————————	
France	————————		
India	————————		
Russia	————————		
USA	————————————————————————————		

Figure 1. Use of wall-mounted teaching materials.

Thus, for example, in all the Russian classrooms, the wall material consisted mostly of permanent rules, injunctions and reminders, in relation to matters like posture and handwriting. In the Indian classrooms these permanent messages were moral rather than procedural. In most of the English classrooms the walls were used very much as a semi-permanent showcase for children's (and teachers') work, and in this matter the word 'display' as used by English teachers exactly fits the function since high priority was attached to the quality of presentation. In France, however, we found a wider range: from rules and reminders to the much more transitory collections of 'work in progress' where words, problems, information, drawings and so on were pinned up temporarily, referred to over the next day or so, added to and then taken down and replaced by others. Here the classroom was less a showroom or gallery than a workshop or studio. In the United States we tended to find an eclectic mix of all three – children's finished work on display, work in progress, exhortations and pocket homilies, usually relating to attitudes and relationships, and, in every classroom, the Stars and Stripes and the Pledge, focus for an unvarying daily ritual.

It will be noted that such a procedure gives a somewhat flat picture: it is, by definition, one-dimensional. Thus, even in so apparently mundane and example as wall-mounted materials my brief description hints at additional, cross-cutting dimensions: 'transient-permanent', for example, and 'moral-procedural'. The continuum, then, is a staging post in the analysis, not its terminal point.

Nevertheless, even with this very basic example we can see that the cross-cultural continuum serves two functions. The first is to identify, on a given dimension of pedagogy, the range of practices across all five countries and all the classrooms observed in those countries, together with – assuming the totality of classrooms across these five countries to represent a fair diversity of educational thinking and practice – a range of possibilities to inform our larger debate about pedagogy *per se*. The second function is to help in our attempts to tease out *cultural universals* or *invariants* in teaching from the cultural *specifics* or *variables*. The fact that on this particular dimension there were both similarities within each of the five cultures, and striking differences between them, is helpful in the context of comparative study. From such comparisons we can venture hypotheses about how the classrooms are perceived in relation to teaching and learning in each of the countries, and how these perceptions relate to prevailing policies, theories of pedagogy, professional roles and so on. Had there been no country-specific clustering the dimensions would still have supported the first, 'universal', pedagogic analysis. This is not an exact science, and though I have used the word 'cluster', I stress that I am not referring to the statistical procedure of cluster analysis. Having said that, those parts of the data which are quantified or which it is legitimate to quantify (word-counts and time-analyses for example), can perhaps be clustered in this formal sense.

From this simple application of the cross-cultural continuum procedure, we can see how it can be used in the context of some of the other dimensions uncovered and/or used in the fieldwork. We can construct continua – that is to say representations of significant between-lesson variation – in respect of aspects of teaching as diverse as lesson length (Figure 2), how lessons are structured (3 and 4), the balance of oral and written work (5), the character of the pedagogical language and of teachers' questions (6 and 7) the breadth of a lesson's focus (8), the relative emphasis on subject-matter and affective/behavioural issues (9), the range and manner of delivery of the lesson's messages (10), and the view of knowledge which pervades the whole (11).

LESSON LENGTH: MINUTES	20	30	40	50	60	70	80	90
England								
France								
India								
Russia								
USA								

Figure 2. Length of lessons.

LESSON STRUCTURE A	Formulaic, fixed	Developmental, flexible
England		
France		
India		
Russia		
USA		

Figure 3. Structure of lessons (A).

LESSON STRUCTURE B	Short, regular episodes	Irregular, mixed length episodes
England		
France		
India		
Russia		
USA		

Figure 4. Structure of lessons (B).

BALANCE OF ORAL/WRITTEN	Mostly oral	Oral/writing/reading balance	Mostly reading/writing
England			
France			
India			
Russia			
USA			

Figure 5. Balance of oral and written work in lessons.

PEDAGOGIC LANGUAGE	Precise, formal, technical	Imprecise, conversational, vernacular
England		
France		
India		
Russia		
USA		

Figure 6. Pedagogical language.

TEACHERS' QUESTIONS	Mainly closed	Mixture of closed/open	Mainly open
England			
France			
India			
Russia			
USA			

Figure 7. Teachers' questions.

LEARNING TASK FOCUS	Narrow	Broad/diffuse
England		
France		
India		
Russia		
USA		

Figure 8. Learning task: breadth and diffuseness of focus.

TEACHING EMPHASIS	Subject-matter emphasis	Affective/behavioural emphasis
England		
France		
India		
Russia		
USA		

Figure 9. Balance of emphasis on subject-matter and affective/behavioual issues.

TEACHING MESSAGES	Linear, cumulative	Multiple, complex, simultaneous
England		
France		
India		
Russia		
USA		

Figure 10. Manner in which teaching messages are conveyed.

VIEW OF KNOWLEDGE	Codified, rule-bound, received	Uncodified, negotiable, reflexive
England		
France		
India		
Russia		
USA		

Figure 11. View of knowledge informing lessons.

Taken dimension by dimension – and Figures 1-11 represent only a selection of those used – the procedure can add significantly to our understanding of pedagogy (or perhaps I should say, to my understanding, when I map the continua onto my earlier English classroom data in areas like the use of time, pupils' task-related behaviour and teacher-pupil discourse).

By moving onto the next stage and taking dimensions together, however, we begin to see teaching in the round and open up some of its tensions and dilemmas, including those tensions in matters of value which reflect the wider culture. We also find that particular combinations of positioning on the dimensions recur, and from these we can construct pedagogic paradigms. The paradigms are descriptive rather than normative, and imply a way of pointing up essential contrasts in teaching which go well beyond the one-dimensional polarities to which we are daily treated by politicians and the press.

Let me give you a couple of examples to take this out of the realms of the abstract. We have a number of lessons which despite their different contexts and content share the following combinations of characteristics, or placings on the continua:

Paradigm A
- short and unvarying lesson length (30-45 minutes) (Figure 2)
- clear and formulaic structure (Figure 3)
- clearly-demarcated and relatively brief stages or episodes, bounded by introduction and recapitulation (Figure 4)
- a succession of prescribed and clearly-bounded learning tasks, each broken down into small steps (relates to Figures 4 and 8)
- a clear sense of pace, imposed by the teacher and sustained throughout
- unambiguous and unvarying routines and rules of procedure which are both followed are rarely referred to
- a limited range of messages conveyed, and most of these directly related to the lesson's subject-matter (Figures 8 and 10)
- simple physical organisation
- a mixture of oral and written work, both of them structured and proceduralised, with use of appropriate technical terminology (Figures 5 and 6, touching on 7)
- limited variation in learning outcomes

We have another group of lessons which, again in very different contexts, share the following:

Paradigm B
- extended lesson length (1-1½hours) (Figure 2)
- discernible but loose structure (Figure 3)
- longer sub-stages, with ragged boundaries between them (Figure 4)

- routines and rules of procedure which are frequently mentioned, often renegotiated, and sometimes contested (touches on Figures 9 and 11)
- one or two broad learning tasks which are each treated as unitary, rather than broken down into small steps (Figures 4 and 8)
- little sense of pace: the speed of teaching and learning shaped by events as they happen rather than by the teacher's advance planning
- complex physical organisation
- a wide spectrum of messages conveyed, ranging from content and classroom procedure to personal and interpersonal values (Figures 8 and 10)
- a predominance of written work, with oral encounters conversational rather than structured (Figures 5 and 6, touching on 7)
- wide variation in pupil outcomes

If this were a study of school and classroom effectiveness you would probably expect a pretest-posttest programme of such teaching tracked over a year or two to show that the second group of lessons was less effective than the first, for they appear to fall short on several of the more familiar effectiveness indicators. Indeed, the first group is closely aligned to Rosenshine's classic (1987) model of effective direct instruction. However, my purpose in presenting them in this form is to make some rather different points. First, these are extremes: in between are lessons which combine elements from both ends of the various continua. Second, in only two of the five countries, India and Russia, was there a high degree of consistency and predictability in the way the various continua combined.

The first list is in fact characteristically Russian or indeed continental: we observed this formula in nearly all of the Russian classrooms, in both Moscow and southern Russia, and Level 1 interviewees in Moscow – at the Ministry of Education and the Russian Academy of Education – confirmed its national prevalence. Indeed, in her interview with me the Russian Federation's Director of Primary Education was happy to trace its pedigree back in an unbroken line through the vicissitudes of perestroika, the Soviet system and Tsarist autocracy to Jan Komenski (Comenius): history is indeed a necessary adjunct of comparativism. The second list, however, though derived from several Michigan classrooms, can be contrasted with other very different combinations from the same three school districts in that same state. Similarly, lessons observed and recorded in Michigan, northern England and southern France tended to combine between-lesson consistency on some continua with inconsistency on others, less so in France than in England and Michigan, but with much greater pedagogical variation in France than is implied by that over-used image of the Minister of Education with his stopwatch. By and large, the further west we travelled, the greater the variation in pedagogy. The variation says as much about values as about effectiveness, and it is to this matter that I shall turn shortly. First, however, to another of my initial problems, that of the parts and the whole.

The Parts and the Whole

Taking the lesson as the basic unit of analysis, preparing narrative accounts and attending to matters like lesson structure, alongside specific pedagogic elements like planning, task-related behaviour, organisation, time on task and discourse, will take us some way to achieving that balance of dissection and reconstruction for which I argued earlier. However, the more I revisit the Five Cultures lesson tapes and transcripts the more I find that in my quest to make sense of the totality of what I have observed and recorded on each occasion I need analogies and metaphors of a kind which the social sciences simply cannot provide.

Eliot Eisner (1974), has long argued the applicability of artistic, especially visual, modes of analysis and evaluation in educational settings, and some ethnographers make considerable use of the techniques and conventions of literary criticism, of different literary genres and of devices like metaphor and metonymy. There is an important debate here about the conventional contrast between so-called 'scientific' and 'non-scientific' research accounts and the way that ostensibly factual accounts deploy literary conventions to assert the realism of what they portray (Atkinson, 1994).

The language of the classroom is an obvious candidate for scrutiny within a literary-critical paradigm, as an alternative to computer word-counts on the one hand and ethnomethodological analysis on the other. However, in my search for ways of understanding the whole, as opposed to the parts, I find a different art-form, that of music, even more persuasive. I do not have space to work through my emerging framework for analysis in detail, but the essence – and I invite sceptical readers to suspend disbelief for one moment – is as follows.

Teaching, like music is *performance*. That performance can be preceded by *composition* (lesson planning) and in execution is thus an *interpretation*, or it can be partly or completely *improvisatory*. The performance of teaching can be in planning *orchestrated* and in execution *conducted* – with varying degrees of competence and persuasiveness, with participants staying together or losing their way, and with consequences which may move, excite, bore or alienate. In both its planning and execution teaching is bounded and constrained, as is music, by *time*, which far from being a one-dimensional measure as implied by that familiar variable 'time on task' is in fact many-faceted. Time in teaching comprises *time intended* and *actual time spent*, and in each of these we have *pulse, tempo* or speed, and *rhythm*. The critical temporal variable in teaching is, I would suggest, not the current official preoccupation (in respect of literacy and numeracy for example) with overall *time intended* and *spent*, but the *internal time* of a lesson, its *tempo* or *pace*, or its ratio of time taken to content encountered, allied to lesson *dynamics*, that subtle admixture which generates (or destroys) the energy and commitment which children give to the task in hand.

Similarly, a lesson can be dominated by one or more clearly-discernible *themes, melodic lines* or indeed *leitmotifs*, and these can be *harmonically* sustained or they can be woven together in a *contrapuntal* relationship; or the lesson can descend into cacophony. The whole is bounded by *form* – and in teaching, as in music, there are many forms, from the single, loose programmatic movement, to the formal episodic structure of the classic central European lesson plan, framed by *introduction* and *recapitulation* and punctuated by *rondo-form* recalls of the main theme. (Is it a coincidence that Central Europe is a centre of gravity for both musical and pedagogical form?) Beyond form in this sense are the larger musical structures and genres, and we have in our data exemplifications of lessons orchestrated and conducted as *operatic* episodes (in a Russian village school) and lessons bearing a strong resemblance in their reiterative, ritualistic and antiphonal character, and their priest-acolyte relationship (as in many of the Indian classrooms) to sacred music or religious ritual. Indeed, my Bombay colleague Denzil Saldanha, having viewed some of the Indian tapes, sees this as a definite cultural continuity from religious to secular India rather than merely a convenient analogy.

If this were indeed an exercise in analogy it would be interesting but little else. However, having worked hard to understand teaching over many years I find the perspective a genuinely useful one in tackling the problem of relating the parts and the whole as I have outlined it. Especially, I find that this approach to the concept of *form* illuminates the relationship between the structure and organisation of teaching and its meaning; that *tempo* takes us beyond the familiar process variables of 'time for learning', 'opportunity to learn' and 'pupil time on task'; while *melody, harmony, polyphony* and *counterpoint* help me to unravel the way the messages of teaching – whether explicit or implicit, congruent or incongruent, are developed and relate to each other over the course of a single lesson. For this, the musical metaphor is a useful adjunct to the more commonly-evoked dramatic distinction between *text* and *subtext* (in the same way my use of musical form can usefully be set against visual-spatial principles like *proportion, balance,* and *perspective*).

Together, these concepts also help me to unpack some of the differences between the lessons I have observed and recorded in the five countries. Thus, to gloss Figures 3 and 4 for example, there is a clear contrast in the data between on the one hand those lessons whose themes will vary from one lesson to the next but whose length, tempo and form remain predictably and reliably the same, and on the other hand those lessons which pursue the more ambitious but risky strategy of multiple and even conflicting themes within a many-layered structure and a rambling time-frame, sometimes succeeding because of the skilful way they are orchestrated and conducted, sometimes losing pace, coherence and the attention of the pupils.

Again, risking comparison across the five cultures, the form of the lessons we observed became more variable and complex as we moved west. Moreover – and this is perhaps where this kind of analysis can engage usefully with school effectiveness research – the increased complexity was at two distinct levels: the level of *organisation* (as noted in English primary classrooms by researchers like Bennett, Galton, Mortimore and myself), and the level of *message* and *meaning* (the theme initiated in Figures 9-11).

Let me elaborate this notion of layered complexity. In no lesson that I have ever observed is there not a powerful leitmotif of values relating to, for example: the extent to which knowledge is open or bounded, provisional or uncontestable (Figure 11); how ideas should be handled; the kinds of authority the teacher and the curriculum embody; how individuals and groups should relate to each other; and what counts as success in learning. However, we found four sharp contrasts across classrooms and cultures in respect of such message systems: first and most predictably, in their substance, for knowledge, the teacher's authority and so on were viewed and presented very differently in different cultural contexts; second (Figure 9), in the relative emphasis given to subject-matter and affective and behavioural issues; third, in the extent to which such messages were either secure and therefore implicit, or less secure and therefore perforce explicit and frequently reiterated; fourth, in the manner in which the messages were conveyed (Figure 10). In respect of the last two, the sharpest constrasts, as in so much else, were between most of the Russian lessons and many of the Michigan ones. In the one context the substantive messages about the nature of knowledge, teaching and learning and about behavioural norms and expectations were unambiguous yet also – bar the occasional brief reminder – tacit; in the other context they were the subject of frequent reminders by the teacher and often intense encounters ranging from negotiation to confrontation.

In this you may wish to detect the contrast between lately-abandoned totalitarianism and the confusions of the world's most self-conscious democracy. However, when I add that the Michigan classrooms also exhibited the greatest organisational complexity, you will see how this kind of analysis can refresh the parts of teaching which process-product and school effectiveness research cannot reach. Here we had a combination of organisational complexity and a contrapuntal and sometimes cacophonous message system, with classroom exchanges veering back and forth between negotiation over the learning task and negotiation over behaviour, and some marked inconsistencies between each. It was not – as usually argued – the organisational structure *per se* which led to the general lack of pace in learning and the high levels of pupil distraction that we observed in some of the Michigan lessons, but the high level of negotiation to which the teachers were committed, and the consequently problematic and confusing nature of the messages which were sometimes conveyed. The organisational complexity simply exacerbated this.

Holistic analysis of this kind, therefore, offers not just the academic luxury of another way of characterising teaching but, for those of us who are also concerned with the quality and improvement of education, new ways to understand how and why some lessons and some teachers are more effective than others. I do not dispute the importance to the improvement of teaching of isolating variables like 'high expectations', 'clarity of presentation', 'advance cognitive organisers', and 'ability grouping' (Creemers, 1996), but I do feel that an equally strong case can be made for assaying alternative, more integrative paradigms.

The Macro-Micro Relationship

The other imperative in comparative classroom research that I identified was that of finding a way to relate events in the classroom to the society of which it is a part. The normal formulation of this imperative as the 'macro-micro problem' can be misleading if it is taken to imply that schooling and society are separate social systems. The reality, whether we are interested in the formal relationship between national policies and school administration, the less predictable relationship between educational policies and lessons as planned and presented, or the complex and subtle ways in which cultural values are manifested in pedagogy, is that culture must be understood and researched as intrinsic and pervasive rather than, as it tends to be in school effectiveness research, extraneous. In the same way that attending to pedagogic form – whether you do it through the constructs of music, drama, anthropology or the physical sciences – is a way of re-unifying and making readily communicable what we more commonly tend to leave dissected, so the explication of the values in teaching is as essential a part of the search for its educational meaning as is conventional analysis of subject-matter and how it is packaged and presented.

We can proceed on the basis of social theory, grand or grounded. We can enlist Gramsci (1971), Bourdieu (1977), or Apple (1990) to provide one kind of explanatory framework through theories of hegemony, cultural capital and cultural reproduction. This will situate what we observe in classrooms in a very specific way as part of an irresistible historical and political tide in which the individual teacher or child is relatively powerless. Or we can use the postmodernist preoccupation with fragmentation, pluralism and individualism to set the classroom and the state in a much less certain relationship (Giroux, 1992). Or again, as economic globalisation induces governments like that of the United Kingdom (UK) to define the function of state education in ever more instrumental terms, we should perhaps provide the corrective of a more reflective and critical analysis of the relationship between education and the economy (Halsey, 1997).

I am, as they say, still working on this, but at this stage I can venture a couple of thoughts. The first is a comment on economic instrumentalism, very much the current doctrine. Like Peter Robinson (1997 and in this volume), Levin & Kelly (1997) have argued that "the general notion that the competitive economic position ... [of the UK] can only be sustained if we can outcompete students from other countries in scores on achievement tests is naive and hardly supported by the empirical data". Not only are the advocates of educational borrowing from the Pacific Rim having to think again as they watch some of the vaunted economies in that region disintegrating, but analysis of classroom practice tends to underscore the naivety of the supposed linear and causal link between a particular form of pedagogy in primary schools (the 'interactive whole class teaching' currently commended by ministers and their advisers), test results and economic prosperity, for the international ubiquity of whole class teaching means that the correlation can go any way one wishes. There is, in fact, *no* correlation between whole class teaching as such and pupil performance, still less between whole class teaching and national economic performance (Alexander, 1996). The macro-micro relationship in education, even in statist regimes and command economies, is much more tenuous than this. If we wish to unearth what in teaching really drives pupil learning we should concentrate less on those generalised organisational strategies that happen to catch the untutored eye and more on the generic features such as teacher-pupil discourse whose impact on cognition is clearly supported by psychological evidence.

My second observation is that theories of hegemony and cultural reproduction begin to crumble when you study pedagogy within countries undergoing substantial change or losing their collective sense of direction. I can exemplify this, once again, in the contrasting contexts of Russia and the USA.

In many Russian classrooms I observed, and both teachers and officials confirmed in interview, a continuity and stability in pedagogic values and practices from Soviet days which contrasted markedly with post-Soviet policies and rhetoric and with the economic and social dislocation of the world outside the school. There was a strong emphasis on rules, deference to the teacher, and individual striving for the collective good. There was a sense of pride in the school and a sense of occasion about each lesson.

In Michigan, I found teachers explicitly working to counter a range of what they saw as undesirable values and tendencies prevalent in the community and wider society, especially rampant individualism, materialism, intolerance, violence and economic instrumentalism. The pursuit of this objective introduced considerable and usually unresolved tensions into their teaching as on the one hand their discourse and classroom rituals and routines were heavy with the rhetoric of caring and sharing while their moral posture of tolerance meant that much of the pedagogic content of their teaching, especially in the area of children's writing, was dominated by the contrary language and mores of mass television – from O.J. Simpson to the Simpsons.

These contexts were very different, but neither of them was readily amenable to the simple hegemonic concept of pedagogy. In the Russian schools there was a formal commitment to post-Soviet values. At the same time, no visitor could be other than acutely conscious of the tensions, especially in Kursk, a city with which both Brezhnev and Rutskoy had been strongly associated (our first visit was only a year after Yeltsin's assault on the Rutskoy faction in the Moscow White House) and where Communist Party allegiance and nostalgia were still very strong. In both cases, the wider societal context was one of dislocation and value-dissensus. Parents of the Moscow and Kursk children were trying to survive acute financial hardship and the degeneration of civic infrastructures. The Michigan parents and teachers were anxious about the collapse of traditional values and their children's personal safety (a concern shared by many of the Russian teachers). The schools' responses to this shared problem, however, were very different. In enacting continuity of educational practices and their underlying values from Soviet days, the Russian classrooms provided a context of stability to which pupils responded positively and which parents appeared to endorse. In contrast, by appearing simultaneously to oppose and condone the prevailing cultural values some of the Michigan teachers created only moral confusion. And out of that moral confusion came procedural and behavioural problems, loss of classroom control and a diminution of the teacher's ability to promote learning.

These examples test the explanatory value of theories of hegemony and cultural reproduction, and point up just how problematic it can be to explicate the macro-micro relationship in the context of school and classroom research. The postmodernist option in the two contexts exemplified looks decidedly tempting, though I could also provide contrasting examples, especially from India, France and England, which would clearly exemplify Giroux's claim (1992) that pedagogy is a "technology of language, power and practice that produces and legitimates forms of moral and political regulation that construct and offer human beings particular views of themselves and the world".

The examples should also remind those who define pedagogy in terms of technique alone not only that the value context is important and powerful, but that value-congruence and value-dissonance, though they are not readily factor-analysed, are undoubtedly significant contributory elements in effective or – should we now say? – harmonious teaching.

Conclusion

At the beginning of this chapter I described my own route into comparative research as the inevitable next stage in a long-term engagement with the policy and practice of English primary education. I identified two national educational ailments to which comparative research appeared to offer the hope of an antidote. One was the corrosive power of the traditional/progressive polarity in primary education; the other was the persistence, against the current of modernisation claims, of the 19th century proto-industrial primary curriculum and its associated values. The fact that international research has now been enlisted by policy-makers and their advisers to support rather than to challenge these archetypes shows how far we still have to go to secure a proper open debate about this vital stage of education. Viewed sociologically rather than pathologically, however, the persistence of this view of primary education at all levels of the system, not least among teachers, also supports theories of hegemony and cultural reproduction, and particularly Apple's view (1990, p. 123) that "control and domination are vested in commonsense practices and consciousness as well as by overt economic and political manipulation".

I then identified six important issues in classroom research which seemed to be in their own way as much in need of resolution, and used my current five-country study of primary education to provide perspectives on – if not solutions to – each of them. The issues were:

- the over-sharp opposition of quantitative and qualitative methods and of the claims and counter-claims associated with each;
- the question of whether the important research criterion of generalisability should continue to be framed as an exclusively statistical construct, and of whether other criteria for authenticating intensive classroom data and making it generally applicable could be agreed; this matter seemed particularly pressing given the logistical and cultural constraints on making valid international comparisons in the area of pedagogy;
- the need to balance the scientific – or perhaps scientistic – urge to dissect, deconstruct and factor-analyse teaching with equal attention to matters of overall form and meaning, and to find a new language

and new modes of analysis for making sense of the totality of teaching encounters;

- the related challenge of finding ways to build on the technology of precoded observation schedules and ethnographic fieldnotes to find ways of capturing an even wider spectrum of the sights, sounds and behaviours of which teaching is constituted; again, this is a particular need in comparative classroom research where opportunities for revisiting and replication are likely to be limited;
- the question of how one examines and charts the macro-micro relationship in comparative research, especially the way in which one situates schools and classrooms within the context of culture and values and examines how a culture permeates the language and actions of teachers and pupils;
- the overarching question of pedagogy, or teaching, itself: how one defines and conceptualises it; the extent to which it can properly be characterised as craft, art or science;[1] and how one separates its universals or invariants from those of its variables which are culture-specific; how far, indeed it is appropriate to talk of 'cultural models' of teaching (Clarke, 1996). This, too, is no longer a merely academic question now that international educational comparison has been politicised and pedagogic cherry-picking has been adopted as a legitimate way to improve teaching quality and raise educational standards.

In addressing these questions, I emphasised the importance of building up rich datasets which include video and photography and maximise the opportunity for revisiting teaching as it happens. I showed how one might attempt to balance atomistic and holistic data and data analysis. I suggested that the idea of the 'cross-cultural continuum' could counter the current 'best buy' approach to international comparison while also helping to tease out further the cultural invariants and variables in teaching. I voted teacher-pupil discourse as the pedagogic 'text' most in need of detailed study (certainly it is the text which in this particular project is gaining most attention). I argued that we should try to find additional metaphors, analogies and constructs for making better sense of the overall structure, form and meaning of teaching, and to this end I tentatively invoked the constructs of music, another kind of composition and another kind of performance, but in many respects closer to teaching than we may realise. And I illustrated the problematic nature of the macro-micro relationship, once one moves beyond the familiar comparativists' preoccupation with systems and structures and studies teaching at the level of values.

Because the project is large and space is limited, I have not gone into detail. I have referred only to Level 2 (the school) and at that level only to a small proportion of the classroom data, and I have barely mentioned what to me is one of its most important strands, the comparative analysis of classroom discourse.

Readers will have to judge whether the questions I have identified are worth worrying about, and, if so, whether my commentary sheds any light on them. I end with two general observations about the policy context of comparative classroom research in this country, as it now stands.

Comparative research is currently being used to buttress the laudable and necessary commitment to raising standards in education, and especially primary education. Indeed it was this trend as much as any which prompted the programme of seminars on which this and its companion volume are based. Comparative classroom research, our concern in this section of the book, can identify important preconditions for effective teaching. But it can and should be used far less selectively and uncritically than it has been so far. Taken in the round, comparative research not only offers pointers for raising educational standards; it also challenges some of very assumptions on which the current drive for standards are based. For example:

- The assumption that the relationship between pedagogy, attainment in literacy and national economic competitiveness is direct, linear and causal (attainment and economic performance being multi-factorial, the reality is much more complex).
- The assumption that whole class teaching, internationally, is a correlate only of educational success (its international ubiquity means that it is associated with all levels of educational and economic attainment and therefore correlates with none).
- The assumption that a concern with children's development and ways of learning is an ideological aberration, and a peculiarly English one at that (it is not – it is of increasing concern to policy-makers, as well as educators, in countries as diverse as France, Russia and India, and for that matter, Japan and China).
- The assumption that the key temporal variable in pedagogy is *time on task* (my project indicates that *pace* and *episodic structure* deserve equal attention) and the linked argument that increasing time on task will therefore raise standards (it may, but not without attention to the way time is used).
- The assumption that the way to raise standards in literacy and numeracy is to downgrade the rest of the curriculum (the QCA international database on curriculum and assessment prepared by Joanna Le Metais and Ralph Tabberer [1997 and this book's companion volume], as well as studies like my own, readily puncture that one).
- The assumption that reading and writing can be detached from talk and should constitute the exclusive focus for the development of

literacy. (Our data show, especially in France and Russia, a considerable counterbalancing commitment to *oracy*, and the development of spoken language as an adjunct, not merely an alternative, to writing. Because half of our lessons are language/literacy lessons, we shall have quite a lot to say about this important aspect of primary education at a later stage in the analysis.)

- The assumption that the pedagogic power of classroom interaction resides chiefly in teacher-initiated question and answer sessions, or so-called 'interactive whole class teaching' (my video and transcript material uncovers a much more extensive spectrum of discourse, and indicates a much broader concept of effective interaction).

The other point I want to make concerns 'effectiveness', since May 1997 the official adjunct to 'standards'.[2]

While it is clear that the monopoly by one kind of research of a concept as important as school effectiveness is neither tenable nor helpful, I am not one of those who dismisses the dominant paradigm as of no value. On the contrary, studies such as ISERP have added usefully to our understanding of the relationship between teaching processes and outcomes, and the steadiness of commitment in these studies to answering the basic question 'What school and classroom conditions *really* make a difference to pupil learning?' must be applauded. However, it is time that we confronted four fundamental weaknesses of the paradigm, the more urgently because of the way it appears to have seduced government ministers and officials.

First, the school effectiveness enterprise as currently conducted manages to defy both logic and common sense by making culture peripheral to cross-cultural analysis. In this matter, though I note David Reynolds's apparent conversion in this volume to the idea that a culture is not merely – as it was in Reynolds & Teddlie (1995) – a self-contained 'system' existing apart from the 'social system' and the 'educational system', I am not convinced by it, since it runs counter not just to the rest of the school effectiveness literature, but also to its methodology.

Second, for inherent methodological reasons school effectiveness research is unable to engage with the purposes, meanings and messages which elevate pedagogy from mindless technique to considered educational act. Though I count this a weakness, and a serious one, others count it a strength, because they can use it to justify devising a uniform, all-purpose, context-free and content-neutral model of effective teaching and imposing it on England's 20,000 primary schools and 182,000 primary teachers.

Third, in as far as what comes out of such research depends in an exact way upon what you put in, there is considerable arbitrariness in the list of variables which the dominant school effectiveness paradigm includes and excludes – see, for example, the frequently-cited model of

Creemers (1994, 1997). This is aggravated by the self-referenced and therefore self-reinforcing character of much of the school effectiveness literature.

Fourth, the claim that this particular branch of educational research is a discipline in its own right is surely premature. It has as yet little of the internal dialectic of conflicting theories and methodologies which give a discipline the hard edge of scepticism which is essential to its vitality, and it displays scant interest in the debatable lands between one discipline and another which expose the strengths, limitations and potential of each. Moreover, it is validated less by the usual disciplinary mechanism of rigorous internal critique than by the patronage which it happens to enjoy among those seeking academic legitimation for their policy agenda.

In a climate which is more than usually hostile to educational research and to the theory and speculation which are its proper and essential companions, gaining acceptance for a richer spectrum of pedagogic analysis is bound to be difficult. In this paper I hope that I have shown how it is possible to strengthen and extend our understanding of teaching by invoking radically different ways of studying and defining it. However, even though I have consistently stood for a line of enquiry which seeks to understand teaching in order to improve it, I have no illusions about the prospects – for the time being, at least – for the work described here, for I know precisely, from the way my Leeds research was exploited by both the political and professional communities in 1991-1992 (a process charted in Alexander 1997), the ingredients which make such exploitation more or less likely.

The difference between 1997-1998 and 1991-1992 is worth pointing up. In 1992, once the political and media dust of the Leeds research and the subsequent government initiative on primary teaching had settled, we were left with two principles of cardinal importance: first, an acknowledgement by the then UK Secretary of State that "questions about how to teach are not for Government to determine"; second, strong advocacy of the principle of 'fitness for purpose' – classroom-based pedagogical decisions carefully tailored to context, grounded in a broad repertoire of strategies and techniques and informed by a principled understanding of subject-matter, learning and teaching (Alexander et al, 1992, paras 1 and 86-128).

By 1998, the first principle had given way to direct government intervention in pedagogy, while the second had been replaced by the minute-by-minute prescriptions of the literacy and numeracy hours (DfEE, 1998a; 1998b). Here we had, in a single pedagogical formula imposed on every primary school, classroom, teacher and child in England [3], not just the antithesis of 'fitness for purpose', but the apparent rejection of much – diversity, dialectic, history, values and meaning – that is central to the idea of 'culture'. The rejection was the more resounding for being justified as a distillation of the best of international practice.

Acknowledgement

The fieldwork for the project Primary Education in Five Cultures was undertaken with a grant from the Leverhulme Trust. The British Council gave additional financial and administrative support in France, India and Russia, and the University of Warwick supported the translation and transcription of the video and audiotapes. Karen Mills was my co-researcher in each country and generated all the video and photographic data. She and Michele Schweisfurth assisted with the preliminary data analysis. Full acknowledgement of the help given by many dozens of people in the field will be made in the forthcoming book about the project.

Notes

[1] I trust that by now my view on this is clear. The familiar question "Is teaching an art or a science?" forces the issue needlessly and inappropriately. Gage's classic discussion of "the scientific basis of the art of teaching" (Gage, 1978) remains one of the best antidotes to this kind of polarisation.

[2] The UK Labour Government elected in May 1997 appointed a Standards Minister and a Standards Task Force, and established a Standards and Effectiveness Unit within the Department for Education and Employment.

[3] The literacy and numeracy hours were presented as *recommended* strategies, but their architects made it clear that schools would be expected not so much to opt into the strategies as to make a convincing case for opting out.

References

Alexander, R.J. (1984) *Primary Teaching*. London: Cassell

Alexander, R.J. (1988) Garden or jungle? Teacher development and informal primary education, in W.A.L. Blyth (Ed.) *Informal Primary Education Today: essays and studies*. London: Falmer Press.

Alexander, R.J. (1995) *Versions of Primary Education*. London: Routledge.

Alexander, R.J. (1996) *Other Primary Schools and Ours: hazards of international comparison*. Warwick: University of Warwick Centre for Research in Elementary and Primary Education.

Alexander, R.J. (1997) *Policy and Practice in Primary Education: local initiative, national agenda*. London: Routledge.

Alexander, R.J., Rose, A.J. & Woodhead, C. (1992) *Curriculum Organisation and Classroom Practice in Primary Schools: a discussion paper*. London: DES.

Alexander, R.J., Willcocks, J. & Nelson, N. (1996) Discourse, pedagogy and the National Curriculum: change and continuity in primary schools, *Research Papers in Education*, 11, pp. 81-120.

Apple, M. (1990) *Ideology and the Curriculum*. London: Routledge.

Archer, M. (1979) *The Social Origins of Educational Systems*. London: Sage.

Atkinson, P. (1990) *The Ethnographic Imagination: textual constructions of reality*. London: Routledge.

Ball, S.J. (1994) *Educational Reform: a critical and post-structural approach*. Buckingham: Open University Press.

Bennett, S.N. (1976) *Teaching Styles and Pupil Progress*. London: Open Books.

Bennett, S.N., Desforges, C., Cockburn, A. & Wilkinson, B. (1984) *The Quality of Pupil Learning Experiences*. Hove: Lawrence Erlbaum.

Bourdieu, P. & Passeron, J-C. (1990) *Reproduction*. London: Sage.

Broadfoot, P. (1996) *Education, Assessment and Society: a sociological analysis*. Buckingham: Open University Press.

Broadfoot, P. & Osborn, M., with Gilly, M. & Bucher, A. (1993) *Perceptions of Teaching: primary school teachers in England and France*. London: Cassell.

Brown, P., Halsey, A.H., Lauder, H. & Wells, A.S. (1997) The transformation of education and society, in A.H. Halsey, H. Lauder, P. Brown, A.S. Wells (Eds) *Education: culture, economy and society*. Oxford: Oxford University Press.

Clarke, P. (1996) *Cultural Models of Teacher Thinking and Teaching*. Harvard: University of Harvard.

Creemers, B.P.M. (1994) *The Effective Classroom*. London: Cassell.

Creemers, B.P.M. (1996) *Effective Schools and Effective Teachers: an international perspective*. Warwick: University of Warwick Centre for Research in Elementary and Primary Education.

Department for Education and Employment (1998a) *The Implementation of the National Numeracy Strategy: the final report of the Numeracy Task Force*. London: DfEE.

Department for Education and Employment (1998b) *The National Literacy Strategy: framework for teaching*. London: DfEE.

Edwards, D. & Mercer, N. (1987) *Common Knowledge: the development of understanding in the classroom*. London: Methuen.

Eisner, E.W. (1979) *The Educational Imagination*. London: Collier Macmillan.

Eisner, E.W. (1985) *The Art of Educational Evaluation*. Lewes: Falmer Press.

Fuller, B. & Clarke, P. (1994) Raising school effects while ignoring culture? local conditions and the influence of classroom tools, rules and pedagogy, *Review of Educational Research*, 64, pp. 119-137.

Gage, N.L. (1978) *The Scientific Basis of the Art of Teaching*. New York: Teachers College Press.

Galton, M. (1998) *Reliving the ORACLE Experience: back to basics or back to the future?* Warwick: University of Warwick Centre for Research in Elementary and Primary Education.

Galton, M. & Simon, B. (1980) *Progress and Performance in the Primary Classroom*. London: Routledge.

Giroux, H. (1992) *Border Crossings: cultural workers and the politics of education*. London: Routledge.

Gramsci, A. (1971) *Selections from the Prison Notebooks*. New York: International Publishers.

Hargreaves, D.H. (1996) Teaching as a research-based profession: possibilities and prospects, Teacher Training Agency Annual Lecture, 1996.

Hargreaves, D.H. (1997) In defence of evidence-based teaching: a rejoinder to Martyn Hammersley, *British Educational research Journal*, 23, pp. 405-419.

Lawton, D. (1983) *Curriculum Studies and Educational Planning*. London: Hodder & Stoughton.

Levin, H.M. & Kelly, C. (1997) Can education do it alone? in A.H. Halsey, H. Lauder, P. Brown & A.S. Wells (Eds) *Education: culture, economy and society*. Oxford: Oxford University Press.

Lockheed, M.E. & Verspoor, A.M. (1991) *Improving Primary Education in Developing Countries*. Washington: World Bank in conjunction with Oxford University Press.

Luxton, R. & Last, G. (1997) *Underachievement and Pedagogy*. London: National Institute for Economic and Social Research,

Mortimore, P., Sammons, P., Stoll, L., Lewis, D. & Ecob, R. (1988) *School Matters: the junior years*. London: Open Books.

Neill, S.R.StJ., (1991) *Classroom Non-Verbal Communication*. London: Routledge.

Osborn, M. (1997) Children's experiences of schooling in England and France: some lessons from a comparative study, *Education Review*, June.

Pollard, A. (1985) *The Social World of the Primary School*. London: Routledge.

Pollard, A., Broadfoot, P., Croll, P., Osborn, M. & Abbott, D. (1994) *Changing English Primary Schools: the impact of the Education Reform Act at Key Stage One*. London: Cassell.

Reynolds, D., Creemers, B.P.M., Nesselrodt, P.S., Schaffer, E.C., Stringfield, S. & Teddlie, C. (1994) *Advances in School Effectiveness Research and Practice*. Oxford: Pergamon.

Reynolds, D. & Farrell, S. (1996) *Worlds Apart? A Review of International Surveys of Educational Achievement Involving England*. London: OFSTED.

Reynolds, D. & Teddlie, C. (1995) *World Class Schools: a preliminary analysis from the International School Effectiveness Research Project*. Newcastle-upon-Tyne: University of Newcastle-upon-Tyne School of Education.

Robinson, P. (1997) Literacy and numeracy and economic performance, (Working Paper 888). London: Centre for Educational Performance, London School of Economics.

Rosenshine, B. (1987) Direct instruction, in M.J. Dunkin (Ed.) *The International Encyclopaedia of Teaching and Teacher Education*. Oxford: Pergamon.

Sammons, P., Hiliman, J. & Mortimore, P. (1995) *Key Characteristics of Effective Schools: a review of school effectiveness research*. London: OFSTED.

Schaffer, E.C., Nesselrodt, P.S. & Stringfield, S. (1994) The contributions of classroom observation to school effectiveness research, in D. Reynolds, B.P.M. Creemers, P.S. Nesselrodt, E.C. Schaffer, S. Stringfield & C. Teddlie, *Advances in School Effectiveness Research and Practice*. Oxford: Pergamon.

Simon, B. (1983) The study of education as a university subject in Britain, *Studies in Higher Education*, 8, pp. 1-13.

Tizard, B., Blatchford, P., Burke, J., Farquhar, C., & Plewis, I. (1988) *Young Children at School in the Inner City*. London: Lawrence Erlbaum.

Tobin, J.J. & Davidson, D.H. (1990) The ethics of polyvocal ethnography: empowering vs textualising children and teachers, *Qualitative Studies in Education*, 3, pp. 271-283.

Tobin, J.J., Wu, D.Y. & Davidson, D.H. (1989) *Preschool in Three Cultures: Japan, China and the United States*. New Haven: Yale University Press.

Watson, G. & Seiler, R.M. (1992) (Ed.) *Text in Context: contributions to ethnomethodology*. London: Sage.

Woods, P. (1995) *Creative Teachers in Primary Schools*. Buckingham: Open University Press.

Robin Alexander

Woods, P. & Jeffrey, B. (1996) *Teachable Moments: the art of teaching in primary schools*. Buckingham: Open University Press.

Commentary: interpreting classroom practice around the globe

MAURICE GALTON

Anyone who has had the privilege of visiting schools in different countries generally begins by focusing upon the more obvious differences and similarities. Visiting Pacific Rim countries such as Taiwan, Hong Kong and Singapore, it is the size of the schools and the size of the classes which, initially, capture one's attention. On the other hand, when going to the remoter parts of Canada or to the Australian outback the problems faced by teachers in isolated small schools are reminiscent of those experienced in rural areas in the United Kingdom (UK). Beyond this superficial view, then it is usually the seating and curriculum that become the focus of attention. Almost invariably, although not always, larger classes are associated with children sitting in rows, particularly once the fifth grade is reached, while the main feature of the isolated rural school is the delivery of a differentiated curriculum by one teacher to groups of children from across a wide age and ability band. More detailed discussion about the curriculum may well centre upon the place of aesthetic subjects and the relative dominance of the three Rs.

Once these matters have been dealt with, interest usually shifts to questions of pedagogy, where the visitor may well discover that there are more similarities than appear at first sight. What a teacher says and does in front of a whole class may not differ appreciably from what the same teacher says or does when involved with a group of pupils or an individual child. Indeed Cuban (1984) has documented "a seemingly stubborn continuity in the character of instruction" as a result of his study of a hundred years of American pedagogy. Similar conclusions have been reached by researchers in other countries. For example the balance between questions and teacher statements consistently hovers between 12% and 16% in primary classrooms in countries with diverse political and cultural backgrounds, such as the former East German Democratic Republic and India (Doneau, 1994) as well as in the UK (Galton et al, 1980). Of these questions a relatively small proportion will be concerned with challenging pupils' ideas. Even fewer questions will emanate from pupils (Alexander, 1992; 1995).

In our own recent work at Leicester, the replication of the original Observation Research and Classroom Learning Evaluation (ORACLE) study indicates that despite a shift in the amount of whole class teaching from 19% in 1976 to 35% in 1996, the relative proportion of teacher questions to teacher statements across the two decades differs by less than 1% and is in line with Doneau's estimates (Galton et al, 1998). Even in some of the economically successful Pacific Rim countries similar difficulties can occur when teachers attempt to foster enquiry. Cortazzi, for example, quotes a teacher from Brunei who makes the following comment about his pupils:

> *In the schools in Brunei, it is typical that only a few students*
> *ask questions in the classroom. This is due to the students'*
> *background and culture. They expect to be quiet and*
> *respectful when confronting their elders, trained not to speak*
> *a lot or argue with them. Some teachers prefer silence in*
> *classroom, not violating the classroom culture, which is*
> *silence and listening to the teacher. (Cortazzi, 1998, p. 47)*

This practice appears to contrast sharply with the cultural perspective in China where Cortazzi quotes the highly influential 13th century thinker, Zhu Xi, who maintained that:

> *'if a student cannot raise any questions in his teaching the*
> *teacher should teach him. If a student raises many questions,*
> *however the teacher should help him'. Progress is made*
> *through such shifts. (Cortazzi, 1998, p. 47)*

The point which Cortazzi seeks to make is that similarities and differences in classroom practice come about mainly for reasons of culture and expectations. In other words, the peculiarities and similarities of different systems are not to be attributed to broad generalised criteria such as interactive whole class teaching, however loosely that term is defined. According to Cortazzi's analysis, whole class teaching in the UK will therefore not be the same as whole class teaching in China and the successes of one country cannot, therefore, be easily transferred to another. For this and other reasons, therefore, comparative studies of the kind advocated by David Reynolds and his International School Effectiveness Research Project (ISERP) team are unlikely to yield significant or useful findings on pedagogy (Reynolds & Teddlie, 1995, and Reynolds in this volume).

First, following Cuban (1984) and others, the observed overall variations in pedagogy are likely to be so small that the proportions of variance in test score attributed to these pedagogic differences will be negligible compared to other factors. Indeed Creemers (1997) one of Reynolds's co-investigators, has attributed between only 2% and 4% of the variation in pupil performance to classroom process factors. Second, even if such differences can be demonstrated internationally and it has been argued by Gage (1985), using a medical analogy, that insignificant differences when applied across large populations can nevertheless have an educational effect, the consequences of the cultural diversity and the difficulty in affecting reasonable control across the different samples are likely to render any conclusions highly problematic. In addition, the high costs of mounting cross-national presage-product studies, such as the ISERP school effectiveness research project, generally means that the sampling frame will always be very limited. As Alexander (1996) notes, the ISERP project only managed to survey 12 out of the 25,000 primary schools in the UK and the same number out of the 80,000 elementary schools in the USA. Even if collaborative networks of the kind designed by ISERP avoid some of the major problems of comparability and of generalisability identified by Westbury (1993) and Maehr & Maehr (1996) due to variations in grade and in ability range within national samples, many problems still remain due to the timing of test administration and the construct validity of the tests used (Galton, 1988).

If, therefore, empirical studies which look at effects of practice across differential cultures are to continue to have a place in comparative research, then, as Cortazzi (1998) suggests, it is perhaps more useful to start looking at different cultural groups within one educational setting so that for example one might study a sample of pupils from Pacific Rim countries who had spent time in schools in the UK as well as in their mother tongue country.

In looking at a future research agenda, I believe that the way forward is to engage in more intensive, highly focused and localised studies in more restricted settings. Rather than take the broad brush approach, as advocated by David Reynolds, where one tries to isolate general variables and then carry out experimental studies to see if the effect of these variables under controlled conditions can be maximised, it may be that a more effective strategy would be to target specific aspects of pedagogy and look at these in very narrow cultural settings. Those advocating a broad brush approach seem to imply that we know nothing about effective teaching and its relationship to specific kinds of learning. But a cursory glance at successive editions of the *Handbook of Research on Teaching* from the first edition (Gage, 1963) to the eagerly awaited fourth volume (now in press), would testify to the progress which has been made during four decades of research. We know about the effectiveness of direct instruction for teaching procedures (Rosenshine, 1987) and the value of co-operative learning for developing concepts (Bennett, 1992; Cohen, 1994). More recently, we have come to realise the importance of scaffolding tasks as an aid to developing metacognition and thereby ensuring transfer in learning (Palinscar & Brown, 1984; Rosenshine et al, 1996). Studies of teachers working within other cultural settings suggest that effective practitioners apply the same principles as their Western European and North American colleagues but within different contexts, and that choice of context is largely determined by cultural imperatives, particularly ideas of collective responsibility and public attitudes to child rearing (Biggs, 1994; Watkins & Biggs, 1996).

Thus the research of Cortazzi & Jin (1996) into the use of teachers' questions in China and in the UK would be an exemplar of the suggested approach, as would Alexander's on-going research, discussed in this volume, on the analysis of discourse in whole class and other organisational settings across a range of countries. In a similar manner, the detailed study by Tobin et al (1989) of pre-school teachers' responses to videotaped extracts of critical incidents appears to offer another useful perspective on cultural variation. For example, Tobin's account in this volume of the way pre-school teachers from Japan and the USA reacted to a situation in which a boy pupil acted aggressively towards another male pupil, graphically illustrates how strongly cultural norms influence the structure of classroom organisation. The expectations of parents in the USA that teachers should actively engage with a disruptive child in an effort not only to control that child's behaviour but to inculcate within the individual an ethical rationale for improving behaviour, was regarded by the Japanese teachers as a premature attempt to treat pupils as adults rather than allowing them to enjoy being children. In contrast, American teachers, perhaps mindful that failure to act against the aggressive child might result in a legal claim from the dissatisfied parents of the victim, viewed the Japanese teachers' preference for leaving the children to sort out such disputes for themselves on the grounds that "they will never learn to play together if I interfere" as a dereliction of duty.

In such circumstances, to tell an American teacher, or for that matter his or her British counterpart, particularly those working in inner city schools where classroom control can often be the major concern, to engage in more whole class teaching inevitably means there will be a conflict between the teacher's management of the children's learning and his or her management of children's behaviour.

We have observed such conflict in our recent replication of ORACLE (Galton et al, 1999). As a result of pressures from OFSTED and from spokespersons from the various Task Forces – pressures which have been described by one commentator as a 'reign of terror' (Brighouse, 1997) – we have seen a 16% rise in the proportion of whole class interaction since 1976. However, much of the task-related activity during this whole class teaching has been interspersed with regular routine exchanges with individual children. Most of these routine interactions are not concerned with serious disruption as described by Tobin et al (1989), but are likely to be neutral in tone and to do with instructions to 'sit up straight' or to 'stop fidgeting' or to 'listen'. In this context 'listening' is perceived by pupils as an instruction to 'sit up straight and look at me (the teacher)'. Such interactions, which disrupt the flow of the lesson, therefore mainly consist of teachers' attempts to nip disruptive behaviour in the bud. In contrast pupils in Singapore and other Pacific Rim countries will often see it as their collective responsibility to deal with a fellow classmate who shows signs of lacking concentration.

Given this emphasis, noted by Biggs (1994) and others such as Cortazzi (1998), on the willingness of pupils in these countries to provide each other with mutual support, studies of co-operative learning would also appear to be a potentially rewarding area for future cross cultural research. Indeed such research is likely to be welcomed by both governments and the teaching profession, since commentators such as Morris have noted:

> *At the very time when English teachers are being urged to adopt the methods of their allegedly more successful Asian counterparts, the latter are being urged to become more like their English colleagues. Countries such as Singapore and Hong Kong are looking to increase the proportion of cooperative group work within the curriculum and to encourage a greater degree of critical thinking. (Morris, 1998, p. 4)*

Even in the UK, there is still a great deal that can be done in this area, particularly in multi-cultural settings as illustrated by the work of Cowie et al (1994). For this reason, in our own work we are carrying out a joint project into co-operative learning with the National Institute of Education (NIE) in Singapore, based on a mixture of qualitative and quantitative approaches. This arrangement, based on a 'memorandum of understanding', corresponds to the kinds of detailed in-depth study that I wish to advocate in contrast to the relatively large scale empirical studies, often involving unrepresentative samples, and concerned only with presage variables such as teacher opinions and product measures such as standardised tests. Much useful work can be done on a comparatively small scale and at minimal cost. For example, I have two doctoral students, one in the UK and one in Hong Kong, who are presently replicating part of the research of Tobin et al (1989) with their own nursery classes.

I have argued, therefore, that we now have a sufficient body of knowledge about what constitutes an effective pedagogy to identify key areas for future research such as the use of different kinds of questions, explanations and scaffolds for different learning tasks involving various knowledge demands. The challenge now is to see how these general principles work effectively in different cultural contexts. The expectations that both teachers and pupils bring to such activities are clearly important, as Cortazzi (1998) demonstrates. In my opinion, detailed intensive studies in which different aspects of specific teaching strategies are looked at across two or three contrasting cultural settings are more likely to advance our knowledge of what is and is not transferable between one country and another.

References

Alexander, R.J. (1992) *Policy and Practice in Primary Education*. London: Routledge.

Alexander, R.J. (1995) *Versions of Primary Education*. London: Routledge.

Alexander, R.J. (1996) *Other Primary Schools and Ours: hazards of international comparison*. Warwick: University of Warwick Centre for Research in Elementary and Primary Education.

Bennett, N. (1992) *Managing Learning in the Primary School*. Association for the Study of Primary Education. Chester: Trentham Books.

Biggs, J. (1994) What are effective schools? Lessons from East and West, *Australian Educational Researcher*, 21, pp. 19-40.

Brighouse, T. (1997) Leading and managing primary schools: the changing world of the local education authority, in C. Cullingford (Ed.) *The Politics of Primary Education*. Buckingham: Open University Press.

Cohen, E. (1994) Restructuring classrooms: conditions for productive small groups, *Review of Educational Research*, 64, pp. 1-35.

Cortazzi, M. & Jin, L. (1996) Cultures of learning: language classrooms in China, in H. Coleman (Ed.) *Society and the Language Classroom*, pp. 169-206. Cambridge: Cambridge University Press.

Cortazzi, M. (1988) Learning from Asian lessons: cultural expectations and classroom talk, *Education 3 to 13*, 26(2), pp. 42-49.

Cowie, H., Smith, P., Boulton, M. & Laver, R. (1994) *Co-operation in the Multi-Ethnic Classroom*. London: David Fulton.

Creemers, B. (1997) *Effective Schools and Effective Teachers: an international perspective*. Warwick: University of Warwick Centre for Research in Elementary and Primary Education.

Cuban, L. (1984) *How Teachers Taught: constancy and change in American classrooms, 1890-1980*. New York: Longman.

Doneau, S. (1985) Soliciting in the classroom, in T. Husen, & N. Postlethwaite (Eds) *The International Encyclopaedia of Education: research and studies*. Oxford: Pergamon Press.

Gage, N. (Ed.) (1963) *Handbook of Research on Teaching*. Chicago: Rand McNally.

Gage, N. (1985) *Hard Gains in the Soft Sciences, the Case for Pedagogy*. CEOR Monograph. Bloomington: Phi Delta Kappa.

Galton, M. (1998) The real lessons from the Pacific rim: what do the tests measure? *Education 3 to 13*, 26(2), pp. 50-61.

Galton, M., Hargreaves, L., Comber, C. & Wall, D. (1999) *Inside the Primary Classroom – 20 Years On*. London: Routledge.

Galton, M., Simon, B. & Croll, P. (1980) *Inside the Primary Classroom*. London: Routledge & Kegan Paul.

Maehr, M. & Maehr, J. (1996) Schools aren't as good as they used to be: they never were, *Educational Researcher*, 25(8), pp. 21-24.

Morris, P. (1998) Comparative education and educational reform: beware of prophets returning from the Far East, *Education 3 to 13*, 26(2), pp. 5-9.

Palincsar, A. & Brown, A. (1984) Reciprocal teaching of comprehension-fostering and comprehension-monitoring activities, *Cognition and Instruction*, 2, pp. 17-175.

Reynolds, D. & Teddlie, C. (1995) *World Class Schools: a preliminary analysis from the International School Effectiveness Research Project*. Newcastle-upon-Tyne: Department of Education, University of Newcastle-upo- Tyne.

Rosenshine, B. (1987) Direct instruction, in M. Dunkin (Ed.) *Teaching and Teacher Education*. Oxford: Pergamon.

Rosenshine, B., Meister, C. & Chapman, S. (1996) Teaching students to generate questions: a review of intervention studies, *Review of Educational Research*, 66, pp. 181-221.

Tobin, J.J., Wu, D.Y.H. & Davidson, D.H. (1989) *Preschool in Three Cultures: Japan, China and the United States*. New Haven: Yale University Press.

Watkins, D. & Biggs, J. (Eds) (1996) *The Chinese Learner: cultural, psychological and contextual influences*. Hong Kong: ACER.

Westbury, I. (1993) American and Japanese achievement – again, *Educational Researcher*, 22(3), pp. 21-25.

Postscript

MICHELE SCHWEISFURTH

The seminar on *Comparative Research in Classrooms and Schools* provided a rare opportunity for a range of generators, users, and observers of research to reflect upon shared critical concerns about the methodology and contribution of school- and classroom-based comparative research. In the discussions which followed each of the day's presentations, and in the final plenary session, some familiar themes of comparative education were revisited. What is the relationship between education and its cultural context? Which classroom research methods are sensitive enough to embrace both? And how may the subsequent findings be 'used' by policy-makers, considering the culturally-embedded nature of the data?

These are questions which comparativists have long been asking, and attempting to answer. At this meeting, the issues raised by the seminar papers, and the interpretations and contributions by the diverse audience, have allowed new perspectives to emerge. We hope that these have helped to refresh the debate about 'learning from comparing', and to make some of us contemplate the way we think about and talk about comparative education research.

During the discussion following Joseph Tobin's paper ('Method and meaning in comparative classroom ethnography'), Michael Crossley reminded us of Michael Sadler's much-quoted adage for comparativists: "The things outside the schools matter even more than the things inside the schools, and govern and interpret the things inside" (Higginson, 1979, p. 49). In seeking what Christine Agambar called "the Holy Grail of correlates and multilevel analyses" some research isolates classrooms from their cultural context, as the researchers overlook influences on what takes place in classrooms, or assume that what will work in one national context will work in another. This is a criticism often aimed at international school effectiveness studies, some of which extend beyond their context generalisations about correlations between classroom variables and student achievement. Such an approach over-simplifies the issues.

The highly-contested topic of pupil-teacher ratios is one example that was raised (by Joseph Tobin); the eager willingness of cost-conscious policy-makers to transfer the logic of larger classes belies, as Peter Lang noted, the complexity of the different forms of interaction, governed in part by cultural factors, which are required in the different situations. It is certainly not a straightforward question of changing class sizes without regard for the nature of teacher-student relations, modes of discourse and pedagogy. Other culture-bound phenomena within which practice is embedded include the degrees of respect and trust granted to teachers by parents and wider society; views on how children are best prepared for the next stage of development, and ultimately for adult citizenship; and the place and nature of creativity. As more than one participant pointed out, these are all underpinned by values, which "penetrate almost every element of educational experience" (Robin Alexander).

But culture is itself not a fixed or consistent phenomenon. It is recent demographic changes interacting with long-standing values and traditions which have helped to shape practice in Chinese and Japanese pre-schools: the "narrowing world" (Joseph Tobin) of children in single-child families has created greater need in schools for communication between older and younger pupils. And, even within one, supposedly monocultural, society such a need is met differently by the "microculture" (Graham Vulliamy) of individual schools. In Japan, the rules regarding children handling babies vary between institutions; importantly, however, the reasoning behind the practice is mutually comprehensible among members of the culture. In addition, as David Johnson pointed out, variations in material conditions over time or between groups or areas within a culture can problematise the "snapshot effect" of much research. Deprive a group of people of resources, or change their living conditions, and earlier generalisations regarding their educational situations decay very quickly. Nor (Robin Alexander) does culture conveniently respect imposed national boundaries, and this creates questions about appropriate units for analysis. In researching in South Africa, as an obvious example, the state borders are less meaningful than the lines drawn between racial groups.

The complexity and inter-relatedness of school and culture, and the shifting changes and continuities within culture itself, make context-sensitive research of education both problematic and imperative. The discussion surrounding "the methodological conundrums of this vast area of enquiry" (Patricia Broadfoot) was wide-ranging. Consider the inter-dependence of variables, such as how pupil-teacher relationships interact with wider values about authority and with the nature of classroom discourse, for example. Given these tightly-meshed dependencies, where is the researcher's best starting point? Maurice Galton suggested that variables should not be brought in by the researcher from the outside, but should emerge from close study of the subject within its context. The advantages of gaining a variety of perspectives were also highlighted: showing classroom videotape to various audiences, for example, created "polyvocal" (Joseph Tobin) data which inductively revealed differences between cultures, and revealed similarities, and differences too, in perspectives within cultures. Between cultures, the similarities are at least as interesting as the differences. If universalities are to be found across cultures in the field of education, these would be useful tools for analysts, practitioners and policy-makers alike. While avoiding the temptation to uncouple classrooms from their contexts, the question was considered, following Robin Alexander's paper ('Culture in pedagogy, pedagogy across cultures'): can universal pedagogical procedures and principles be gleaned from this inter- and intra-cultural diversity? What exists internationally in education? What varies depending on the context?

More contested was the use of experimental 'borrowing' of practices from other national schooling contexts, such as the Barking and Dagenham experiment with the implementation of a model of whole-class interactive teaching. Marilyn Osborn raised the issues of ethics and the Hawthorne effect in experimentation, and Maurice Galton pointed out the difficulties of identifying and isolating appropriate variables. However, as David Reynolds pointed out, experimentation is not unique to large research projects conducted systematically: schools and teachers regularly conduct smaller-scale experiments with the education of their own students. He also noted the potential that "tinkering with the surface" has for "revealing deeper structures".

When discussing the uses of comparative education research, the most commonly understood means of application is through 'borrowing' or transfer of educational policies or practices from one setting to another. Like experimentation, 'borrowing' already exists, and has done throughout the history of education. However, it infers very narrow kinds of generalisability, and ways in which research can feed into decision-making.

The practice also tends to ignore the cultural context; however, as participants asked in various ways, how can information which is so relative to the intricacies of its environment be useful? Innovative research strategies, many of them qualitative (Joseph Tobin's and Robin Alexander's research are examples) require new ways of informing: ways which demand more flexible notions of application than do the isolation of key variables from an education system, statistical generalisation regarding their effects, and their wholesale transfer from the studied to the target system. The more indirect mode of mediation and application, and "feeding into the policy process" (Rosemary Preston), recalls

Lawrence Stenhouse's suggestion that comparative education research be used to "tutor our judgement", and its value as such a tutor was endorsed in various ways by commentators during the seminar.

Graham Vulliamy flagged up the difference between "ecological validity" and "population validity", ascribing the value of depth to the former. This linked with the case made by Robin Alexander for validating comparative classroom research procedures against the criterion of cultural authenticity rather than treating statistical generalisability as the only proper test. Robin Alexander expressed his belief that close-grained study of classrooms can act as "a window onto culture", and he used musical metaphors to signify more subtle aspects of classroom life than the traditional language of research would allow.

The notion of 'users' or 'end-users', based on a product model of research, is also limiting, as Martin Hughes noted: he preferred the term 'engagement' to signify the relationship between the researcher and those empowered to apply research. And Joanna Le Metais suggested seeing the process of learning from cross-cultural research as a "journey of travelling together" not "handing out Christmas gifts". These are potentially powerful metaphors which highlight the importance of considering not only how we conduct and apply research, but also how we talk about it. Rosemary Preston too raised the critical issue of discourse: the language used in formulating research and in disseminating and discussing it can constrain those involved, and result in compromised positions and reductionism. As Chris Jones noted: there are never simple statements in comparative education, but this complexity can exacerbate rather than discourage the quest for simplification.

The problem is, as Christine Agambar admitted in her commentary, that users of research, pressed for time and results, feel they need a 'hard view' supported by 'soundbites'; however, "complex interactive studies are difficult to encapsulate". Policy-makers also have the tendency to resort to "firefighting" (David Johnson), rather than using research to contribute to a thoughtfully-constructed vision. However, Graham Vulliamy believed that policy-makers are now more sceptical of superficial correlations, and are becoming interested in processes as well as products. In any case, as we were reminded, the audience for comparative education research need not be only those who have the power to use it in policy formulation. Practitioners, for example, by being exposed to a "widened repertoire of the possible" (Joseph Tobin), can develop a greater self-consciousness of action and more reflective practice.

Patricia Broadfoot referred to the growing sophistication in comparative education, and the discussions at the seminar on classroom research are testimony to this. In the comparative study of education, as greater and greater complexity is uncovered, as diversity reveals itself in smaller and smaller units, as we need to travel deeper and deeper into culture and classrooms to understand their relationship, and as our discourse strains to accommodate these intricacies, the recurrent question remains: how can what we are learning be used, and not abused? Continuing the debate and discussion could only help.

PART THREE

Comparing Pupil Achievement

Comparing Pupil Achievement

PATRICIA BROADFOOT

I suppose we should be pleased. At last the potential of Comparative Education has been recognised. It has established itself in the eyes of policy-makers as an important mechanism for both judging the health of a particular education system and for learning about ways to improve it. If 20 years ago the future of the field itself seemed in some doubt as specialist appointments to university posts dwindled and courses were axed, now the commitment to 'learning from comparing' has arguably never been stronger.

How to account for this change in fortune? Is it merely a manifestation of the vagaries of fashion which, as with clothes, come and go in response to the influence of particular leading 'designers'? Is it a response to the growing internationalisation of our collective culture which makes us more ready to look beyond our own shores for educational ideas as much as for markets and political liaisons?

Clearly, as this volume as a whole makes clear, both these factors are important in helping to transform and relocate comparative research at the heart of contemporary educational debates. But perhaps most significant of all in bringing about such a change, is the current international obsession with measurement; the assumption that it is possible to describe, compare and evaluate all the different aspects of educational activity. We live in an age dominated by such rationalist assumptions An age that assumes it is desirable to measure the quality of education using quantitative techniques and one that is willing to invest very considerable resources in so doing in the belief that such studies will elucidate whether the education system is both providing value for money and the necessary infrastructure of skills to ensure future economic competitiveness on the international stage. Thus countries around the world are putting in place mechanisms for both the *intra-national* comparison of standards – of schools, of regions and even, sometimes of individual teachers – as well as *inter-national* comparisons of relative standards.

Arguably, however, as Hilary Steedman suggests in her contribution to this volume, this enthusiasm for comparison between countries has overtaken the instruments available for doing it. We are trying to reach Mars with a rocket built for going to the moon. Our technology is at best dangerously meaningless; at worst, pernicious, in its effects. Like all technologies, international surveys are neutral in themselves and it is *the use to which the products are put* which requires extreme caution if the overall effect is to be beneficial. Arguably one of the most important contributions that comparativivsts can make in today's climate is to provide the steering wheel and the brakes for the pantechnicon of international comparisons of student achievement; to guide the technology into potentially fruitful directions and to illuminate the hazards that attend careless and even reckless driving

In this third section of the book, the various papers offer a critical analysis of what is currently one of the most prominent features of the comparative educational landscape. They address the issues thrown up by the recent surge of interest in international comparisons of student achievement, the rationale for such studies and the aspirations that inform them. By means of detailed, scholarly analysis of the strengths and weaknesses of different approaches, the chapters challenge us to adopt a healthy scepticism about the value of such studies when they are not combined with a careful and expert awareness of their limitations.

It is pertinent to question at a little more length the reasons behind the current upsurge of interest in international comparisons. One important agenda which Steedman addresses is the search for a common language to describe educational standards across countries. In a world which is likely to be increasingly characterised by the mobility of labour across national borders. there is a widely felt need for an international qualifications framework which would provide transparent descriptions of an individual's competencies to facilitate selection. This aspiration is itself a clear expression of the rationalist discourse currently informing the whole business of assessment, qualifications and selection. It assumes, for example, that competencies are portable when the evidence suggests they are not. As Steedman argues, even a relatively simple and unambiguous competency such as bricklaying is likely to vary according to features of the context in which the skill is being performed.

The picture is further muddied by a host of more arcane technical limitations which impact on the process of comparing. Steedman's example of the International Standard Classification of Education (ISCED) scale which purports to measure proportions of the population completing various levels of education across a range of countries shows clearly how dangerously flawed such analyses can be. Robinson makes a similar case in relation to the Third International Mathematics and Science Study TIMSS study. In his contribution to this book, Robinson draws attention to the similar tendency by economists to engage in the uncritical use of comparative data and their tendency to focus on the potentially misleading, and dangerously simplistic, procedure of ranking means in league tables of educational performance whilst ignoring the key issue of statistical significance.

In mounting a trenchant critique of comparisons based on huge econometric data-bases and their naive or maybe at times wilful, misuse, both Robinson and Steedman highlight the need to ask fundamental questions about the assumptions underpinning such surveys. What is the link between educational standards achieved and national economic performance? Where are we trying to get to as a nation? What do educational qualifications represent – a guarantee of specific competencies or a testimony to the ability to learn?

Responding to the first of these questions, Robinson provides a devastating critique of 'human capital theory' which purports to link educational productivity to national levels of educational achievement. He provides extensive international data to demonstrate the, at best, weak, correlation between national attainment data in mathematics and Gross National Product. Referring to the much vaunted success of the 'Asian Tiger' economies in recent decades he argues that "any notion that the impressive economic growth rate of these countries in the decade up to 1997 is a product of past superior attainment in Mathematics is not borne out by the evidence. Indeed the relative improvement in the Mathematics attainment of Hong Kong students has *followed* economic growth and not precipitated it". Indeed it may be, he suggests, that the correlation, if it exists at all, is the other way, with poverty and inequality leading to poor educational performance.

Any challenge to the almost common-sense assumption that there is a causal link between the educational level of a population and its economic productivity, immediately prompts a search for alternative explanations of economic success. Why do some countries, such as the USA, do relatively badly in international educational surveys and yet have very strong economies and visa versa? Any attempt to answer this question immediately highlights the key role played by the broader national context. It challenges the ready assumptions of policy-borrowing that suggest we can improve educational performance simply by adopting techniques and practices that appear to work well in other national contexts. For, whatever the innovation in question, its effects will only endure if it is linked to a more fundamental understanding of learning and how this, in turn, is influenced by the prevailing culture.

This is the core argument that informs the chapters by Broadfoot, and by Osborn and Planel in this book. Drawing on their comparative study of the influence of national culture on pupil attitudes, classroom practice and learning outcomes in England and France – the Quality in Educational Systems Trans-nationally (QUEST) project – these chapters offer explicit evidence for the way in which measured student performance reflects culturally-informed perspectives and practices which condition the content and practice of learning in profound ways. If the chapters by Steedman and Robinson provide an almost irresistible critique of the *limitations* of large-scale international comparisons of achievement, those by members of the QUEST team offer guidance for fruitful new developments. In asserting the need to retain the cultural integrity of the educational project, such that pupil attitudes, teachers' values and practices and broader social traditions are understood as an inseparable unity, they remind us of the essentially humanistic nature of decisions about what is to be learned, how and for what purpose.

Thus questions about how to raise educational standards are fundamentally linked to culture and to the values that inform it. They need to be prefaced by a sustained debate about national educational goals. Decisions made at this level can then serve, as Steedman suggests, as the base line for establishing key thresholds of achievement, the content and skills assessed in public examinations and key vocational competencies. Without such a debate, we cannot gauge the success of the education system in its own terms and can only flounder in the relativistic and flawed judgements of international comparisons or the arbitrary benchmarks of a national assessment system.

Recent developments have presented the field of comparative education with a unique opportunity to contribute to contemporary policy debates. Policy-makers are hungry to learn from other countries. But they are impatient with academic scruples and timescales. They want hard data and clear guidance But they also want effective tools and defensible methodologies. Those willing to learn will find clear guidance in this collection of papers. Those who are less willing ignore them at their peril.

Measuring the Quality of Educational Outputs: some unresolved problems

HILARY STEEDMAN

Introduction

The aim of this chapter is to contribute to discussion of how measurement of the quality of educational outputs might be improved. Section 1 provides a brief review of the background to the recent increase in interest in the measurement of educational outputs and Section 2 examines important differences in the way individual countries define and collect data on qualifications. Section 3 reviews the appropriateness of the International Standard Classification of Education (ISCED) framework as the basis for classification of data on qualifications. It illustrates the difficulties that arise from the use of ISCED with reference to *Education at a Glance* (OECD, 1997) and *Education across the European Union: statistics and indicators* (EUROSTAT, 1997). Section 4 proposes further ways of assessing the quality of educational outputs.

Current Approaches to the Measurement of Educational Outputs in Growth Economics

From the mid 1980s onwards there has been renewed interest on the part of economists in investigating the determinants of economic growth (Romer, 1986; Lucas, 1988; Rebelo, 1991). In particular, more recent theory has sought to establish a significant role for human capital in determining the rate of economic growth. This has led in turn to a renewal of efforts by economists to measure the human capital resources of countries or geographical areas.

Inevitably, this has proved a time-consuming and difficult task. Economists working in this field are principally interested in gathering a large number of observations over time from a large number of countries in order to apply sophisticated econometric analyses to the data on human capital. It may be too crude to summarise the requirements of economists in this field as 'quantity not quality'. Nevertheless, the assembling of a sufficient number of observations over time for as many countries as possible is a prime objective of such studies. Development economists pioneered early efforts to construct education data sets which could be used to compare measures of education across a range of countries. Lee & Psacharopolous (1979) give an account of these attempts and conclude that, especially in the case of developed countries, the lack of an established link between for example, enrolment rates and economic growth probably results from the failure to measure and compare the quality of education outputs. Data sets relating to education in a large number of countries over a continuous time span were subsequently constructed by Psacharopolous & Ariagada (1986). Seeking to improve on the use of enrolment rates as an indicator of human capital, this study took as the essential building blocks or unit of measurement, years of education. This approach had the disadvantage of failing to differentiate between the value of years of education at different levels of the education system. In this, and in a in number of other respects, the work of Barro & Lee (1993) represents an advance in refinement in educational measurement across a large number of countries in that it does not merely estimate stocks of total years of education of the population but distinguishes between years spent at different levels of the education system and, in the case of a subset of countries, between incomplete primary and complete primary and between incomplete secondary and complete secondary education.

Barro & Lee make clear the limitations of their data which arise from fundamental problems of missing or unreliable observations. They also refer to unreliability of data collection methods in a number of countries and to problems arising from reliance on country data collected by non-standardised methods. However, an implicit assumption of the Barro & Lee work is that education designated by a country as being at a given *level* of the educational structure can be assumed to result in a similar degree of accumulation of human capital in each country. Barro & Lee do not seriously question the assumption made in their work that the *quality* of education at the same level across countries can be considered comparable (Sala-i-Martin & Mulligan, 1995). Increasingly, however, education and training in industrialised countries is characterised by diversification of the school population at around age 15/16 into different tracks with different goals and outputs.

Among economists investigating economic growth, there has, as yet, been little success in conclusively showing the significance of the part played by human capital. While Mankiw et al (1992) and Barro (1991) have found human capital variables significant in cross-country regressions, DeLong & Summers (1991) claim that once equipment investment is taken into account, other variables, including human capital, add little explanatory power. Oulton & Young (1996) also found that neither the level nor the growth rate of the Barro–Lee 'years of education' was significant in explaining the growth rate of GDP.

One reason why the human capital variable has not been shown to have more significance in such models may be that methods of measurement are still not sufficiently sophisticated to capture the crucial differences between different countries' stocks. More recent work (Hanushek & Kim, 1995; Sala-i-Martin & Mulligan, 1995) takes up the challenge of attempting to capture quality differences both within and between countries in stocks of human capital. Hanushek & Kim propose a measure of human capital which involves weighting school enrolment data by a factor derived from the results of the International Evaluation of Educational Achievement surveys carried out at intervals since 1961. Sala-i-Martin & Mulligan use prices (wage data at different points in time by educational level in different US states) as a proxy for skills. Gemmell (1996) criticises previous work including that of Barro (1991) for using school enrolment rates as a proxy both for stocks of and investments in human capital. Gemmell proposes a human capital measure which is capable of distinguishing between stocks and flows (although, he is obliged by lack of data on stocks by educational level to use enrolment rates in 1960 as a proxy for stocks). Unlike Sala-i-Martin & Mulligan and Hanushek & Kim, Gemmell does not address the question of quality differences at given levels of education although he does distinguish enrolments by level – primary, secondary and tertiary. It is not the aim of this paper to evaluate the overall validity of these studies, but it is interesting to note that both Hanushek & Kim and Gemmell claim to have detected a stronger relationship between growth and the indicator used for human capital than had been found in studies using a simpler measure.

Measurements of the Output of Educational Provision

Quality differences assume particular importance when we consider the growth in demand for the measurement of human capital from a different source and for a different purpose, namely the demand from governments for a means of assessing and comparing internationally the performance of publicly-funded systems of education by comparison of their outputs. In OECD countries interest in such comparisons has increased at the same time as interest in comparing the outputs of the education system *within* countries – between schools, local authorities etc. has grown. This concern with cost-efficiency derives from intensifying competition for increases in public spending from a largely fixed (in real terms) public expenditure budget. All this takes place in the wider context of the expansion in the role of codified knowledge in advanced economies. The central role now played in economic growth by knowledge-based innovation puts pressure on governments to ensure a flow of well-qualified entrants to the labour market. The combination of these international competitive pressures and internal budget constraints leads national governments to feel under increasing pressure to ensure that public resources for education are used as effectively as possible.

Intra-country comparisons help to identify the extent to which education systems in some areas within a country are under-performing. However, with intensifying global competition, governments now consider that performance of educational provision in line with an internally-determined norm is no longer a satisfactory measure of efficiency and effectiveness. Inter-country comparisons based on measured outputs are also required to determine whether the standard achieved is the optimum possible. The two types of comparison are related to the extent that both stem from a desire to ensure that resources devoted to education are used in such a way as to produce the optimum outcomes.

Both economists and governments are, therefore, broadly speaking, working within the same paradigm in their concern with the measurement of human capital. In both cases interest in educational outputs arises from structural changes in the functioning of world markets (more intense global competition) allied to technological change in the production of goods and services which requires a more highly-educated labour force. However, in practice, their interests and approaches diverge – growth economists are concerned principally with human capital as an *input*, that is, one among a number of independent variables influencing economic growth. Until now, they have had little interest in how efficiently or inefficiently those inputs have been produced. Governments and policy makers view stocks of human capital as *outputs* of educational provision – that is, as a dependent variable – and their questions largely concern relative efficiency in the way resources devoted to education are used.

The comparison of the quality of the outputs of different patterns of educational provision is essential to the internal and international skills audits sponsored by or carried out by governments. Many of the approaches to the measurement of human capital adopted by growth economists will therefore be too crude for skills audit purposes. For example, the use of prices as a proxy for skill levels across national labour markets with differing levels of supply and demand does not provide the measure of embodied human capital needed for efficiency studies. However, as the earlier part of this section indicates, growth economists are increasingly interested in refining stocks and flows data by reference to measures of relative quality and it is at this interface that the two different exercises may have a common interest.

The continuing diversification of the output of the educational system at the higher levels (upper secondary and tertiary education) has made inter-country comparisons a more complex undertaking. But qualitative differences in the attainments of different groups of students at the upper levels of the educational structure are of prime importance to governments. They are important because governments are anxious to ascertain how far the investment they are making from the public purse in the education and training of young people is producing skills and knowledge which will enable their manufacturers and businesses to remain competitive.

Once a concern for the quality of a *diversified range* of outputs from education and training systems has been introduced, many of the standard tools and procedures that had served a useful purpose in an earlier age prove to be ill-adapted to new demands. This is particularly the case with the methods used by a number of countries to collect data on stocks of qualifications in the population and with existing taxonomies of educational levels – in particular the International Standard Classification of Education (ISCED). Problems arising from the methods used by different countries to record data on education level attained and definitions of educational achievement are discussed in Section 2. The difficulties these create for the allocation of qualifications to the ISCED scale and the inherent limitations of the ISCED scale are discussed in Section 3.

Collecting Data on Individuals' Highest Level of Education and Defining 'Attainment'

All European Union member countries carry out sample surveys of their populations (usually known as Labour Force Surveys) at least every two years and often more frequently. One of the questions in this survey is designed to yield information on the highest level of education attained by individuals of working age. But important differences persist in the measure of 'highest educational level' used by different countries and these differences present major problems when deciding how to allocate different countries' stocks of education to the ISCED scale.

Some countries measure educational output in terms of school stages reached and/or 'completed'. Others measure it in terms of qualifications obtained. Some do both. Of course, a great deal depends on what is meant by 'being at' or 'completing' a level. If a level is only counted as 'complete' or 'reached' if the individual concerned has passed a formal test or assessment, then the problem largely disappears. But this is certainly not the case in Sweden, for example, where all those who remain to the end of their ninth school year are counted as having completed lower secondary education whatever their school marks.

By contrast in France, the certificate based on the examination taken at the end of lower secondary schooling, the *Brevet*, is not awarded to all who complete the *troisième* year nor is this the case for similar examinations in Germany or in the United Kingdom (UK). In all those countries where highest *qualification levels* are the measure of educational attainment, only those who gain the recognised qualification at, for example, the end of compulsory education, are counted as having completed that level. Those who complete in the sense that they are enrolled for the whole school year but who do not gain the qualification, are recorded at the next level of qualification down. But if these same individuals had been questioned using say the Danish or Swedish system of national classification they would have been recorded in terms of the level reached regardless of what their marks had been in any examination at the end of secondary schooling. Table I provides an overview of the differences between EU countries on this question.

In addition to the fundamental problem of whether we are measuring inputs (years of education) or outputs (qualifications awarded) there are other significant differences in the reporting of qualifications as follows:

1. In some countries (e.g. France) only state validated qualifications are reported and qualifications gained through independent training providers are not recorded. In the UK, by contrast, qualifications awarded by bodies such as City & Guilds are recorded,
2. In some countries (e.g. Belgium) only qualifications awarded within the educational system are reported and vocational qualifications awarded by the Ministry of Employment are not recorded.
3. In some countries e.g. Germany, all recorded qualifications require passes in a range of core subjects. In the UK, by contrast, the criterion for classification in the 'some 0-level' or 'some A-level' category was, until recently, a single '0' or 'A' level pass.

Variations between countries in the definition of educational level and attainment by individuals thus constitute an unresolved problem for all those concerned to ensure that international comparisons of educational attainment are as accurate as possible. International organisations such as the OECD and EUROSTAT charged with publishing statistics showing educational attainment across a range of countries are particularly affected. Currently, the notes issued with their main publications, respectively *Education at a Glance* and *Education across the European Union* fail to point out the extent of the differences of definition between countries.

	Both measures used in one survey	Education measured by qualification obtained	Education measured by level
Belgium	X	Mostly X	Some X
Denmark	X	Some X	Mostly X
Germany		X	
Greece (b)	X	X	X
Spain		Mostly X	Some X
France (a)		X	X
Ireland	X	X	X
Italy	X	Mostly X	Some X
Luxembourg	X	Mostly X	Some X
Netherlands (b)	X	Some X	Mostly X
Austria (b)		Mostly X	Some X
Portugal (b)	X	Mostly X	Some X
Finland	X	X	X
Sweden (b)	X	Some X	Mostly X
United Kingdom		X	

(a) But two measures available for whole population
(b) In this case much depends on what is meant by 'completed level of education'. If this is a defined level and if completion depends on reaching that level then this classification could also be considered qualification dependent

Table I. Differences between EU countries in criteria used to assess educational attainment in national sample surveys.

The Classification of Educational Outputs

Once national data has been collected, international organisations and others constructing international comparisons must make decisions about the allocation of the national categories used to an agreed international classification. Chief among the tools currently used for the classification of educational outputs is the ISCED. The ISCED categories are as follows:

ISCED 0 Education preceding the first level (pre-primary)
ISCED 1 Education at the first level (primary)
ISCED 2 Education at the lower secondary level
ISCED 3 Education at the upper secondary level

ISCED 5 Education at the tertiary level, first stage
ISCED 6 Education at the tertiary level, first stage, leading to first degree
ISCED 7 Education at the tertiary level, second stage, leading to a
postgraduate degree.

The ISCED was developed by UNESCO more than 20 years ago to
provide a framework for the international classification of education
defined as "organized and sustained communication designed to bring
about learning". It was originally envisaged that the classification could
be used for a number of purposes, principally the classification of
courses of education, but other uses envisaged included the
classification of stocks of educated individuals in the population
(Unesco Office of Statistics, 1975).[1] Despite the broad definition of
education quoted above, the ISCED classifies "courses, programmes and
fields of education according to their educational content", educational
content being defined as having two dimensions – level and subject
matter.

It can be seen from the description above of the work carried out by
Barro & Lee using the ISCED levels as the basic building blocks, that
where comparisons are primarily global and quantitative, the
categorisation of years of education according to ISCED level can give
some useful information concerning the weighting of different years of
education in the calculation of human capital accumulation. However,
when advanced industrialised countries try to use the ISCED
classification for a very different purpose, namely to assess the *total
performance* of their educational system, the limitations of ISCED
become more obvious, and the need for a revised taxonomy of
educational outputs more apparent. Healy & Nordin (1995) have made
similar points concerning the limitations of the ISCED taxonomy as a
result of work for the OECD Study Group B which develops indicators
for the domain of education and labour market destinations. In 1997 a
UNESCO working party set up to consider the growing problem of the
existing ISCED classification issued a draft paper containing proposals
for a new ISCED scale (UNESCO, 1997).

The new ISCED classifications proposed in the draft paper
constitute an improvement over the current classification since they
recognise the increasing tendency for pupils to follow courses with
different standards and different curricula particularly in upper
secondary education. But they will not begin to resolve the problems
arising from the different data collection and reporting conventions
among European countries summarised in Section 2 above.

For the present, however, the 1975 ISCED scale given above is still
in use. In practice, one of the main problems of this scale has been that
the generality of its definitions allows too many different interpretations
of what is understood as an 'educational level'. An egregious example of

this is the differing interpretations of the ISCED 2/3 cut-off point which has resulted in differences between EUROSTAT and OECD education statistics.

In *Education at a Glance* 1997 Annex 1 we find the typical cumulative years of schooling by level of education for all the countries examined. For the UK, the typical cumulative years of schooling for primary education are given as 7 which, with a starting age of 5, indicates that primary schooling in the UK finishes at age 12. Lower secondary education takes ten years from the start of compulsory schooling, finishing at age 15. It is difficult to recognise here the reality of the British system, where primary education normally finishes at age 11 and compulsory schooling at age 16. Even more confusing is the fact that two years earlier in *Education at a Glance* 1995, for the UK, the typical finishing age of lower secondary education is given as 14, two years before the end of the compulsory period of education.[2] Most, but not all the other countries in the Table set the beginning of upper secondary education in the year in which compulsory education ends, i.e. end on to compulsory education. All the EU countries do so, except Belgium (where education is compulsory to 18) which gives 15 as the start of upper secondary education, Spain – where upper secondary education is given as starting at 14 with compulsory education until age 15, and Austria – where upper secondary education is given as starting at 14 with compulsory education until age 16.

When we turn back to the ISCED definitions developed by UNESCO, we can see that the definition of ISCED 3 depends upon two criteria. First, it is based upon some eight years of previous schooling. With a modal starting age for education in Western Europe of 6, it could be argued that ISCED 3 could start at or around age 14. Yet the other criterion is that some significant subject specialisation should occur – here the definition fits most closely the education that usually occurs at a later age than 14 in most European countries. While most countries have changed their definition of ISCED 3 to reflect later starting ages of upper secondary education the UK government has adhered more closely than most OECD countries to the letter of the original ISCED 3 definition. But the decision of the UK government to specify a lower starting age than 16 for the start of upper secondary education has important consequences for the reporting of educational levels which are explained in the following paragraphs.

Annex 1 in *Education at a Glance* forms the basis for a further table, Table A2.1 which shows the percentage of the population 25-64 years of age that has completed a certain level of education. Here, the UK emerges as one of the very highest qualified populations aged 25-64 in the EC, second only to Germany and well above France, Belgium and the Netherlands. This does not reconcile well with the comparisons of skills in France, Germany and the UK carried out elsewhere where France and

Germany have been shown to have higher stocks of qualified individuals than the UK (Green & Steedman, 1997; Steedman et al, 1997).

Another glaring inconsistency revealed by OECD figures for the UK is with figures produced by the Office of the National Council for Education and Training Targets (NACETT). NACETT has calculated a figure for the workforce, *not* the population in England, qualified to A-level, (G)NVQ3 or equivalent of 40% for the same year (1995), 35 percentage points lower than the figure of 75% given for the total UK population aged 25-64 in the OECD table at ISCED Level 3 (see Table II). Even allowing for differences of definition, (the NACETT figure excludes qualifications which do not lead to some form of higher education) the enormous disparity between these two figures looks extremely odd.

If we look more closely, we can see that much turns on the definition of upper secondary education. If lower secondary education is defined as ending at age 14-15 and upper secondary education in the UK as starting at 15-16, then O-level/GCSE can be classified as a qualification awarded in the course of upper secondary education. Whereas NACETT classifies O-level/GCSE to a category below the category containing A-level and equivalent qualifications, the UK authorities have classified O-level/GCSE to the same category as that containing A-level qualifications for the OECD international comparisons. O-level/GCSE is one of the largest categories of qualification, and shifting it from one level to another therefore makes a lot of difference.

However, the GCSE is quite unambiguously a qualification usually obtained within the compulsory period of schooling in England and Wales (indeed, it constitutes the assessment of the final stage of compulsory education in certain subjects). In this respect, it most closely resembles the French *Brevet*. This French qualification is assigned to ISCED 2 (in Table A2.1 in *Education at a Glance*, p. 38). Under no circumstances does the GCSE constitute a qualification acceptable as an entry qualification to higher education (except in the very archaic sense of being a matriculation requirement). It is therefore not possible to argue that the GCSE belongs in ISCED 3 by virtue of being a qualification widely accepted as an entry qualification to the next stage of education. My own view is, therefore, that it would be more accurate to assign GCSE to ISCED 2 if only to achieve some consistency with the National Targets.

The problem of the classification of GCSE becomes particularly acute when we look at other sources of international comparisons of educational levels of the population. The statistical office of the European Union (EUROSTAT) publishes an annual volume of educational statistics entitled *Education across the European Union: statistics and indicators*. In these publications, GCSE passes are treated differently than in *Education at a Glance*.

Section E of *Education across the European Union* presents Tables which give percentages of the population aged 25-59 by highest ISCED level of education attained. Table E4 is a close counterpart to Table A2.1 of *Education at a Glance* discussed above. The EUROSTAT definition of ISCED 3 is different from the UNESCO definition adopted by OECD. In the EUROSTAT definition of ISCED 3 'data include population with attainment in general education less than ISCED 3 but with an additional vocational qualification'. This definition means that UK O-level holders are back in ISCED 2 and only those who hold a vocational qualification in addition to O-level are classified to ISCED 3. This definition gives us a very different allocation of the UK population to the ISCED levels. Table II summarises both allocations.

	OECD (b)	EUROSTAT
<ISCED 3	24	47
ISCED 3	54	31
>ISCED 3	21	22

(a) For EUROSTAT, aged 25-59, for OECD men aged 25-64, women aged 25-59; (b) Figures add to <100 because of rounding

Table II. UK population aged 25-64(a) by highest ISCED level of education attained 1995.

It can be seen from Table II that, as a result of using different definitions of the ISCED 3 category for the UK, there are serious inconsistencies between OECD and EUROSTAT in data on stocks of education by ISCED levels. OECD figures show the UK as having 75% of the population at ISCED 3 and above while EUROSTAT shows just over half the population at that level.

Assessing the Quality of Education and Training Outputs

This paper has so far dealt primarily with the problems raised by current methods of presenting educational outputs. It is clear that procedures currently adopted by international bodies are not yet sufficiently coordinated to serve as a basis either for growth economists or for use by economists assessing educational efficiency in a comparative context. In this concluding section, therefore, I suggest some ways in which progress might be made towards a better understanding of the content and standards of educational qualifications which could act as a resource for statisticians' decisions about the allocation of qualifications to different levels of the international classification system.

A useful starting point in the process of establishing equivalences of qualifications across countries is the fact that all countries having some educational provision have also developed a set of generic categories in order to classify this provision. Once curricular pathways became diversified so that a variety of curricula and assessment were available, individuals gaining a given recognised qualification no longer necessarily studied the same subjects nor took the same test. Judgements of equivalence between subjects (e.g. between passes in different subjects at GCE A-level in England and Wales) then had to be made. Without such judgements, the output of the educational system would have lost its usefulness as a signalling device within the education system and on labour markets. As a result, *within* most countries, there is a long-standing tradition of making judgements about equivalence of qualifications between different qualifications awarded by that country's education system.

Even where the range of coverage or the standards required in two sets of qualifications are not identical, the performance of individuals with two different sets of qualifications may still be considered similar enough for these different sets of qualifications to be bracketed together as equivalent. This happens in almost all countries, not least in Britain, where we have probably a larger range of qualifications than in any other country. Thus, in the past, equivalences have been agreed for the purposes of university entrance or for entrance to lower level courses between, in England, BTEC and GCE qualifications. In France, the newer Baccalaureate qualifications have been granted equivalence with the older more traditional qualification which dates from the 19th century. In the USA, the GED examination is accepted within the education system (although not on the labour market) as conferring the equivalent of a High School Diploma.

The step from agreeing intra-country equivalences to establishing their validity is a large one. Nevertheless, for advanced industrialised economies the different types of qualifications in these countries fulfill similar roles. Except at the very highest levels, almost all qualifications fulfill two purposes. First, they attest fitness to proceed to the next stage in an established cursus or level within the education and training system. Second, they are recognised by employers as signalling sets of general or specific skills required in employment. The fact is often overlooked that most advanced industrialised countries have very similar structures of educational progression and a similar categorisation of qualifications with regard to labour market entry. These categories, when found across countries, can form the basis for an analysis and comparison of qualifications themselves.

Using these generic categories as a starting point, standards of attainment of students at comparable stages of education in a variety of countries can be investigated in a number of ways. Evidence from the investigation of quality of educational attainment can then be used to inform decisions about the allocation of qualifications to international classification levels. No one method of investigation of quality should be relied upon for such judgements. However, a more reliable way of proceeding is to draw upon evidence from all available sources and methods of comparing between countries and to see how far consistency and convergence of views on standards emerge from this process. To the extent that a judgement on standards is similar regardless of the methodology used, that judgement can be taken to be robust. This procedure is already well-known and tested in qualitative social science research and known as 'triangulation' (Miles & Hubermann, 1984).

The sources on which we can draw are a) international comparisons of educational achievement; b) reports compiled by teams of experienced educationalists; c) published work comparing syllabuses and examination papers; d) reports commissioned from independent experts comparing examination papers, and e) experiments in which the same examination questions are set in the national examinations or evaluation exercises of two or more countries.

Alone, each of these methods has weaknesses. International surveys have to contend with two major problems. First they have to ensure that the tests set, test at least part of the curriculum covered in the countries surveyed and that sufficient common questions nevertheless emerge. Second, it is necessary to ensure that in each country a representative sample of the population to be surveyed is drawn and tested. All recent international surveys have been the subject of some criticism on both these counts.[3]

Reports by visiting groups of experts are inevitably limited by the number of institutions that can be visited and the amount of documentation that can be evaluated within a short time scale. Nevertheless, when such surveys are undertaken by experts (such as the British HMI [Her Majesty's Inspectors of Schools]) having a long and wide experience in their own countries, such judgements carry considerable weight (HMI/DES, 1991; 1993).

The third method, comparing examination papers taken nationally or guaranteed as being of a similar standard throughout the country, overcomes two of the problems that arise for international testing programmes. First, the curriculum tested in the examinations considered is the one taught. Second, the students tested in those examinations are a whole population and not a sample. However, curricula and therefore examinations do differ from country to country and judgements must be made about whether the questions set or the skills developed are sufficiently similar to be able to say that students are performing to similar levels. The methodology of such studies has been much advanced by painstaking and detailed work recently carried out in the USA (Britton & Raizen, 1996). See also the other chapters in this section.

A fourth approach is to set identical questions in the national examinations of two or more countries which certify successful completion of a given level of education. This is the approach that was adopted in a recent attempt to assess basic mathematical competence in Swedish and English 16-year-olds (Wolf & Steedman, 1998), This approach requires time and patience and may yield only a limited range of common questions. It requires the support and approval of national governments. However, it overcomes many of the problems of the first three approaches set out above.

Whatever view comparativists may take of the comparison of stocks and flows of qualifications in different national populations we may be sure that national governments and international and supranational organizations will continue to use these as a basis for inter-country comparison. There will be important consequences for national education policies. In my view the contribution of comparative education should be:

- to try to ensure that the comparisons made are as fair a reflection of embodied competence as is possible given the resources available.
- to work to improve the quality of the information base used to establish educational equivalence and the transparency with which such work is undertaken.

Acknowledgements

An earlier version of this chapter was published in July 1996 as Discussion Paper No. 302 by the Centre for Economic Performance, London School of Economics and Political Science. Detailed and helpful comments were received on this and later drafts from a number of sources, in particular the Analytical Services Branch of the Department for Education, Anne West, Centre for Educational Research, LSE, Nicholas Oulton, Bank of England, Allan Nordin, Statistics Sweden, Laurent Freysson, EUROSTAT, Thomas Healy, OECD and participants at an Economic and Social Research Council-sponsored seminar held at the Graduate School of Education, University of Bristol in March 1998. Errors are of course my own.

The research reported here was supported by the Nuffield Foundation. The Centre for Economic Performance is financed by the Economic and Social Research Council.

Notes

[1] Healy & Nordin (1995) attribute the difficulties currently encountered in using the ISCED classification for comparing stocks of education to the fact that the classification was set up to classify and compare courses of education. However, UNESCO do make clear that they envisaged that ISCED could also be used for stock comparisons.

[2] The start of upper secondary education is also given as 14 for the UK in the UNESCO *Statistical Yearbooks* as far back as 1983. UNESCO defines upper secondary as corresponding to ISCED level 3 and this same definition is used by OECD. In the UNESCO *Statistical Year Book*, UK upper secondary education lasts for four years from 14-18. Moreover there are differences in this respect between England and Scotland.

[3] For a full account of the main problems see Nagy (1995).

References

Barro, R.J. (1991) Economic growth in a cross-section of countries, *Quarterly Journal of Economics*, 106(2), May, pp. 407-443.

Barro, R.J. & Lee, J.W. (1993) International comparisons of educational attainment, National Bureau of Economic Research Working Paper No. 4349.

Britton, E.D. & Raizen, S.A. (Eds) (1996) *Examining the Examinations: an international comparison of science and mathematics examinations for college-bound students*. Kluwer Academic Publishers: Boston.

DeLong, J.B. & Summers, L.H. (1991) Equipment investment and economic growth, *Quarterly Journal of Economics*, 106(2), May, pp. 445-502.

EUROSTAT (1997) *Education across the European Union Statistics and Indicators*. Brussels/Luxemburg: EUROSTAT.

Gemmell, N. (1996) Evaluating the impacts of human capital stocks and accumulation on economic growth: some new evidence, *Oxford Bulletin of Economics and Statistics*, 58, pp. 9-28.

Green, A. & Steedman, H. (1997) *Into the Twenty First Century: an assessment of British skill profiles and prospects,* Special Report. London: Centre for Economic Performance, London School of Economics and Political Science.

Hanushek, E.A. & Kim, D. (1995) Schooling, labour force quality and economic growth, Rochester Center for Economic Research, Working Paper No. 411, University of Rochester, September .

Healy, T.J. & Nordin, A. (1995) Concepts and definitions, in CERI/OECD *Education and Employment*. OECD: Paris.

HMI/DES (1993) *Education Observed: aspects of vocational education in France*. London: HMSO.

HMI/DES (1991) *Aspects of Vocational Education and Training in the Federal Republic of Germany*. London: HMSO.

Lee, K-H. & Psacharaopoulos, G. (1979) International comparisons of educational and economic indicators revisited, *World Development*, 7, pp. 995-1004.

Lucas, R.E. (1988) On the mechanics of economic development, *Journal of Monetary Economics*, 22, pp. 3-42.

Mankiw, N.G., Romer, D. & Weil, D.N. (1992) A contribution to the empirics of economic growth, *Quarterly Journal of Economics*, 107(2), May, pp. 407-437.

Miles, M.B. & Hubermann, M. (1984) *Qualitative Data Analysis: a sourcebook of new methods*. Beverly Hills: Sage.

Nagy, P. (1995) International comparisons of student achievement: examining the tests and the data. Paper presented at the Annual Conference Canadian Society for the Study of Education, Montreal, June.

OECD Review of National Policies for Education (1991) *Education in Belgium: the diverging paths*, pp. 97-117. OECD: Paris.

OECD (1997) *Education at a Glance*. OECD Indicators. OECD: Paris.

Oulton, N. & Young, G. (1996) How high is the social rate of return to investment? *Oxford Review of Economic Policy*, 12(2), pp. 48-69.

Psacharaopoulos, G. & Ariagada, A.M. (1986) *The Educational Attainment of the Labour Force: an international comparison*, Report No. EDT 38. Wahington: Education and Training Department, The World Bank.

Rebelo, S. (1991) Long-run policy analysis and long-run growth, *Journal of Political Economy*, 99, pp. 500-521.

Romer, P.M. (1986) Increasing returns and long-run growth, *Journal of Political Economy*, 94, pp. 1002-1037.

Sala-i-Martin, X. & Mulligan, C.B. (1995) Measuring aggregate human capital, Discussion Paper No. 723, Economic Growth Center, Yale University.

Steedman, H. & Green, A., Brtrand, O., Richter, A, Rubin, M. & Weber, K. (1997) *Assessment, Qualifications and Standards: the UK compared to France, Germany, Singapore and the US: a technical report.* London: Centre for Economic Performance, London School of Economics and Political Science.

UNESCO (1975) *ISCED Handbook: United Kingdom (England and Wales).* Paris: UNESCO Office of Statistics.

UNESCO (1997) *International Standard Classification of Education* (Draft Paper 151 EXI8 Annex II). Paris: UNESCO.

Wolf, A. & Steedman, H. (1998) Basic competence in mathematics: Swedish and English 16-year-olds, *Comparative Education*, 34, pp. 241-259.

The Tyranny of League Tables: international comparisons of educational attainment and economic performance

PETER ROBINSON

One of the first acts of the new United Kingdom (UK) Labour Government in 1997 was to set ambitious national targets to improve standards of literacy and numeracy in schools. The setting of national targets to boost the attainment of skills and qualifications began under the previous Government, which set targets for the level of qualifications to be attained by the adult workforce and by new entrants to the workforce.

Behind this target-setting agenda is a belief in the importance of educational attainment for economic performance. Britain's relatively poor showing in international tests in mathematics, for example, is assumed to have direct implications for the performance of Britain's economy compared with other countries, in terms of the level of and growth rate in average living standards. The relatively good performance of, for example, some Asian countries in international tests is believed to explain, in some large part, their economic success. Many politicians and their advisers hold these truths to be self evident.

With the attainment of British schoolchildren in the 'basic' skills being such a contentious political issue it seems warranted to try and un-pack some of these assumptions. One might hope that these assumptions may themselves be subject to greater questioning anyway after several 'Asian Tigers' ran into economic difficulties in 1997. Intuitively many people believe that there is a link between educational attainment and economic performance. This paper is not an attempt to suggest this intuition is misplaced. It may well be sound. However, it is a link which is relatively hard to demonstrate empirically.

The chapter looks at evidence from international studies on the attainment of students from different countries in international tests of literacy and numeracy and science. It then tries to see if levels of attainment are in any way correlated with economic performance. The measure of economic performance used here is the overall level of economic wellbeing, commonly measured in terms of gross domestic or national product (GDP or GNP) per capita. It is widely believed that high and/or improving standards of literacy and numeracy will lead to a higher level of per capita GDP/GNP.

There has been a great deal of empirical work which has tried to establish links between various educational indicators and economic growth. There is some measure of agreement amongst economists and others involved in economic development that a reasonably high level of enrolment of children in primary and secondary education is a necessary condition for poorer countries to reach a rate of economic growth which will allow them to converge with the living standards of the advanced industrial economies (see for example Barro, 1991). However, any agreement on the links between education and economic growth tends to stop there (see for example the review by Ashton & Green, 1997).

Countries which have had near universal enrolment in primary education and high levels of enrolment in secondary education over at least two generations will have negligible levels of functional illiteracy in the adult population. Once the vast majority of the adult population are functionally literate, which has been the case in all the advanced industrial countries for many years, any link between the attainment of literacy and numeracy and economic performance is very hard to demonstrate.

In the public policy debate in the UK, the existence of a link between economic performance and levels of literacy and numeracy in the industrialised countries is sometimes taken for granted. Britain's relatively poor showing in international tests in mathematics is frequently referred to, with the presumption that this in turn is linked with economic performance. It is worth asking whether empirical analysis backs this presumption.

Numeracy and Economic Performance

In 1995, 40 countries took part in the Third International Mathematics and Science Study (TIMSS) (Keys et al, 1996). These included most of the OECD countries, plus several of the East Asian countries which grew very rapidly up to 1997, several former Eastern bloc countries and a few poorer developing countries. In England, 3579 students aged around 14 years took the tests and scored slightly below the mean for all 40 countries participating.

The mean scores for the 40 countries are shown in Table I. This is a rather lengthier version of the 'league table' of countries, which is so loved by journalists and politicians. In this list England lies 24th. One presentational trick frequently used is to report selectively only a small number of countries so that England can be shown to lie 17th out of 20 countries or 9th out of 10, so giving the impression that the relative performance of English students is worse.

However, there is a much more fundamental objection to the use of such 'league tables'. Ironically, the debate over international comparisons of numeracy tends to lose sight of the important concept of statistical significance. The results reported in Table I are based on tests administered to samples of young people and are therefore subject to a margin of error. Small differences in scores between different countries' students could have arisen by chance. Fortunately, the publications which contain the results usually report sample sizes and standard errors and even whether or not any comparison between two countries reveals a difference in scores which is statistically different. So Table I also reports whether the mean score of the students in each country in these maths tests was significantly higher (+), significantly lower (-) or not significantly different from the scores of the English students.

This allows for a more meaningful understanding of the relative performance of the sample of English 14-year-olds. The students in 19 countries scored significantly higher than those in England and students in 11 countries scored significantly lower. For nine countries (including Scotland) the scores of their students were not significantly different from the scores of the English students. One could still conclude that the English (and Scottish) students performed less well than might have been hoped for, but this way of presenting the results is far more satisfactory than a crude league table.

There is of course a direct parallel here with the debate over school league tables. If we reviewed two primary schools each with 40 children taking the Standard Assessment Tasks (SATs) in mathematics at the end of Key Stage 2, we might find that one school had 60% of children (i.e. 24) scoring at level 4 or above while the second had 65% of children (i.e. 26) at or above this level. Given the very small size of the cohort taking the tests in the two schools, rigidly to rank one school above the other in a league table would constitute innumeracy of the highest order.

Table I also indicates the level of per capita GNP in each country expressed as an index number, with England set at 100. These estimates of per capita GNP are in terms of 'purchasing power parity' and attempt to estimate the real purchasing value of the average income in each country. As estimates, these levels of per capita GNP are also subject to a margin of error, conventionally assumed to be at least plus or minus five percentage points. What this means is that the per capita GNP of the Netherlands and Sweden is not significantly different from that of the UK. This margin of error means that it is also dangerous to use these estimates of per capita GNP rigidly to rank countries into a league table of economic success.

	Mean score	Significance[1]	GNP per capita[2]
Singapore	643	+	122
Korea	607	+	57
Japan	605	+	118
Hong Kong	588	+	125
Belgium (Fl)	565	+	113
Czech Republic	564	+	50
Slovak Republic	547	+	34
Switzerland	545	+	140
Netherlands	541	+	104
Slovenia	541	+	35
Bulgaria	540	+	24
Austria	539	+	109
France	538	+	110
Hungary	537	+	35
Russia	535	+	26
Australia	530	+	101
Ireland	527	+	76
Canada	527	+	111
Belgium (Fr)	526	+	113
Thailand	522	=	39
Israel	522	=	85
Sweden	519	+	95
Germany	509	=	109
New Zealand	508	=	88
England	506		100
Norway	503	=	113
Denmark	502	=	111
USA	500	=	144
Scotland	496	=	100
Latvia	493	=	18
Spain	487	-	77
Iceland	487	-	111
Greece	484	-	61
Romania	477	-	23
Lithuania	477	-	18
Cyprus	474	-	NA
Portugal	454	-	67

Iran	428	-	31
Kuwait	392	-	138
Columbia	385	-	30
South Africa	354	-	29

Notes
[1] + indicates that the mean score for that country was significantly higher than for England – indicates that the mean score was significantly lower = indicates that the mean score was not significantly different when compared with England
[2] GNP per capita measured in terms of purchasing power parity. Estimates have a margin of error of +/- 5%.

Table I. Levels of attainment in mathematics for 40 countries. Sources: Keys et al, 1996; World Bank, 1996.

One feature of Table I worth highlighting is the collection of countries clustered around England, with their students having mean scores in the maths test which were not significantly different from those of English students. These countries include the USA, Germany, Norway and Denmark, all with per capita GNPs significantly higher than in the UK. One of the more amusing features of the debate in recent years was the decision of Sig Prais, long a critic of British performance and a fan of the German model, to disown Germany as a country from which Britain might learn, in the light of the poor performance of German students in TIMSS (Prais, 1997).

In previous international tests in mathematics, English (and Scottish) students have tended to score at around the average for those countries participating. These tests are reviewed in Reynolds & Farrell (1996). For example, in the International Assessment of Educational Progress 2 (IAEPM 2) carried out for 13 year olds in 1990, students in England scored significantly less well than students in six other countries, significantly better than students in six other countries and not significantly different from students in seven other countries. These are not the results reported in Reynolds & Farrell (1996) who simply report mean scores without any indication of their statistical significance.

The key question to answer is whether there is any link between doing well in these international tests and relative economic performance? Students from the – until recently – fast growing East Asian countries, Singapore, South Korea and Hong Kong, along with Japan, were the top four performers in the mathematics tests carried out in 1995. This is taken as a clear indication of the link between doing well in these tests and economic performance. However, the students in a number of former Eastern bloc countries such as the Czech and Slovak Republics and Bulgaria also performed well. On the other hand, as has already been noted, students in the USA and Germany had mathematics scores which were not significantly different from those of the English students. In many international tests students in the USA tend to come out with scores which are often close to those of the English students, which raises a puzzle because the USA remains the world's most successful major industrial nation with the highest level of per capita GNP.

Clearly, in order to establish whether there is any systematic link between doing well in these international tests of attainment in mathematics and overall economic performance, we need to hunt for a correlation between the scores for all the countries participating in the tests and levels of per capita GNP, rather than just quoting the results for one or two countries and then alleging that this 'proves' that a link exists.

Strictly speaking we would like to have the results from tests of attainment for a large sample of countries from some time ago, which could then be correlated with subsequent growth rates in per capita GNP. This would allow one to test the hypothesis that high standards of attainment in the generation entering the labour market in say 1960 helped to foster *subsequent* economic growth. This is the logic behind the work of Barro (1991) who has tried to demonstrate the link between, for example, primary and secondary enrolments in 1960 and subsequent economic growth. However, this kind of work tends to be hindered by limitations in the available data.

In practice we only have data for a large number of countries for the attainment in numeracy of young people in 1995, which can then be correlated with levels of GNP in the mid-1990s, even though current levels of GNP are of course the result of growth over previous decades before the current generation were in the labour market. Nevertheless in the public debate the attainment of today's generation of young people is set alongside the current 'league table' of countries ranked by per capita GNP and a link is presumed. It is this presumed link which can be tested using a large sample of countries.

Figure 1 looks at the correlation between performance in the international mathematics test in 1995 and per capita GNP tor 39 of the 40 participating countries in the Third International Mathematics and Science Study (excluding Cyprus for whom reliable GNP data were not available).

It can be seen that the correlation between attainment in mathematics and per capita GNP for these 39 countries, although in the right direction, is so weak as to be meaningless. Figure 1 is in effect a scatter diagram showing almost no correlation. One can experiment with the data, for example by excluding obvious outliers such as Kuwait with its poor attainment in mathematics but its oil wealth; or by excluding the former Eastern Bloc countries and/or the developing countries. No experimentation produces any better results. There is effectively no correlation between doing well in the international tests of attainment in mathematics in 1996 and overall economic performance as measured by per capita GNP.

Figure 2 shows the correlation between mathematics attainment in 1996 and economic growth over the previous decade for 36 countries, though why good attainment amongst 13 year olds in 1996 should have allowed faster economic growth over the previous decade is unclear. Again the relationship is so weak as to be meaningless.

Figure 3 reports perhaps a more meaningful experiment. It takes the scores for 13 year olds in 16 countries which took part in the Second International Mathematics study in 1982-1983 and correlates them with economic growth over the subsequent decade. Again the result is a scatter diagram showing no correlation. Perhaps this Figure is the most convincing and interesting, because two of the fast growing Asian economies over this period, Hong Kong and Thailand, took part in the Second International Mathematics Study.

However, in 1982-1983 the 13-year-olds in these countries did *not* have significantly higher scores in mathematics than the 13-year-olds in England. Any notion that the impressive economic growth rates of these countries in the decade up to 1994 is a product of past superior attainment in mathematics is not borne out by the evidence. Indeed the relative improvement in the mathematics attainment of Hong Kong students has *followed* economic growth and not precipitated it.

This illustrates one of the important features of research in this area. Even if we find a correlation between an educational indicator and economic performance this implies nothing about causation. For example, higher education enrolments are likely to rise with the increase in average living standards as college seems to be something that higher income households like to 'consume' . In this case high income countries will have high college enrolment rates, but it could be wholly wrong to conclude that high enrolment rates have caused a high level of per capita GNP, rather than the other way around.

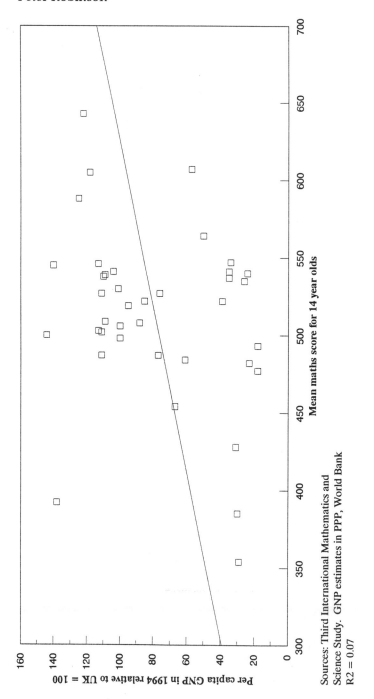

Sources: Third International Mathematics and
Science Study. GNP estimates in PPP, World Bank

R2 = 0.07

Figure 1. The correlation between mathematics attainment in 1996 and average
living standards in 1994.

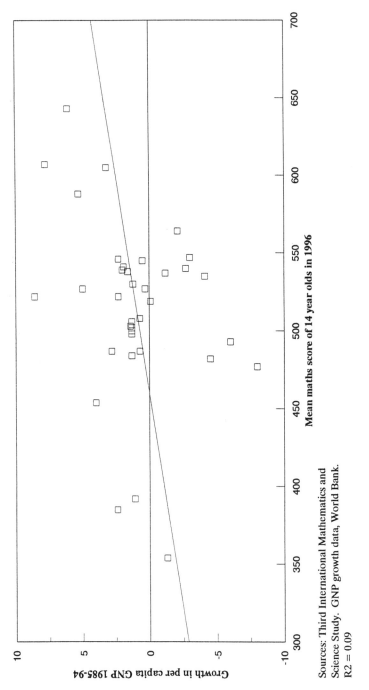

Figure 2. The correlation between mathematics attainment in 1996 and economic growth 1985-1994.

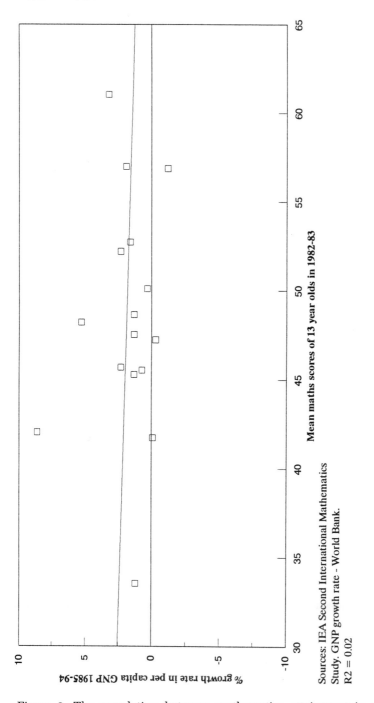

Figure 3. The correlation between mathematics attainment in 1982-1983 and economic growth 1985-1994.

Figure 4 looks at the link between the mean achievement scores of 13-year-olds in 12 countries in the First International Mathematics Study in 1964 and economic growth over the period 1965-1989. For the first time there is a significant positive correlation between mathematics attainment and economic growth, but only for this smaller sample of OECD countries. However, in this study the mean achievement score of the English students was very close to the average for the whole sample of countries. The score of the English students in 1964 should have 'bought' the UK an economic growth rate close to the average for this sample of countries. Amongst these 12 countries then the UK's below average economic growth rate over the whole period 1965-1989 cannot be 'explained' by poor attainment in mathematics.

Although the correlation in Figure 4 looks impressive, it is only for 12 OECD countries, and excludes any Eastern bloc or Asian or developing countries. Moreover, the two countries in Figure 4 with the poorest attainment scores and poorest economic growth rates, Sweden and the USA, were in 1964 the richest countries in the sample. The country with the best score and growth rate is Japan, which in 1964 was the poorest country in the sample. Any apparent link in Figure 4 between economic growth and mathematics attainment could easily be explained by the process of catch-up, as relatively poorer countries grow quickly so as to converge on the richest countries which in the meantime are growing relatively slowly. Indeed 'catch-up' has always been the most widely accepted explanation amongst economists for the impressive economic growth registered by some Asian countries up to 1997, the corollary being that once the gap had been closed such countries growth rates would subside. This is exactly what appears to have happened to Japan.

Overall then the evidence linking mathematics attainment with either the level of or growth rate in per capita GNP is very weak. The only significant positive correlation is for 12 OECD countries which took part in the First International Mathematics Study in 1964. In this study the mean attainment for the English students was close to the average for all 12 countries, so that the UK's below average economic growth rate over the subsequent quarter of a century cannot be put down to below average attainment in mathematics.

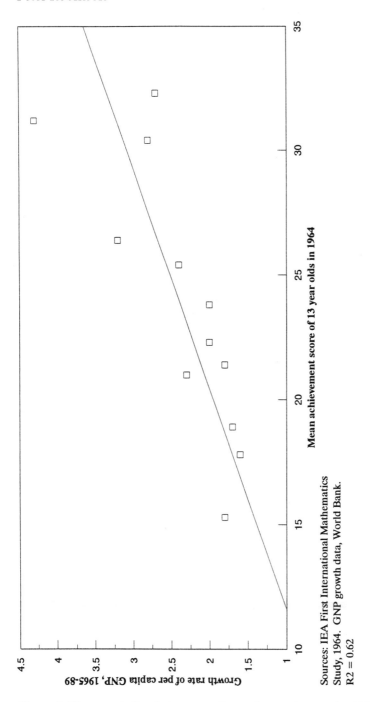

Figure 4. The correlation between mathematics attainment in 1964 and economic growth 1965-1989.

Science Attainment and Economic Performance

The results of the science tests administered as part of the Third International Mathematics and Science Study in 1995 are as interesting as the results of the mathematics tests. In science, the English (though not Scottish) students had scores well above the mean average for all 40 countries, scoring significantly higher than students in 25 other countries, with scores not significantly different from students in 10 other countries, while in only four countries did students do significantly better than the English. *Indeed England's relatively good showing in science was much more clear cut than its relatively poor showing in mathematics.*

Not that attainment in science is linked to economic performance either. Figure 5 illustrates the absence of any meaningful correlation between attainment in science and levels of per capita GNP. No amount of experimentation with the data can produce a significant correlation.

In conclusion, although English students tended not to perform particularly well in the international tests of mathematics attainment in 1995, but did very well in the international tests of science attainment, neither is correlated in any meaningful way with economic performance as measured by the level of or growth rate in per capita GNP.

However, the relatively good performance of English students in the science tests in 1995 is itself of considerable interest as a control for assessing explanations put forward for the less impressive showing of English students in mathematics in 1995. There might be a temptation to put the relative under -performance in mathematics down to systemic problems in English education or indeed English society. Some might allege that the results in mathematics are disappointing because of the under – resourcing of English schools or because of large class sizes. But why would these resource handicaps not show up in poor science scores as well, especially given that science is a more resource intensive subject? Others might point to the relative lack of status of teachers in the English education system, or to an anti-education bias in English culture, or to the effects of the creaming-off of students to the independent sector. But why should all these factors not impact on relative science attainment too?

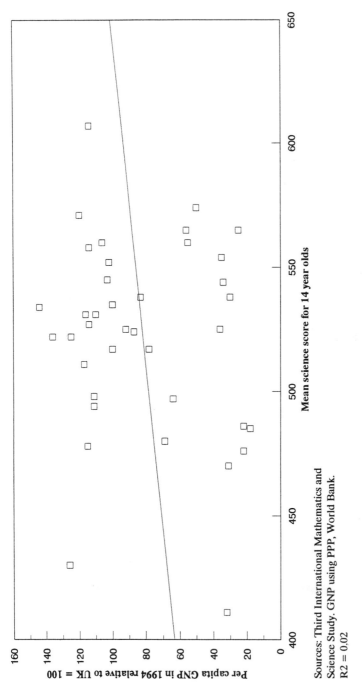

Figure 5. The link between science attainment and living standards for 38 countries.

The relatively good performance of English students in science has to move the debate decisively away from general assertions about the inadequacies of the English education system for explaining the below par performance in mathematics. Instead of general worries about English education as a whole we are left with specific questions about the structure and delivery of the mathematics curriculum. In one sense this is good news. It should be easier to identify and remedy any concerns with respect to one part of the curriculum than to try and turn the whole education system upside down.

Literacy and Economic Performance

International comparisons of attainment in literacy are much rarer than comparisons of attainment in mathematics and science. However, in the Autumn of 1997 the results of British participation in the International Literacy Survey were made available (Carey et al, 1997). This involved a sample of 3811 adults aged 16 to 60 in Britain. Unfortunately only the results from seven other countries were available at this time for comparison with the British results.

	Level 1		Level 2	
	%	Compared to Britain	%	Compared to Britain
Canada	17	=	23	=
Germany	14	-	13	=
Great Britain	22		17	
Netherlands	11	-	15	=
Poland	43	+	3	-
Sweden	8	-	32	+
Switzerland (French)	18	=	10	=
Switzerland (German)	19	=	9	=
USA	21	=	21	+

Notes: + indicates that the proportion for that country was significantly higher than for Britain; − indicates that the proportion was significantly lower; = indicates that the proportion was not significantly different when compared with Britain. Carey et al (1997) report that the proportion of Swiss adults at level 4/5 is not significantly different when compared with Britain, though the reported standard errors would suggest that significantly fewer Swiss adults were at level 4/5 than in Britain. The higher proportion of USA adults at level 4/5 is only just significant.

Table II. Levels of attainment in prose literacy for eight countries.

Table II reports the proportion of the sample in each country with prose literacy skills at level 1 (indicating very basic skills in using information from texts) and at level 4/5 (requiring high level skills in drawing inferences from dense text). The table also indicates whether the proportions achieving these levels in the other countries were significantly different from the proportions achieving these levels in Britain.

Only limited conclusions can be drawn. There were significantly fewer adults in Sweden, the Netherlands and Germany who were at level 1 when compared with Britain. There were significantly more adults in Poland who had only a limited grasp of prose literacy. The proportion of adults in Canada, Switzerland and the USA at this lowest level were not significantly different: from Britain. Again the concept of statistical significance is vital here. Some reporting of these results has suggested that the United States, Canada and Switzerland had fewer adults with lower scores in prose literacy than Britain. Such statements are not statistically valid.

Only Sweden clearly had a significantly higher proportion of adults performing at level 4/5 when compared with Britain. The proportion of adults in the USA at level 4/5 was only barely significantly higher than in Britain. Only Poland had significantly fewer adults at level 4/5 than in Britain. For Canada, the Netherlands, Germany and Switzerland, the proportion of adults at level 4/5 in prose literacy was not significantly different from Britain.

To sum up, only adults in Sweden clearly performed significantly better than adults in Britain in terms of prose literacy. Only adults in Poland performed significantly worse. For the other countries there is relatively little differentiation, though for the USA, Canada and Britain there was a somewhat greater dispersion of scores.

Is there any correlation between doing well in these literacy tests and economic performance? With only eight countries any formal assessment is somewhat redundant. But we can observe that Sweden has a level of per capita GNP which is no higher than in the UK, so that it is not clear that the higher levels of literacy of Swedish adults deliver any economic payback. The USA and Switzerland have the highest levels of per capita GNP in this sample of countries but literacy scores amongst their adults which generally are not significantly different from adults in Britain. Admittedly Poland has the lowest level of per capita GNP and the poorest standards of prose literacy, but one would really need a much bigger sample of countries before one concluded much from this.

The results of the survey of literacy in eight countries reported here, along with a number of other studies in the UK, have identified some individuals who have 'literacy problems'. This is absolutely *not* the same as saying that these people are 'illiterate'. Functional illiteracy is very rare in the UK and in all the advanced industrial countries. In the

OECD countries some adults have problems with their reading or spelling or writing, but this is not the same as the functional illiteracy still widespread in many developing countries. In the UK less than 1% of the adult population is functionally illiterate (Brooks et al, 1995).

The World Bank (1996) has data for most countries on the proportion of the adult population which is functionally illiterate. Significantly, amongst the Asian Tigers, adult illiteracy rates were still quite high in the mid-1980s. For example, Singapore and Hong Kong had, in 1985, adult illiteracy rates of 14 and 12% respectively, rising to 20% for women. So their impressive economic progress in the following decade does not appear to have been hampered by levels of adult illiteracy significantly higher than in the advanced industrial economies, including Britain.

The Dispersion of Scores and Income Inequality

There have been suggestions of a possible connection between the greater dispersion of literacy scores in Britain and the USA, and the greater degree of income inequality in those countries, compared with, for example, Sweden or the Netherlands or Germany. This is an avenue worth exploring further. The TIMSS results showed that the science scores for the English students were also significantly more dispersed than in many other countries, though this was *not* the case with the maths results. Reviews of the results of previous international maths tests have raised concerns about the greater dispersion of scores in England. However, this focus shifts the terms of the debate decisively away from international comparisons of educational attainment and some link with living standards, and towards a concern with the labour market prospects and incomes of those individuals with poor basic skills. Arguably this is precisely where the debate should be focused (Robinson, 1997).

Of course, the greater income inequality in the UK and the USA may have much more to do with the institutions of the labour market and with the progressiveness of the tax and benefits system, as with a possibly longer tail of adults with poor basic skills. Making the link between increased wage dispersion in these countries and the dispersion of attainment in basic skills raises a whole different set of research issues. It is very difficult to establish a link between inequality and the dispersion of scores in TIMSS. Even if a correlation was to be found, there is a possibility that causation could run either way. Despite the attempts of UK Government ministers to claim otherwise, poverty and income inequality have a significant impact on educational attainment, so that in, for example, the UK, the higher dispersion of scores in some international tests could be the result of greater inequality and not the cause.

Conclusions

English students tend to perform less well when compared with students in a range of other countries in international tests in mathematics. On the other hand the evidence linking mathematics attainment and the level or growth rate in per capita GNP is very weak. It follows that there is no evidence that boosting national attainment in mathematics would improve national economic performance. The ill-conceived notion that it would should not perhaps be allowed to influence the debate as much as it appears to.

A good control for assessing explanations of the relatively poor showing of English students in international tests in mathematics is the very good relative performance of these same students in science. This alone suggests that any generalisations about the inadequacies of English schooling are unfounded. Instead we are left with specific concerns about the structure and delivery of the mathematics curriculum.

In international tests of adult literacy the performance of British adults is about average, with only Swedish adults consistently doing significantly better. There is no way of demonstrating a link between levels of attainment in literacy and relative economic performance.

If Britain were a student in school receiving their end-of-term report it might well read "... doing very well in science and about average in literacy, but with some unevenness of performance in both subjects, and with some overall weaknesses in mathematics". However, this student would definitely not be on line to get a statement of special educational need, though from the rhetoric which accompanies the discussion of these international tests this is often the impression which is left.

There is another subtext to this debate over educational attainment and economic performance. Barely hidden beneath the surface of the writings of many policy makers on this topic is a degree of 'panic' about Britain's relative economic performance. It seems to be widely assumed that Britain is remorselessly slipping down the international 'league table' of economic prosperity. This assumption gives a justification to the hunt for scapegoats for this alleged problem. In the past the scapegoats have included the City of London and the alleged anti-industrial bias of English culture. The current favourite scapegoat is the education system.

However, if one starts from the premise that Britain's underlying economic growth rate compares reasonably well with other countries at a similar stage of economic development and that the faster growth of some other countries primarily reflects a process of catch-up, then one is not looking for scapegoats. This may help explain the cautious tone of this chapter. Economically, Britain is not about to be relegated to some lower league of economic performance.

This is not to argue that we should not be continuously looking at aspects of our economic performance and asking what can be done to sustain a reasonable rate of growth in living standards. It also does not imply that we should not want to think hard about the strengths and weaknesses of the English education system, though this should not be done solely or even mainly from the perspective of what is best for the economy. However, it does suggest that what could be a sober and informed debate about English education is in danger of being drowned out by the simplistic and often shrill rhetoric which seems to dominate policy making in education.

References

Ashton, D. & Green, F. (1997) *Education, Training and the Global Economy.* Cheltenham: Edward Elgar.

Barro, R.J. (1991) Economic growth in a cross-section of countries, *Quarterly Journal of Economics*, 106(2), pp. 407-443.

Brooks, G., Foxman, D. & Gorman, T. (1995) *Standards in Literacy and Numeracy, 1948-1994*, NCE briefing new series 7. London: National Commission on Education.

Carey, S., Low, S. & Hansbro, J. (1997) *Adult Literacy in Britain.* London: The Stationery Office, Office for National Statistics.

Keys, W., Karris, S. & Fernandes, C. (1996) *Third International Mathematics and Science Study.* Slough: National Foundation for Educational Research.

Prais, S. (1997) How did English schools and pupils really perform in the 1995 international comparisons in mathematics, *National Institute Economic Review*, No. 161, July, pp. 53-68.

Reynolds, D. & Farrell, S. (1996) *Worlds Apart? A Review of International Studies of Educational Achievement Involving England.* London: HMSO for OFSTED.

Robinson, P. (1997) *Literacy, Numeracy and Economic Performance,* Special Report. London: Centre for Economic Performance, London School of Economics.

World Bank (1996) *World Development Report.* New York: Oxford University Press.

Comparative Research on Pupil Achievement: in search of validity, reliability and utility

PATRICIA BROADFOOT

International comparisons of educational standards have become fashionable because governments around the world are becoming increasingly convinced that high levels of knowledge and skills in the working population are the key to future economic competitiveness. Whether this is indeed the case – and the contribution by Peter Robinson to this volume must call such widespread assumptions into question – is arguably less important than the fact that governments believe it to be so; that although education is expensive, it is also the key to future national prosperity. Thus, for both these reasons, it must be made to work efficiently and effectively. One of the most obvious starting points for ascertaining both the relative and the absolute effectiveness of the system is to establish the level of national standards and to compare these with those of competitor nations. To this end many countries have in recent years, set up national assessment systems to generate nationally-specific data concerning student achievement. Many have also become involved in one or more international comparative studies such as the recently-published Third International Mathematics and Science Study (TIMSS) (Keys et al, 1996).

In many countries, such as France, Australia, Canada and New Zealand, (Broadfoot, 1992; Masters & Forster, 1997; Anderson & Bachor, 1998; Crooks, 1997) these national assessment systems have been designed to generate diagnostic data concerning student achievement. Such data both provide government with information concerning the impact of social, environmental and school level variables on student achievement and give teachers information about individual pupil performance that they can use to support learning in the classroom. In other countries, such as England, national assessment systems, whilst also being intended to fulfil these needs, are primarily designed to provide summative achievement data as the basis for 'league tables' of institutional performance. Their aim is to encourage the operation of market forces in education. In this latter case, it is assumed by the United Kingdom (UK) Government that providing consumers with information about school standards in the form of league tables of national assessment results, will provide a degree of inter-institutional competition that will act as a stimulus to the achievement of higher standards across the system – a philosophy which is borrowed from the market-place.

When comparisons of pupils' achievements are published – whether this is on an international basis or on an intra-national basis between local institutions and authorities, it inevitably prompts a good deal of speculation and debate concerning the cause of an apparently poor position in the league table. Indeed, trenchant criticisms have been made about the equity of such a procedure. In England, for example, the publication of 'league tables' of the results of pupils in English and maths at the end of primary school on a school by school basis, prompted a furore of criticism concerning the validity and utility of publishing de-contextualised raw scores as a measure of school quality. Indeed, such objections have fuelled the search for so-called 'value-added' measures which measure the progress made by individual pupils in an institution rather than raw outcome scores. However the logic of this quest continues to be be-devilled with technical problems (Thomas et al, 1997). International comparative studies of pupil achievement which are typically of a 'snapshot' design, have also given rise to much controversy, both technical and educational (for example, Goldstein, 1995; 1996; Bracey, 1996; and Stedman, 1997),

Curriculum content will also clearly affect student learning outcomes both in terms of the emphasis within a particular subject and in terms of the number and range of different subjects studied. As Winter, 1998 has shown, the allocated instructional time (AIE) for a particular subject such as maths can vary substantially both within schools and across countries, with very significant effects on learning outcomes.

Technical critiques have emphasised the problem of comparing 'like with like'. Despite the most careful efforts to match pupil samples in terms of age, gender and socio-economic characteristics, significant differences undoubtedly remain in, for example, the numbers of children who have repeated years in different countries and are thus older than the putative sample, and in those with 'special needs' who are included or excluded. Stedman (1997) for example, argues that student achievement in the United States has been represented unfairly because results for a whole age cohort have been compared with those of small élites in other countries. Furthermore, he argues, social inequality in terms of opportunity to learn caused by variability in local school funding results in a far from standardised national picture – a point which was made by Husen (1983) in the early days of such international studies but is one of the many sources of variability which remain salient as influences on the comparability of the data gathered in such studies.

The importance of such conceptual and methodological problems is well illustrated in a study by O'Leary et al (1997). Their comparison of the results of two international maths and science surveys – International Assessment of Educational Progress (IAEP) and TIMSS – which were conducted four years apart, showed significant differences in the rankings achieved by several countries. Not only do such variations make it very difficult for policy-makers to know what action to take, they also call into question the reliability of the data themselves and hence the utility of the whole exercise. They raise what must be very real concerns about both the equity and the utility of international comparisons of educational standards and indeed of similar intra-national, inter-institutional comparisons based solely on the comparison of test scores (Brown, 1998).

But, whilst there has been a good deal of public and academic debate concerning the equity of such comparisons at a *methodological* level and a similarly impassioned debate about the desirable and undesirable impact of the *results* of such exercises, there has been surprisingly little informed discussion about the *cause* of the different levels of achievement identified to the extent that the data can be depended upon. In comparison with the very substantial research funding that has been devoted to conducting tests of learning outcomes, relatively few enquiries have been conducted to explore in a more systematic and in-depth way *why* it is that national systems of education appear to be differentially effective in achieving their goals.

This is not to say that policy-makers and others are not only too ready to jump to conclusions in this respect and to seize on particular measures such as more whole class teaching or greater provision of homework as the panacea for redressing apparent underperformance. Reynolds & Farrell's, (1996) study of UK learning outcomes in comparison with those of the so-called 'Asian tigers', for example, was seized upon by both Government and the media and has had a substantial influence on subsequent policy decisions. It is the argument of this chapter that while governments around the world are showing increasing interest in international comparisons of students' achievements and in the institution of national assessment systems, is testimony to what has become an increasingly general concern among governments with raising standards, this interest has not been matched by the development of understanding concerning how and why the various policies adopted to achieve this end are likely to achieve their intended goals. This is both surprising and regrettable given that the achievement of higher standards in education ultimately depends on pupils *learning* more effectively.

The Context for Quality

Theories abound concerning how schools may be made more effective. In England, for example, the passing of the 1988 Education Reform Act marked a commitment on the part of the British Government to turning its back on tradition by introducing stronger central Government control of the content of the curriculum. Coupled with a freer rein being given to individual institutions to allow them to respond to the demands of the market, this was seen as the most likely way to raise educational standards. In France, by contrast, the passing of the equally momentous 'Loi Jospin' in 1989 also marked a significant break with tradition in the commitment made on the part of the French Government to strengthening the autonomy of individual schools and teachers. It was anticipated that this approach, plus the extending of teachers' professional skills, would be the most likely way of raising educational standards.

These diametrically contrasting policy-initiatives reflect the different political stances currently prevailing in England and France. They are mirrored by a range of similarly-targetted, policy initiatives currently taking place in other countries as Governments seek to respond to the perceived challenges of the 21st century. The significant differences in the policy responses being made to common international pressures reflects the fact that education is a cultural project. It takes place against a background of national institutional and ideological traditions as well as other influences such as race, gender and the local environment.[1] Thus, for example, a comparison of the effectiveness of English teaching in the European Union (Bonnet, 1998) highlights the key role played by variations in national culture in either encouraging or inhibiting both motivation and achievement.

Motivation to learn in particular, emerges from research findings as particularly subject to cultural influences. The six country Student Learning Orientations (SLOG) project, (1987) found considerable variations in this respect, particularly in the balance between intrinsic and extrinsic motivation and the crucial link between 'continuing motivation' and the impact of assessment (Maehr, 1976), All too often it is assumed by policy-makers and others that the examination 'carrot' will motivate children to try harder. However, the extent to which this is true varies from culture to culture and as Kellaghan et al (1996) point out, "current assumptions about the role of examinations in motivating students fail to take into account differences in the personal characteristics of students and the contexts in which they live" (p. vii).

In the same way, it is also assumed by policy makers in countries such as the UK and the USA that 'naming and shaming' by means of national and international 'league-tables' of performance will motivate institutions to try harder. But, the apparent failure of 'high-stakes' institutional assessment to have an effect on standards (Stake, 1991) is further testimony to the fact that the link between effort, learning and performance is considerably more complex than most policy-makers believe (Firestone, 1997). As Bronfenbrenner (1979) and others have shown, what matters most in promoting learning are not necessarily the 'objective' features of a learning situation, but the ways in which these are construed and interpreted by individuals within a particular culture and setting. Thus attempts to put in place policies aimed at improving performance are only likely to be effective if they are informed by an understanding of the culturally-specific relationship between motivation, intervention and outcomes for both individuals and institutions.

Yet, despite the fact that the dangers of 'policy-borrowing' (Phillips, 1989) are now widely acknowledged and that educational practices which appear to be effective in one country will not necessarily achieve the same success in another, this awareness appears not to have inhibited a veritable epidemic of similar policy approaches spreading from one country to another in response to prevailing educational fashions. The current school effectiveness movement is one example of such diffusion in which the emphasis among policy-makers is much more on the nature of the educational intervention itself, rather than its potential impact on a particular educational and social culture despite the fact that researchers involved in the field are themselves increasingly stressing the key role of culture in influencing outcomes (Hargreaves, 1995).[2]

It is the argument of this chapter that comparative studies of learning outcomes, like other policy initiatives, are only a useful policy tool if they are contextualised within an analysis of the national culture, pedagogic traditions and educational priorities of a particular country. Even if de-contextualised comparisons can be developed to a point where they are *technically* defensible in that they are indeed comparing 'like with like', it is hardly equitable to judge the quality of the educational provision of either individual schools or countries as a whole in terms of pupil achievements without reference to the broader social context. Indeed it may well be that differences *between* schools *within* countries are a much more valid and pressing source of concern. However, to the extent that international patterns of differences in student learning outcomes can be established reliably and validly, it is vital to take culture as the starting point for analysis in establishing the nature of the particular pedagogic procedures that may hold the key to enhancing student learning.

Thus this chapter and the one that follows (Osborn & Planel) describe a very different kind of comparative approach to the study of national differences in pupil achievement. Both papers derive from the same ESRC-funded research project - Quality in Educational Systems Trans-nationally (QUEST)[3] – which was designed to link a detailed and careful comparison of pupil learning outcomes with related data concerning culture and classroom practice. This first chapter explores in detail the rationale and associated methodology for a much more qualitative approach to international comparisons of student learning outcomes. The second demonstrates the potential of such a comparative approach by presenting a range of empirical insights which illuminate the link between pupil attitudes to school and education; the pedagogy they experience and the ways these impact on their learning as demonstrated in a variety of assessment tasks. Perhaps even more significant, however, are the data the chapter presents which illuminate differences in *how* pupils set about solving the assessment problems presented and the associated insights these data provide into the impact on learning styles of different curricular and pedagogic emphases.

France and England: similar but different

The focus of the QUEST study is on two countries – England and France – in which the powerful influence of culture in shaping both educational traditions and participants perspectives has already been clearly illustrated in previous research on teachers. These two countries are closely linked in many ways – not least in their history, their common membership of the European Union and their geographic proximity. This reduces the potential impact of broader, political and economic differences on the analysis and hence highlights the specific role played by differences in culture and educational practices. on the learning outcomes being studied. The research revealed that the *national* differences between English and French primary school teachers, were more marked than any intra-national variations based on either the personal characteristics of the teacher, such as age and experience, or the location of the school (Broadfoot & Osborn, 1993).

These previous studies explored the construction of primary teachers' professional identity in England and France. They showed that teachers' priorities, and what they define as their responsibilities, are a function of the national culture and the national educational traditions in which they work (Broadfoot & Osborn, 1987; 1993). This research suggested that French teachers had a narrower, more 'restricted' and more classroom-focused conception of their role which centred on academic objectives, while English teachers saw themselves as having a more 'extended', wide-ranging and diffuse set of responsibilities and goals. These included responsibility for children's social and personal development as well as their academic progress, and also involved responsibilities to colleagues, headteacher, parents and the local community. Striking differences in teaching methods, in classroom organisation and in teacher-pupil relationships were also observed (Osborn & Broadfoot, 1992).

At the time of the first study, in the mid-1980s, French classrooms were often characterised by a didactic, highly authoritarian teaching style in which children sat in rows of desks facing the front of the class while the walls were dominated by teacher displays. Most French primary school teachers seemed to stress the 'product' more than the 'process' of learning. Strong emphasis was placed by the teacher on reaching the correct answer as quickly as possible. Neatness, attractive well set-out exercise books and meticulous pieces of finished work were highly valued. In England, more stress was laid on the learning process and less on the finished product, with teachers differentiating according to the perceived needs of the pupil, arranging different levels and types of work according to what they believed their pupils were capable of. By contrast, virtually all the French teachers had as their main aim that *all* pupils should achieve the same basic standard, in order to meet the set objectives by the end of the year. Work was paced to conform to the level of the middle group. Those who could proceed faster were unlikely to be allowed to undertake work at a higher level.

In England the approach was more active. Children were allowed and encouraged to work cooperatively some of the time and were often free to move around the room, while in France they were expected to work either alone or in a whole class situation and movement around the room was strongly discouraged. Teachers' efforts in France were typically directed towards leading children to one correct answer rather than encouraging them to think independently or divergently as was often the case in England. In France all children were typically engaged in the same activity whereas in England there was a greater variety of activities taking place, a more differentiated pedagogy, more emphasis on teaching for understanding and more positive feedback given to pupils.

However, the education systems of both countries have recently been the focus for major policy changes. In France, the reforms have been aimed at helping teachers to focus more on the learning needs of the individual child. In England, by contrast, the reforms have been aimed at implementing a common National Curriculum and a much greater measure of homogeneity and central control. Further research at this time (Broadfoot, 1998; Osborn, 1997) revealed more diversity in teaching styles and in classroom settings in France than in the past, with some classrooms now seating children in small groups, displaying pupils' work on the walls and being characterised by a more relaxed and informal relationship between teacher and pupil. However, the formal *leçon* continued to predominate. Teachers used the blackboard to present ideas to children and then worked extensively with individual pupils at the blackboard at the front of the class. Other children in the class were asked to comment on the work being done by the pupils at the board. Children then went on to work individually at the tasks set. Although pupils had more freedom of movement, choice of activity and resources available to them than when the earlier study was conducted in the mid-1980s, the overwhelming emphasis on French language and mathematics had not changed nor had the dominating authority of the teacher. In England, likewise, the studies revealed that there have been significant changes in teachers' classroom practice and ways of working which included a more collaborative approach, more whole class teaching, a more coherent approach to curriculum planning and progression and much more emphasis on formal assessment. But here again, the fundamental values of teachers concerning the purpose of education and their role within it, had not changed and were still clearly different from those of their French counterparts.

It was in the light of this previous work on teachers and the need for more contextualised comparisons of pupil achievement, that the QUEST project was funded in 1995 by the ESRC, The QUEST project set out to examine the significance of these observed differences in teachers' priorities and pedagogy for children's attitudes to school, their motivation to learn and, most importantly, their learning outcomes. It was hypothesised that if there are significant international variations in teachers' practice as a result of national cultural influences, this is also likely to be true for pupils. It was anticipated that, as products of a different national culture with all its associated traditions and institutions, children in England would come to school with significantly different attitudes about themselves, about school, and about their country than their counterparts in France. As a result, their expectations for themselves and of their teachers were also likely to be different (Osborn, 1996). It was further anticipated that any such differences in attitude to school would be further compounded by the impact of the very different pedagogical practices and styles which are characteristic of these two countries; that as a consequence of these differences, ostensibly the same pedagogic intervention by a teacher might have a very different effect in England than it would in France, To the extent that this was so, it would have very significant implications for policy. It would also reinforce the point that to be both valid and reliable and hence, useful, international comparisons of pupil achievement need data to be properly contextualised in a broader understanding of the educational and cultural context. This core hypothesis is summarised in Figure 1.

National Culture and traditions
⇩
Pupil attitudes, characteristcs and expectations
⇩
Classroom processes
(curriculum, teaching and assessment)
⇩
Learning outcomes

Figure 1. The QUEST hypothesis.

In response to this need for more contextualised comparisons of pupil achievement, one of the aims of the QUEST study was therefore to compare in considerably more detail than is possible in large-scale international surveys, the strengths and weaknesses of pupils at the end of primary school in the core subjects of language (English or French) and maths. By conducting a detailed examination of the links between learning outcomes, classroom processes and pupil attitudes in these two countries, it was hoped to explain any national differences identified in terms of both pupils' attitudes to learning and characteristic classroom approaches on the part of teachers. This kind of contextualised comparative approach arguably provides both a more equitable basis on which to make judgements about relative quality as well as a more useful one for policy-makers. By the same token, not to do so is both unfair to the efforts of those involved in the education system and potentially seriously misleading.

The QUEST project therefore represents an important new approach to the comparative study of pupil achievement which is one of the most rapidly growing aspects of contemporary comparative education research. It brings to bear the methodological and theoretical insights which have been built up in the field since Michael Sadler's work at the turn of the century drew policy-makers' attention to both the potential and the dangers of international comparisons and associated 'policy-borrowing' (Crossley & Broadfoot, 1992). In the light of a growing international obsession with simplistic and often, deeply-flawed international surveys of student achievement, the QUEST project is a response to the clear need for a sustained comparative study specifically designed to explore national differences in pupils' classroom experience and to establish new, more productive, ways of comparing the outcomes of very different educational experiences. In particular, the project team were concerned to address the following questions:

- In what ways do the performances of pupils in language and maths differ in France and England?
- How significant are these differences?
- What factors underpin any perceived pattern of differences in learning outcomes?

- Are there other patterns of differential performance which are more significant than those between the two countries (e.g. gender, social class)?
- What can an exploration of the both the scale and the nature of such differential performance reveal about the factors that influence learning?

Research Design

The research design of the QUEST study included both quantitative and qualitative approaches to data collection in order to maximise both the breadth and depth of the insights generated. This approach built upon the strengths of the previous comparative studies of teachers referred to above in which the clear patterns of response evident in a large questionnaire survey supported the validity of generalisations about national differences, while classroom studies enabled the processes which underlay these differences to be explored in greater depth. However the design of the current study contained some unique and innovative features, including the assessment of learning outcomes and 'focus group' interviews with pupils.

An overall representative sample of 800 children aged 9 to 11 (400 in each country) was selected from four schools in each of two contrasting regions in each country (16 schools in total, eight in each country). The schools represented a socio-economic and geographic mix and each school was matched as carefully as possible in size, location, and socio-economic catchment area with a counterpart in the other country. Care was also taken to have a roughly comparable proportion of ethnic minority children in the two samples. The regions in which the schools were located (Kent, Avon, Pas-de-Calais, and Bouches-du-Rhone) were chosen both to facilitate access to schools using existing contacts of the research team and to be broadly comparable in terms of geographic, economic, and demographic factors. In addition, a sub-sample of children from four schools in each country was interviewed and observed more intensively as detailed below.

Questionnaires in English and French were developed simultaneously by the bi-lingual, bi-national team with care being taken to ensure conceptual, and, as far as possible, linguistic equivalence. These contained both fixed response and open-ended questions covering perceptions of teaching and the curriculum, understanding of the purposes of schooling, and the extent of children's identification with a 'pupil', a 'school', and a 'national' identity. Extensive piloting and the presence of the researchers during the completion of the questionnaires helped to minimise some of the many problems associated with the questionnaire method in a cross-cultural study.

In each of the classes an extensive range of assessments in maths and language were given to children in the presence of both the researcher and the teacher. These included measures of pupil performance which were representative of a range of questions covered in the 1995 Key Stage 2 National Assessments in England and the 1995 Entrée en Sixième evaluation in France (these are described in more detail in the chapter by Osborn & Planel that follows). Children in both countries completed both types of question, thus ensuring that they were all exposed to forms of assessment characteristic of both countries. The selection of appropriate questions and the application of national criteria for marking them proved to be a challenging and arduous task, The criteria developed for the selection of items emphasised that questions should be representative of the breadth, depth, and levels of the curriculum in each country. All questions had to be within the potential capacity of both sets of children.

In maths, in addition to the examples from the national tests in each country, a third maths assessment was developed requiring problem-solving skills which the team felt were not adequately reflected in the national tests. For much the same reason in language, a grammar exercise was introduced which assessed pupil performance in specific areas of difficulty in the two languages. Two exercises from the English and French tests were also combined in order to assess punctuation and handwriting.

In order to pursue in more depth the insights on pupil perceptions of schooling generated through the questionnaire study, the second strand of data collection was more qualitative in nature involving interviews and observation of a sub-sample of children in each country. In order to encourage children to talk more freely and to exchange ideas about schooling the interviews were conducted as group discussions in groups of three pupils. In order to ensure the inclusion of children from contrasting socio-economic backgrounds two matched schools, one from an affluent and one from an inner city catchment area in each region in each country were selected for more intensive study.

In each of these schools, observation was carried out in classrooms using both open-ended field-notes (to provide a rich account of classroom interaction and to record theoretically significant events, dialogue or activities) and a systematic observation schedule developed for the ESRC PACE project (Pollard et al, 1994), This aimed at providing overall national comparisons of pedagogic strategy and curriculum context as well as of teacher activity, pupil engagement and interaction which would supplement, rather than replace, more qualitative data. In addition, other qualitative data in the form of photographs, teaching documents, and examples of children's work were collected to provide background contextual information.

A small exploratory study of 10 children in each country who had experienced both English and French primary education was also carried out. These interviews have provided some rich data but are intended to generate illuminative insights and to provide a form of triangulation with other pupil data, rather than to lead in themselves to generalisations.

This detailed account of the QUEST project methodology illustrates the very different emphasis of international comparisons of pupil achievement when the primary goal is to *explain*, rather than simply to *document*, national differences. The assessment data are limited in scale and a sample of this size cannot claim to be nationally-representative in a formal sense. However, they nevertheless provide a powerful insight into differences between the two countries in terms of what is being learned; how; by whom and why. The following brief overview of key aspects of the research findings is explored in considerably more detail in the chapter that follows. Both provide powerful support for the more qualitative and culturally-focussed approach to comparing pupil leaning outcomes which this chapter calls for.

The Learning Context

What factors influence children's motivation to learn? What can we learn from a greater understanding of how pupils' experience of and attitudes to school may be influenced by different social and national contexts? The questionnaire responses elicited the finding that although, on the whole, children in both countries felt fairly positive about their schools and their teachers, it was striking that French children were typically much more positive about school, more enthusiastic about teachers, and more likely to see teaching as helpful and useful to them. French children also appeared to be more highly motivated and keen to do well in class.

In England, primary teachers and teaching methods are currently being blamed for many educational and social problems. Yet it seems unlikely that the kind of national differences in pupil motivation which were identified are the result of particular teaching methods or of the personality and skill of individual teachers. Indeed, earlier research shows that English teachers place far more emphasis on meeting the individual needs of children and are therefore typically more concerned than French teachers to make school work interesting in order to engage the motivation of children (Broadfoot & Osborn, 1993).

Rather it is factors outside the classroom that appear to be highly important in explaining these variations including differences in the values and culture of the wider society and family values. In France there exists a clearly visible ladder of progress through school. Educational success and intellectual endeavour are highly valued, prized and understood in the wider society. French pupils appear to be motivated by the long-standing existence of a publicly understood learning pathway in the French education system. Consequently, they would appear to have a clearer perception of the school's main function as one of promoting learning. Furthermore, the clear separation in French pupils' minds of 'work' and 'play', and the explicit and immediate feedback which they receive from teachers concerning success or failure also emphasises the school's educational role. The questionnaire responses also suggested that the French children had absorbed some of the prevailing themes of their society's culture and the language through which key national values are mediated. They had a more positive attitude towards national identity and citizenship which is clearly related to the latter's importance in France – and the emphasis on education as a source of national unity which dates back to Napoleon.

By contrast, the long-standing English preoccupation with choice and diversity in educational provision (Archer, 1979) also has a very significant effect. While in the past decade some steps have been taken in England towards a more overtly *national* experience in primary schooling, there continues to be an overwhelming policy and cultural emphasis on individual school responsibility and identity. The lack of a clearly defined, publicly shared, and collective national educational purpose at primary level appears to be directly correlated with a relatively lower level in pupils' aspirations to do well and to work hard. Such differences reinforce the importance of understanding patterns of educational achievement as related to processes of socialisation into national identity.

Pedagogy and Learning Style

As discussed above, though both England and France are currently putting very considerable effort and resources into changing the nature of teachers' pedagogy in order to meet the perceived national needs and the challenges of the 21st century, it was nevertheless anticipated that the deep-rooted cultural differences in the educational traditions of the two countries would still be manifest in the day to day realities of classroom life.

Thus, the QUEST project hypothesised, for example, that the traditional, formal, didactic style of teaching characteristic of French primary schools would tend to foster a passive, authority-dependent, style of learning among pupils in contrast to England, where a more developmental educational philosophy would typically result in pupils who are capable of being more autonomous in their learning and willing to adopt a more individualistic approach. As Figure 2 sets out, it was anticipated that, to the extent that this is the case, French pupils would typically perform better on tasks that required the careful application of learned formulae and procedures, whereas English children would typically perform better on tasks that required problem-solving skills and creative, independent thinking.

(France)
traditional, formal, didactic teaching
⇩
passive, authority-dependent learning

(England)
developmental, individualistic pedagogy
⇩
autonomous and creative learners

Figure 2. QUEST hypothesis 2.

National Differences in Performance

In the event, these hypotheses proved valid. There were identifiable national patterns in the responses to various test items – differences which, as the analyses of Osborn & Planel make clear in the chapter that follows – provide important insights about the strengths and weaknesses of the different educational approaches pursued in the two countries, Perhaps even more significant however – certainly in terms of the argument of this chapter is that there was no clear 'winner' as Table I makes clear. The data presented in Table I make it clear that, not surprisingly, pupils tend to perform best on the tests that reflect their own country's curriculum priorities and the degree of familiarity of a particular style of test item.

Country		Maths[a]	Maths[b]	Language[a]	Language[b]
England	1996	43.0	39.9	65.1	46.1
England	1997	42.1	36.8	67.8	47.5
	All	42.7	38.8	66.0	46.6
France	1996	58.8	32.4	61.8	44.2
France	1997	61.6	33.2	56.0	42.1
	All	59.7	32.6	59.9	43.5
	Overall average	51.4	35.7	62.9	45

[a] = English-based tests; [b] = French-based tests

Table I. School average scores (expressed as percentages).

But, whilst there is an important message here concerning the overall utility of more large-scale international comparisons, even more significant is what Table I does not show – the detailed *profile* of strengths and weaknesses, attitudes and skills that the study was able to uncover by means of its in-depth, qualitative methodology and the *explanation* for these differences which are embedded in the national values and cultural traditions which give meaning to the actions of teachers and pupils in the classroom. As Osborn & Planel demonstrate, both England and France can claim significant strengths, as well as acknowledging some significant weaknesses. Whilst the English children had access to a wider range of skills, these were often at a lower level. Conversely, French pupils were often at a higher level but in a narrower field.

A brief example may usefully illustrate these points. In one of the maths tests, the children were asked to investigate some statements that they were given about what happens to odd and even numbers in simple computational situations. They were also asked to make general statements of their own about calculations involving odd and even numbers. The children's responses were marked according to six cumulative levels which are here presented, for the sake of clarity, in three different bands.

The results indicate that the English children were better equipped than the French children to take the investigation further. Of the English children, 45% achieved above a level 3 compared to only 26% of the French children. However, against this there was a wider range of achievement among the English children across the levels whereas the French results tended to be similar, with 67% of them reaching the midway point of a level 3, and only 6.5% below a level 3, half as many as the English children.

The potential significance for educational outcomes of national cultural differences is well illustrated in this example in the relatively limited spread of scores in France compared to that of the matched sample of English pupils. The indications are that the French tradition of teaching an undifferentiated lesson in which virtually all pupils are expected to be successful results in most pupils indeed being able to master what has been taught. By contrast, the English differentiated approach gives some pupils the possibility of achieving a much more sophisticated level of mastery whilst others are left far behind.

Moreover, the children's explanations and comments written in the course of pursuing the investigation were revealing about the differences in the English and French learning environments. English pupils were more individualistic and 'freer' in expressing themselves, while French children restricted themselves to the given task in their written responses. They tended to repeat and rework the given test item statements and seemed reluctant to commit themselves to making their own general statements about odd and even numbers.

> *Amurjit: The calculator is true because it give you a lot of help with your maths and I think calculators are true.*

> *Aron: I can't think of nothing OK?*

> *Tony: Odds and evens are sometimes complicated when they want to be but sometimes easy and sometimes just the same.*

> *Alan: Sarah is right because if you add 4 and 4 you get 8 but if you add 1 to one side 5 add 4 you have got one extra because of the one you added on. If you add 2 to one side you get an even number.*

(Examples of English children's responses)

This kind of scrutiny of the *way* in which children set about answering the questions posed, underlines the value of exploring not only *levels* of achievement, but also the kind of problem-solving strategies used by the children, since these latter provide a reflection of the way in which the values of a particular learning culture find expression in practice. The example provides an illustration of Sharpe's (1992) characterisation of French education as 'catechistic' in nature in which the business of learning is centred on acquiring an established body of knowledge rather than thinking through solutions for oneself.

The two accounts which follow describe an English and a French maths lesson. They illustrate the way in which differences in teachers' culturally-derived, educational priorities are expressed in the classroom practices which will ultimately produce the idiosyncratic pattern of national strengths and weaknesses revealed by the tests. As such, they demonstrate the importance of understanding every link in the chain of relationships between educational inputs, processes and outputs as a basis for effective policy-making. Thus, in the English extract, the teacher is anxious for the children to think about the problem and to generate their own solutions to it. In the French context, the teacher's concern is to induct the pupils into the mastery of a particular mathematical operation. The pupils are left in no doubt that there is one right answer to the problem and that the teacher is there as the agent of the educational system to ensure that they are taught the necessary knowledge. For English pupils there is no such clear message, they are at once both empowered as Mathematicians and denied the clear sense of purpose given to the French.

English maths lesson on area of polygons:
Not so much a lesson as direction of tasks for children to do.
They work on their own.

"You can talk to each other to help each other."
Children swap books to mark first bit – so some ensuing
discussion.
Teacher moves around helping individuals.
Gives encouragement and practice feedback.
Maths work on area and angles. Children measure different
angles then move to teachers instruction on angles.
Change from individual work and teacher helping individuals
to teacher instruction; some children not listening but
continuing with own work.
Class lesson follows on, moving a boy with his arms out in
front – moving him round 90°/180° etc. Children volunteer to
move him.
Children put up hands if agree/disagree.
(English maths lesson – extract from fieldnotes)

French maths lesson

Without explanation or contextualisation teacher launches
into the process of multiplying decimals by 1000.
The usual procedure is employed – they have to listen (raising
their arms) to the talk eg 3.3 x 1000 then teacher thumps the
table.
Pupils write the answer. Teacher thumps again and they have
to hold up their answers.
[a little later]
One child is sent to the board to write 'le titre de la leçon' –
proportionality.
Teacher refers to four situations involving proportionality in
earlier lessons.
Teacher questions pupils on how much they remember, a lot
of this is inviting pupils to join in chorally e.g. "on multipli
par le meme nombre." This all refers to p. 158 of the CM2
manual.
All attention is directed to p. 59. One child reads aloud and
the rest follow.
Teacher questions in order to ensure pupils understand what
is required by CM2.
"Allez, on se met au travail." Class descends into silent
concentration while teacher perambulates supervizing –
cajoling, commenting "La – tu fais ton tableau – et puis à

côté ...". Teacher sits down and works at her table.
9.15 Teacher announces that if they have finished copying out
the table and completing it, they can now copy the graph
beside it.
9.35 Teacher then writes on the board for all the children to
copy: 'Il existe 3 procèdes de calcul pour trouver le nombre de
pièces de 50 centimes que l'on obtient pour 5 pieces de lF.'
9.40 Children required now to place the points on the graph
and join with a line. The teacher spends some time
commenting – praise and criticism – then sits down. The
teacher is critical of children who don't remember that
'l'image de zéro est zéro'. Says "c'est completement faux", "on
ne fait pas n'importe quoi" – "on ne place pas ses points an
hasard pour me faire plaisir".
9.50 Teacher raises question of what the point of drawing the
graph is. "On peut continuer la ligne – qu'est-ce que je peux
savoir?" Leads them to see that the graph avoids the need to
do calculations -you can see instantly what the equivalences
are.
Teacher tries very hard to get the class to tell her what she
wants them to conclude but in each case ends up stating the
result herself. "Ça-va? Passons au suivant". Same procedure.
4.55 Teacher tells Sonya (just learnt to read in a specialised
unit) that just because she doesn't understand it does not
mean that she can't copy the graph.
(French maths lesson – extract from fieldnotes)

The Power of Expectations

Although these data are only intended to be illustrative, they make clear that differences in what two populations of pupils are able to do reflect teachers' different, culturally-based, expectations about children's achievements as well as their different views of the goals of education. These culturally-based differences in teachers' perspectives are further reinforced by similarly culturally-informed differences in the thinking that informs policy-making itself. Thus not only in England, do teachers typically expect children to reach different levels according to their individual abilities, and to this end they design their teaching to respond to perceived individual differences and indeed to encourage differentiation, this is also true of the broader educational policy framework in which they operate.

In France there is a strong tradition which is still enshrined in both policy and the national culture more generally, that all primary children are expected to reach a recognised and imposed level, though it is accepted that some children may take longer than others to 'arrive'. Teaching has therefore traditionally not been differentiated.

However our data also revealed some significant 'intra-national' variations which were arguably of equal if not more importance than the differences referred to above. Children in both countries who were at school in 'deprived' areas did significantly less well that their peers in more affluent areas but again, the range of achievement was not as wide in France. Given the explicit emphasis on common expectations in France this is perhaps not surprising but, by the same token, the substantial cultural differences in educational ideology and practice in the two countries which were the focus for this study, warn against any easy assumptions that a change in policy stance in England would necessarily bring about the same effect.

As argued earlier in this chapter, comparative studies of mathematical attainment in particular have been used as the basis for much critical comment by politicians and policy makers regarding the teaching of mathematics in the UK, the USA and a number of other countries. This example illustrates the kind of analysis that the QUEST project is pursuing in trying both to identify and to explain national differences in performance in a more constructive way. In England, for example, in a policy climate which is emphasising the importance of whole class teaching in mathematics (DfEE, 1998) and is critical of more individualistic approaches in the subject, it is important to highlight, where appropriate, the effectiveness of some English approaches to the teaching of mathematics.

Our results suggest that where individual initiative, experimentation and critical thinking are encouraged and valued this leads to pupils being more capable than their peers in some other countries to tackle open-ended tasks with confidence and imagination. By the same token, it is also important to recognise that those countries which are currently seeking to encourage the development of the enquiry and problem-solving skills which are so widely associated with future working life – including those 'Asian tigers' whose results on international league tables are currently the envy of many Western countries – are themselves faced with a considerable up-hill struggle to change teaching and learning approaches and procedures which are deeply ingrained in their national educational culture.

Conclusion

Assessment has long been recognised as a powerful influence on pupils' and teachers' priorities. Increasingly in recent years it has also come to be recognised by Governments as a powerful means of driving the priorities of the education system as a whole. Most recently, many Governments have come to see an important place for international comparative studies of attainment. But in the rush to find out national rankings in such international examinations, important caveats are all too frequently ignored. In a very real sense, the desire to have such results has developed more quickly than the methodologies that can deliver valid and reliable results. Equally, comparativists have perhaps not been as vocal as they should have been in warning of the dangers of simplistic comparisons and the disregard of culture and context.

This chapter has described the rationale for a research study aimed at redressing the balance. It has stressed the importance of ensuring the validity of the assessment data collected in that it provides a comprehensive reflection of curriculum content and pedagogic priorities. Moreover, it has argued the necessity of recognising that the variables underpinning the learning outcomes recorded are as much a function of national cultural traditions as they are of particular teaching strategies. If this is so, it suggests that to be useful, international comparisons of learning outcomes need to include scope for a qualitative exploration of pupils' learning orientations and stances as well as tasks which are more readily amenable to reliable comparison. Lastly, it is important to recognise the inherent danger that high-profile, international studies may obscure significant *intra-national* patterns of differential performance. Perhaps most important of all, however, are not issues concerning the validity and reliability of the comparisons being made of pupils' learning outcomes but rather the use to which the results are put. The challenge facing both the education systems which are the focus for this study is how to get the best of both worlds? Is it possible to envisage an approach to classroom practice that gives clear and common expectations to all pupils yet at the same time empowers them to cope with the unknown with confidence and skill?

Whilst there is no ready answer to this question at present simply to pose it is to underline the folly of making simplistic comparisons of standards based on an uncritical scrutiny of outcomes alone. Governments and the media in particular are quick to seize on apparent evidence that the education systems of other countries are more successful. This is neither true nor useful. Yet as a consequence, all too often governments are ready to assume that the application of those educational policies which appear to underpin the success of other countries will, if implemented, lead to similar levels of success in their own country. In so doing they disregard the key influence of national culture which is embodied in institutional traditions, professional ideologies and learner aspirations and perspectives.

Equity, as well as reason, underlines the importance of establishing both the full range of strengths and weaknesses which are associated with a particular education system and an understanding of the various different sources of those strengths and weaknesses. The penalties for not doing so are serious. They are likely to include a very real demoralisation of teachers. But even more significant is the likelihood that not putting in place policies that capitalise on the strengths of a given learning culture will lead to a failure to achieve the very goals being sought.

Notes

[1] See David Reynolds's contribution in this volume.

[2] The patterns of change in these countries tends to reflect historical grounded cultural associations. For example, New Zealand, Australia and Hong Kong are all seeking to introduce a 'levels-based' national curriculum with specified learning targets, accompanied by a criterion-referenced assessment system. In other countries, the emphasis is more on efforts to break down national homogeneity and, as in France, to encourage teachers to introduce a more individualised pedagogy which can provide for a wider range of student learning outcomes.

[3] The members of the QUEST team are Patricia Broadfoot, Marilyn Osborn and Claire Planel, University of Bristol, and Keith Sharpe and Brigitte Ward, Canterbury Christchurch College. The support of the Economic and Social Research Council for this research is gratefully acknowledged.

References

Anderson, J. & Bachor, D. (1998) A Canadian perspective on portfolio use in student assessment, *Assessment in Education*, 5(3).

ATL (1998) *Take Care Mr Blunket!* London: ATL.

Archer, M. (1979) *The Social Origin of Educational Systems*. London: Sage.

Bonnet, G. (Ed.) (1998) The effectiveness of the teaching of English in the European Union. Report of a colloquium, 20-21 October 1997, Paris, Ministere de L'Education Nationale.

Bracey, G.W. (1996) International comparison and the condition of American education, *Educational Researcher*, 25, pp. 5-11.

Broadfoot, P. (1992) Assessment developments, *French Education Review*, 44, pp. 309-316.

Broadfoot, P. with Osborn, M., Planel, C. & Pollard, A. (1996) Assessment in French primary schools, *The Curriculum Journal*, 7(2),pp. 227-246.

Broadfoot, P. & Osborn, M. with Gilly, M. & Paillet, A. (1988) What professional responsibility means to teachers: national contexts and classroom constants, *British Journal of Sociology of Education*, 9, pp. 265-287.

Broadfoot, P. (1998) *What Makes Primary Education Successful? Perspectives from a Comparative Study in European Education*. New York: Sharpe.

Broadfoot, R., Osborn, M., Gilly, M. & Brucher, A. (1993) *Perceptions of Teaching: primary school teachers in England and France*. London: Cassell.

Bronfenbrenner, U. (1979) *The Ecology of Human Development*. Cambridge: Harvard.

Brown, M. (1999) Problems of interpreting international comparative data, *Oxford Studies in Comparative Education*, 9(1), forthcoming.

Budge, D. (1997) maths failure lingers after curriculum revolution, *The Times Educational Supplement*, 13 June, p. 20, popular report on TIMSS findings.

Crook, S.T. & Flockton, L. (1996) Science: assessment results 1995 National Education Monitoring report 1, 2 (Art) and 3 Graphs Tables and Maps. Education Assessment Resource Unit, University of Otago, New Zealand.

Crossley, M. & Broadfoot, P. (1992) Comparative and international research in education. Scope, problems and potential, *British Educational Research Journal*, 18, pp. 99-112.

DfEE (1998) *Numeracy Matters. The Preliminary Report of the Numeracy Task Force.* London: DfEE.

Federal Reserve Bank of New York (1998) *Economic Policy Review*, March.

Firestone, W., Winter, J. & Fitz, J. (1998) Different Policies, Common Practice: mathematics assessment and teaching in the United States and England and Wales, paper given to the American Educational Research Association Annual Conference, San Diego.

Goldstein, H. (1995) *Interpreting International Comparisons of Student Achievement.* Paris: UNESCO.

Goldstein, H. (1996) Introduction, *Assessment in Education*, 3, pp. 125-128.

Goldschmidt, P. & Eyerman, T. (1999) International educational performance in the United States: is there a problem that money can fix? Paper submitted to *Comparative Education*, 35(2).

Hanushek, E. (1989) The impact of differential expenditures on school performance, *Educational Researcher*, 8(4), pp. 45-51.

Jones, L.V. (1996) A history of the National Assessment of Educational Progress and some questions about its future, *Educational Researcher*, 25(7), pp. 15-22.

Lees, Lynn Hollen (1994) Educational inequality and academic achievement in England and France, *Comparative Education Review*, 38, pp. 65-87.

Masters, N. & Forset, M. (1997) *Mapping Literacy Achievement: results of the 1996 National School English Literacy Survey.* Canberra: Department of Employment, Education Training and Youth Affairs.

Keys, W., Harris, S. & Fernandes, C. (1996) *Third International Mathematics and Science Study: first national report.* Slough: National Foundation for Educational Research.

Mislevy, R.J. (1995) What can we learn from international assessments? *Educational Evaluation and Policy Analysis*, 17, pp. 419-437.

O'Leary, M., Madaus, G. & Kellaghan, T. (1997) The validity and stability of international comparative findings in mathematics and science: the IAEP TIMSS enigma. International Centre for Research Assessment (ICRA), London, 3-5 July.

Osborn, M. & Broadfoot, P. (1991) A lesson in progress? Primary classrooms observed in England and France, *Oxford Review of Education*, 18, pp. 3-15.

Osborn, M., Broadfoot, P. Planel, C. & Pollard, A. (1997) Social class, educational opportunity and equal entitlement: dilemmas; of schooling in England and France, *Comparative Education*, 33, pp. 375-393.

Osborn, M. (1996) Being a pupil in England and France: findings from a comparative study. Paper presented at the 17th Comparative Education Society in Europe (CESE) International Conference, Athens.

Pollard, A., Broadfoot, P., Croll, P., Osborn, M. & Abbott, D. (1994) *Changing English Primary Schools.* London: Cassell.

Reynolds, D. & Farrell, S. (1996) *Worlds Apart: a review of international surveys of achievement involving England.* London: Office for Standards in Education/HMSO.

Sharpe, K. (1992) Educational homogeneity in French primary education: a double case-study, *British Journal of Sociology of Education*, 13(3).

Stake, R. & Theobald, P. (1991) Teachers' views of testing impact on classrooms, in R. O'Sullivan (Ed.) *Advances in Program Evaluation*, Vol. 1. London: JAI Press.

Stedman, L.C. (1997) International achievement differences: an assessment of a new perspective, *Educational Researcher*, 26(3), pp. 4-15.

Winter, S. (1999) International comparisons of student achievement and the Asian educational phenomenon: a critical analysis, *Comparative Education* 35(2).

Comparing Children's Learning, Attitude and Performance in French and English Primary Schools

MARILYN OSBORN & CLAIRE PLANEL

Introduction and Aims of the Study

In the light of the growing international interest in raising educational standards and in comparing national levels of achievement which was described in the previous contribution, 'Comparative research on pupil achievement', by Patricia Broadfoot, this chapter presents data gathered as part of the QUEST project (Quality in Educational Systems Trans-nationally)[1] which was described in that chapter. It offers a more detailed comparison of primary school learning outcomes in mathematics and language in England and France. It considers, how a qualitative analysis of pupil learning strategies can contribute to the international debate. The overall aim of the research was to examine the interrelationship between the various factors which potentially affect learning. In particular, it sought to investigate pupil learning strategies in mathematics and language in the two countries and to examine the relationship of these to children's educational experiences and attitudes to school in view of significant variations in the teaching approaches and curriculum emphases of primary schools in the two countries.

The QUEST study took as its starting point the notion that the social construction of education is evident both at the level of the structure of the national education system, and in the distinguishing features of the school and classroom practice. Thus the particular classroom/pedagogic techniques reported here may themselves be seen as derived from cultural values built in at a societal level.

In this chapter we first explore the relative strengths and weaknesses of English and French pupils in mathematics and language. Secondly, we link pupil performance in assessments, in terms of achievement and strategies used, to findings on pedagogy and pupil attitudes. Finally, we consider the conclusions and possible policy implications for both the teaching and testing of language and mathematics and international comparisons of achievement more generally.

Methodology

The broad approach of the QUEST project, as described in the preceding chapter was designed to link data on pupils' attitudes to schooling and observation of their classroom experiences with the outcomes from common tests in language and maths taken by children in both countries. In both England and France 400 pupils from eight matched primary schools completed an extensive range of assessments. These included measures of pupil performance which were representative of a range of questions covered in the 1995 Key Stage 2 National Assessments in England and the 1995 Entrée en Sixième evaluation in France (see Appendix). Children in both countries completed both types of question, thus ensuring that they were all exposed to forms of assessment characteristic of both countries. The selection of appropriate questions and the application of national criteria for marking them proved to be a challenging and arduous task. The criteria developed for the selection of items emphasised that questions should be representative of the breadth, depth, and levels of the curriculum in each country. All questions had to be within the potential capacity of both sets of children. The Appendix gives illustrative examples of some of the questions used. A complete set of test papers is contained in our report to QCA (Planel et al, 1998).

Relative Strengths and Weaknesses of Pupil Performance in Language and Maths

The overall conclusions from a test by test comparison of children's scores in the maths and language assessments were that, not surprisingly, pupil performance reflected national curricular content. English pupils performed better at a wider range of maths areas including probability, averages and investigative maths. French pupils performed at a higher level but in a narrower range of maths areas, for example in computation and geometry. Pupil performance tended to reflect national curricular values. English pupils performed better at items which required a more 'hands on' or experimental approach, for example the maths investigation. French pupils performed better at items which required more technical expertise, for example computation. On the whole, pupil performance was negatively affected by the unfamiliarity of another country's national test items.

The performance of English pupils relative to French pupils was strong in the two language tests, although English and French pupils were observed to spend a similar amount of time on language work in the classroom. On the whole English pupils performed better than

French pupils at inferential reading comprehension items (Language 1, Q1 – Q5.3), use of homonyms (Language 1, Q6), punctuation (Language 1, Q7a & Q7b), handwriting (Language 1), spelling (Language 2) and purpose and organisation in story writing (Language 2). French pupils performed better than English pupils in their use of the alphabet (Language 1). Not only were English pupils performing better at the more open ended tasks such as the inferential reading items and story writing but surprisingly they also performed better at some of the more structured tasks, for example the grammar items in Language 1.

It became clear from this overall comparison that a quantitative analysis of overall pupil performance could not answer the questions of 'How?' and 'Why?' English and French pupil performance differed. A qualitative analysis was required to reveal the fundamental strengths and weaknesses in pupil performance between different educational systems and to reveal underlying differences in pupil performance.

English and French Pupil Performance at
Language and Maths: a qualitative analysis

Language

Although the overall results from the two countries suggested that the performance of English and French pupils at story writing (Language 2) was fairly similar (Table I), the qualitative analysis showed that there were important national differences which had been masked by the English national assessment scheme we had been using. French stories were shorter. The weaker French stories were more likely to be very short and in the form of three or four complete, and better punctuated sentences (Figure 1 'L'histoire se passe ...') whereas the weaker English scripts were more likely to be quite long and in the form of a continuous stream, with little or no punctuation (Figure 2 'I opened the door'). French scripts were also more likely to lack consistency in the use of time, place and characters. However they did show a superior use of commas. In the area of style the national emphasis on creativity and imagination in the English context and taught literary strategies in the French context emerged clearly. The stronger English scripts achieved higher scores in style through their use of imaginative vocabulary and descriptive passages, for example,

> *I walked off into the inky darkness of the room Everything was bare except for large flaring torches nailed to the wall. (Boy from school located in high socio-economic status area in Bristol)*

The stronger French scripts scored in their use of literary strategies such as 'lorsque' or 'lors de' instead of 'quand', or, 'à longueur de journée';

syntactic structures such as 'une fois libérée ...'; and expressions such as 'connaître ... comme sa poche', or, 'ni vu ni connu'.

Finally, there were significant difference in the settings and story lines of the English and French scripts. A sample of 100 randomly chosen English and French scripts showed that the preferred English story model was a 'real life' one whereas the preferred French model was closer to a traditional central European folk tale. English stories were more likely to use a 'real life' setting (37 out of 50 English scripts were set at or close to home compared to 15 out of 50 French scripts). English scripts were more likely to centre on 'self as the main character (26 out of 50 English scripts compared to 19 out of 50 French scripts). In contrast French stories, echoing a traditional tale, were often set in a forest or in a former historical period (23 out of 50 compared to only 4 out of 50 English scripts).

	1996		1997	
	English	French	English	French
Overall	46	44	47	42
Average purpose score	47	42	49	42
Average grammar score	42	44	41	38
Average style score	47	48	49	49
Average spelling score	63	46	61	44

Table I. Language 2, 1996 and 1997, average scores.

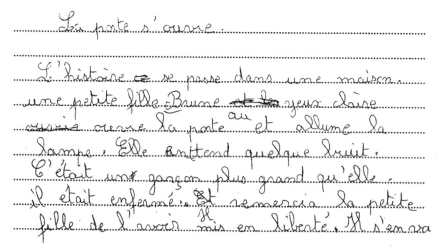

Figure 1. 'L'histoire se passe ...'

The qualitative analysis of English and French story writing scripts thus showed that underlying the seemingly similar quantitative results were two cultural models of the definition of a 'good' story. The performance of English pupils showed relative strength in content and individuality and weakness in form, the converse was true of the French pupils. This suggests that the English definition of a 'good' story includes a relative emphasis on content whereas the definition of a 'good' French story includes a relative emphasis on form.

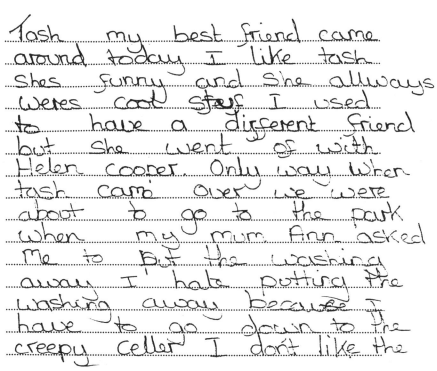

Figure 2. 'Tash my best friend ...'.

Overall results in the performance of English and French children at reading comprehension (Language 1) had suggested that English pupils were doing better than French pupils. The qualitative analysis not only confirmed this finding but strengthened it. It suggested that the English model for reading comprehension emphasised inference. The error analysis of English responses showed that a common English error was to use inference but to fail to directly answer the question. However the French model was more mechanistic, error analysis showed an emphasis on pupils retrieving from the text rather than putting the response in their own words. Other French pupil errors indicated conformity to a model of 'Why ...?' questions and 'Because ...' responses.

The performance of English and French pupils at spelling suggested that despite the relative priority of grammar work in French classrooms (QUEST classroom observation indicated that 15.9% of the French observed classroom time was taken up by grammar compared to 0% of English observed time) English pupils performed better at spelling homonyms (Table II). English pupils also out performed French pupils in spelling in the story writing test (Language 2): more English pupils (25% in 1996 and 26% in 1997 had achieved a level 3 (between 0 and 5 mistakes on the first page) than had French pupils (9% in 1996 and 10% in 1997), Furthermore when a sample of individual pupils' spelling was compared for the same items over the two tests it was found that English children were also more consistent in their spelling.

	1996		1997	
	English % correct	French % correct	English % correct	French % correct
Pupils getting 1-3 out of 9 correct	8	13	5	17
Pupils getting 4-6 out of 9 correct	21	36	24	34
Pupils getting 7-9 out of 9 correct	68	48	69	47

Table II. Grammar items (QUEST item), Question 6.

French spelling errors often involved tense endings. Clearly the performance of pupils in this area, and in spelling in general, is dependent to a large extent on the internal syntactic demands of the language but it was interesting that French pupils also had more problems with the use and manipulation of tenses. Analysis of a sample of 50 English and 50 French story writing scripts showed that French pupils were more likely to be inconsistent in their use of tenses, for example, starting in the past and then suddenly changing to the present (42% of French pupils made at least one such error compared to 24% of English pupils). This suggests that the English emphasis on oral language in the classroom and relatively greater practice of writing diaries, stories, poems, plays and self evaluations (taking up 18.7% of observed QUEST time in English classrooms compared to 1.5% in French classrooms) are not without effect.

Maths

The overall results of pupil performance at Maths C (maths investigation) Table III, and performance at individual French items (from Maths A) and English items (from Maths B) Tables IV, V, VI, VII and VIII showed first that pupil performance reflected national curricular content. English pupils performed better at a wider range of maths areas, including probability, averages, and investigative maths. Secondly, pupil performance reflected national curricular content. English pupils performed better at tasks which required a more 'hands on' or experimental approach. French pupils performed better at items which required more technical expertise. Thirdly, pupil performance was negatively affected by the unfamiliarity of another country's national tests. The qualitative analysis was able to contribute to further understanding of the relative performance of English and French pupils by suggesting not only 'how' they were different but 'why' they were different.

Levels	1996		1997	
	English %	French %	English %	French %
< 3	13.0	8.0	14.0	12.0
= 3	42.0	65.0	45.0	51.0
> 3	44.0	26.0	39.0	35.0

Table III. Maths C (QUEST item), 1996 and 1997.

Number **English items**						
		1996		1997		
Question	**Q type**	**English % correct**	**French % correct**	**English % correct**	**French % correct**	**Strongest**
Q2a	$\square \div 5 = 22$	71.0	68.0	56.0	57.0	French
Q2b	$2\square 8$ $+29\square$	57.0	84.0	54.0	88.0	French
Q3a	323 x $\square$7	31.0	49.0	18.0	55.0	French
Q3b	$\square$ x $\square$ = 42	43.0	50.0	35.0	45.0	French
Q4	Problem	36.0	32.0	33.0	29.0	English
Q5Cc	Problem	38.0	54.0	26.0	50.0	French
Q10a	Decimals	17.0	23.0	18.0	17.0	French
Q10b	Fractions	11.0	3.0	7.0	0.0	English

Table IV. Percentage of English and French correct answers in English number items.

Number French items					
		1996		1997	
Question	Q type	English % correct	French % correct	English % correct	French % correct	Strongest
Q1a	168.75 +42.50	62.0	71.0	63.0	75.0	French
Q1b	463 -167	55.0	83.0	61.0	84.0	French
Q1c	26 2782	19.0	63.0	15.0	65.0	French
Q1d	4.28 x3.5	8.0	49.0	4.0	54.0	French
Q2a	7.14 x 100	28.0	73.0	26.0	70.0	French
Q2b	325.6 ÷ 10	26.0	49.0	24.0	65.0	French
Q7	Problem	48.0	61.0	46.0	61.0	French
Q8	Problem	39.0	56.0	31.0	68.0	French

Table V. Percentage of English and French correct answers in French number items.

Shape, space and measure English items					
		1996		1997	
Question	Q type	English % correct	French % correct	English % correct	French % correct	Strongest
Q6a	Shape from above	18.0	14.0	21.0	8.0	English
Q6b	Shape from above	14.0	10.0	12.0	1.0	English
Q9	Symmetry	64.0	33.0	59.0	41.0	English

Table VI. Percentage of English and French correct answers in English shape, space and measure items.

Shape, space and measure French items					
		1996		1997	
Question	Q type	English % correct	French % correct	English % correct	French % correct	Strongest
Q3a	Drawing a rectangle	88.0	96.0	86.0	94.0	French
Q3b	Above cont.	49.0	75.0	50.0	69.0	French
Q3c	Above cont.	34.0	62.0	32.0	52.0	French
Q4a	Geometric terms	3.0	16.0	9.0	20.0	French
Q4b	Geometric convention	76.0	61.0	69.0	67.0	English
Q5Ca	Perimeter	32.0	29.0	40.0	28.0	English
Q5Cb	Area	67.0	47.0	66.0	56.0	English
Q7	Rectangles	49.9	41.0	45.0	53.0	English

Table VII. Percentage of English and French correct answers in French shape, space and measure items.

		Handling data English items				
		1996		**1997**		
Question	**Q type**	**English % correct**	**French % correct**	**English % correct**	**French % correct**	**Strongest**
Q1	Averages	32.0	14.0	28.0	15.0	English
Q5Ca	Reading a chart	88.0	84.0	83.0	81.0	English
Q5Cb	Filling in a chart	70.0	57.0	67.0	58.0	English
Q7a	Probability	72.0	30.0	65.0	43.0	English
Q7b	Probability	40.0	13.0	65.0	36.0	English
Q7c	Probability	23.0	1.0	21.0	4.0	English
Q8a	Reading a pie chart	30.0	9.0	28.0	13.0	English
Q8b	Reading, estimating	24.0	8.0	14.0	9.0	English
Q8c	Explaining estimation	19.0	2.0	17.0	4.0	English

Table VIII. Percentage of English and French correct answers in English handling data items.

Figure 3. "What other general statements could you make about calculating with odd and even numbers? Say why you think they are true."

When English and French pupil responses to the maths investigation (Maths C) were analysed it was found that English pupils were using more individualistic strategies, as for example in Figures 3 and 4. Although both English and French pupils did explore what happened to odd and even numbers, in a more straight forward way, when they were added, subtracted, multiplied and divided, there were more English pupils who using independent thinking in their investigation. A French response was more likely to show a more mechanistic and routinised approach Figure 5. The strategy of independent thinking, which was revealed by the qualitative analysis to be more characteristic of the English pupils, was well suited to the task of this maths investigation. It explains why the English pupils performed relatively better.

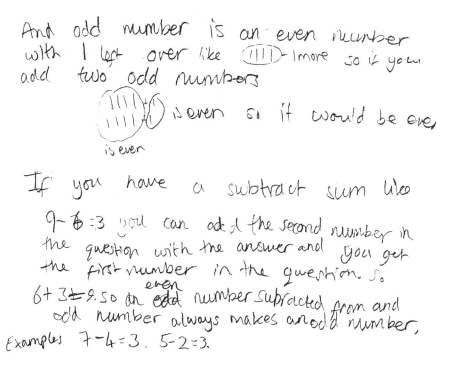

Figure 4. "What other general statements could you make about calculating with odd and even numbers? Say why you think they are true."

The qualitative analysis of pupil performance from a sample of 36 English and 36 French pupils at items in the areas of number, handling data and shape, space and measure (Maths A and B) also showed the same underlying difference of individualism versus mechanism between the two national samples.

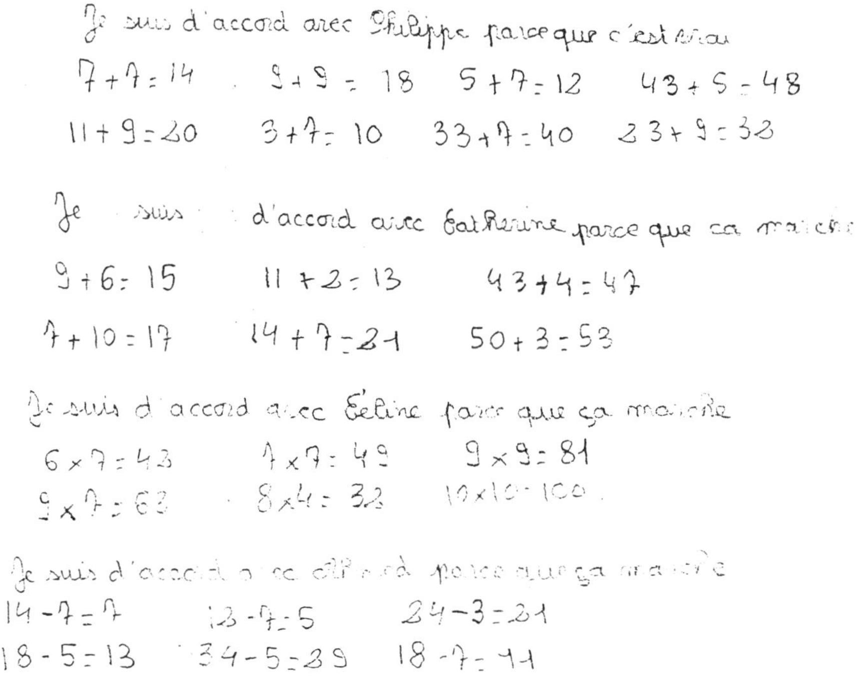

Je suis d'accord avec Philippe parce que c'est vrai

$7 + 7 = 14$ $9 + 9 = 18$ $5 + 7 = 12$ $43 + 5 = 48$

$11 + 9 = 20$ $3 + 7 = 10$ $33 + 7 = 40$ $23 + 9 = 32$

Je suis d'accord avec Catherine parce que ça marche

$9 + 6 = 15$ $11 + 2 = 13$ $43 + 4 = 47$

$7 + 10 = 17$ $14 + 7 = 21$ $50 + 3 = 53$

Je suis d'accord avec Céline parce que ça marche

$6 \times 7 = 43$ $7 \times 7 = 49$ $9 \times 9 = 81$

$9 \times 7 = 63$ $8 \times 4 = 32$ $10 \times 10 = 100$

Je suis d'accord avec David parce que ça marche

$14 - 7 = 7$ $13 - 7 = 5$ $24 - 3 = 21$

$18 - 5 = 13$ $34 - 5 = 29$ $18 - 7 = 11$

Figure 5. "Avec lesquels de ces enfants es-tu d'acord ou pas d'acord? Dis pourquoi tu penses qu'ils ont raison ou tort."

In number, English pupils performed less well because they were more likely to devise their own strategies whereas French pupils relied on processes that they had been taught and in which they had greater expertise and technical skills. When English pupils were faced with arithmetic problem-solving computations such as,

$$\square \div 5 = 22$$

they were less likely to use traditional algorithms than French pupils and where they did so they were more likely to make mistakes. Instead they used tallies, or multiples of 5 Figure 6, or, in one case Figure 7 there was an English pupil who first worked out that 10 x 5 = 50, then did 20 x 5 = 100, and then added a further 2 lots of 5 to make 110.

When confronted by French items which presented the four computations in a traditional horizontal or vertical form the English pupils' errors showed that they had less expertise than the French pupils. In addition, they made more serious errors, for example ignoring place value in 'carrying over':

$$
\begin{array}{r}
168.75 \\
+\ 42.50 \\
\hline
11010.125
\end{array}
$$

In subtraction English pupils made more types of errors and their errors were more serious, for example the lack of understanding in the irreversibility of numbers in subtraction:

$$
\begin{array}{r}
463 \\
-\ 167 \\
\hline
304
\end{array}
$$

this suggested that English pupils were not as well trained as French pupils. The same conclusion can be drawn from the errors made by English pupils in multiplication and division. English pupils, in default of understanding a taught process, were often having to devise their own strategies in long multiplication, for example:

$$
\begin{array}{r}
4.28 \\
\times\ 3.5 \\
\hline
13.40
\end{array}
$$

where an English pupil tried to first multiply decimal numbers by decimal numbers and then multiply whole numbers by whole numbers, so that in the decimal numbers 5 x 8 = 40, 0 and carry 4; 5 x 2 = 10, 10 + 4 = 14, 4 and carry 1 over to the whole numbers. In the whole numbers 3 x 4 = 12, 12 + 1 (the carried over 1 from the decimal number) making 13.

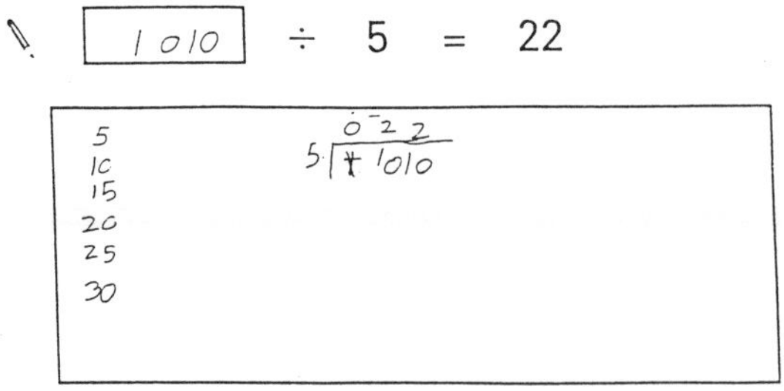

Figure 6. "2a Write in the missing number."

There were less French pupil errors in multiplication and division and they were less diverse. French errors mostly took the form of pupils loosing their way in a process which they knew but were not totally sure of.

```
↘   [ 110 ]   ÷   5   =   22

2 [?] ÷ 5 = 22    10 × 5 = 50
                  20 × 5 = 100 + 2 × 5 = 110
                              ✓
```

Figure 7. "2a Write in the missing number."

The performance of English and French pupils at problem-solving computations where a computation was set up in a language situation showed the same characteristics of English pupils understanding what was required of them but as they were less competent in their use of algorithms they had to develop their own strategies to arrive at a solution. They were often unable to distinguish between efficient and non efficient strategies, for example carrying out repeated addition on 18 lots of 95p and so were more likely to make errors. French pupils used their greater technical expertise and made less errors, for example,

Il y a 83 petits pains qui coutent 3F chacun alors on fait
[There are 83 rolls which cost 3F each so the calculation is]

83	x	3	=		249
petits	3 francs				le
pains					montant

[83 rolls at 3 francs equals 249.]
C'est une multiplication.
[It's a multiplication.]

The better performance of English pupils at handling data was shown by the error analysis of their scripts to be a result of the wider English maths curriculum which includes such items as probability. French errors were more varied and in the case of probability they were less likely to include the language of probability. The poorer performance of French pupils at handling data may also relate to their weaker skill in reading comprehension. English and French pupil errors in shape space and measure also indicated that national performance was related to the degree of familiarity with the type of items.

Such qualitative cross-cultural evaluation of pupil performance can increase understanding about the national frames of reference in learning, in which pupil performance is set. This qualitative analysis of the performance of English and French pupils in language and maths has suggested some of the reasons behind their overall differences in achievement. The scripts showed that English pupils were more likely to rely on individual strategies and solutions. These were their strengths and it was these characteristics that accounted for their greater success in the test of investigative maths and the reading comprehension. The strengths of the French pupils lay in their internalisation of established procedures and it was these strengths which allowed them to out-perform English pupils in the area of number. The qualitative analysis also points to two underlying and contrasting cultural models of pupil learning. The English model could be described as individualised and based on an exploratory approach. It emphasises individual strategies and solutions, and encourages individual self expression. The French model tends towards only one approach, an approach which emphasises conformity, form and technique. These differences in features of pupils' performance and learning strategies are paralleled by differences in classroom processes and pedagogy as the following section suggests.

Classroom Processes, Attitudes to Schooling and Pupil Achievement

One aim of the study was to examine the links between classroom processes and pedagogy, pupil motivation and attitudes to learning and pupil achievement. In this section of the chapter we first give an overall picture of the observed classroom processes, through systematic observation and fieldnotes in a representative sub-sample of eight schools, and secondly consider the relationship between these and pupil achievement. Subsequently we discuss significant differences in pupil attitudes to schooling and motivation in the two countries and consider the relationship of these to the influence of peer culture and to learning outcomes and achievement.

Classroom Processes

Although it would be unwise to generalise too much from a relatively small amount of classroom observation data, the research revealed some potentially important differences and similarities between the two countries. During the time they were observed French children were more likely to be apparently 'task engaged' in the classrooms studied (68% as compared with 57% in England) with English children more likely to be apparently distracted (24% compared with 13% in France).

Children in both countries spent roughly the same amount of time 'managing tasks' such as collecting materials and resources and organising their chapter and books.

These significant differences in task engagement are likely to be associated to some extent with French pupils typically higher levels of motivation across all types of school. However they are more strongly associated with the dominance of the teacher in the classroom setting. Teachers in France were actually 'instructing' (i.e. engaged with children directly on an area of the curriculum) for 33% of the observed time in France, whereas teachers 'instructed' for only 20% of the observed time in England. Overall in England the children spent 60% of their time without directly interacting with the teacher, while the children in France spent only 40% of their time without some form of interaction with the teacher, a finding that reflects the ubiquitous use of the traditional French *leçon* which involves teacher exposition followed by individual practice and a final whole-class evaluation and feedback session.

Conversely there was more child to child interaction in England (39% of observed time as compared with 16% in France) and more of this child-to-child interaction was gender-based in England. Pupils were likely to be task engaged more in France because the teacher was in direct interaction with them more often. This was relatively easy for teachers in France to maintain because of the prevalence of whole class teaching methods (62% of observed time in France as compared with 38% in England) whereas English children spent a greater proportion of their time working individually (51% as against 34% in France) and on group work (8% compared with 0.8% in France which helps to explain some of the higher child-to-child interaction). Typically in France children were not encouraged to interact with their peers while working whereas in England this was tolerated and sometimes encouraged depending on the nature of the task.

However, task engagement was not directly associated statistically for individual pupils with whole class teaching. We tested the hypothesis that for the same individual pupils there would be differences in pupil activity according to pedagogic context (i.e. differences in the proportion of time they appeared task engaged as compared with distracted or managing tasks, according to whether whole class teaching, group work or individual work was taking place). In England there were no significant differences in pupil activity according to pedagogic context.[2] In France also, most of the differences were non-significant, but when pupils were working individually, significantly higher levels of apparent distractedness were observed, compared with those levels of distractedness observed in whole class and group work contexts.[3] This appears to suggest that it is the typical dominance of the teacher in the French classroom setting which keeps pupils apparently on task rather than a high level of intrinsic motivation! It also suggests that more whole class teaching in England would not necessarily result in a higher level of apparent pupil task engagement.

Pupil perceptions from the questionnaire data gathered from the larger sample of 400 pupils in each country confirmed the classroom observation data. English pupils were more likely to say that they felt free to move around the classroom (61 % compared to 34% of French pupils) and 43% of them said that they spent much of their time sitting quietly compared to 73% of French pupils. More French pupils also thought that they spent their time listening and watching the teacher (French pupils 89%, English pupils 67%) and answering teachers' questions (French pupils 89%, English pupils 67%). English pupils thought it was important to have a teacher who spoke clearly, while French pupils thought it was particularly important to have a teacher who wrote clearly, possibly reflecting the preponderance of blackboard work in French teaching.

Our observations, both quantitative and qualitative, point to a possible association between the French teacher's dominance in the traditional *leçon* with its emphasis on repetition until each principle is thoroughly learned and the success of French pupils in computational skills where thorough rehearsal and practice may be important and the aim is that all pupils are brought to a common level of understanding. Conversely, the observation and achievement data together suggest that English pupils who are expected to work more on their own and are given more differentiated work may, as a result be in a better position to develop problem-solving strategies in maths and creativity in writing – where these are likely to be encouraged and less likely to be shouted at or told off if they get things wrong. However, they may be in a worse position when tackling such tasks as computation, if they have not been as thoroughly grounded in skills for tackling these as French children are.

For example, Tall (1993/1996, cited in Harries & Sutherland, 1998) argues that children who fail in mathematics are often actually carrying out a more difficult maths task than those who succeed. Lower attaining pupils in both Tall's study and in our analysis of English pupils were more likely to use primitive mathematical objects and primary processes, for example counting to solve addition problems, or repeated addition to solve problems which could be more effectively solved using multiplication. In Tall's view those pupils who work in this way are consistently carrying out more time-consuming work than other pupils and may be more likely to struggle as a result. The crucial argument for this analysis seems to be that some of this approach may be taught to pupils through classroom teaching or through textbooks, but that failing this, pupils left to work alone may struggle unnecessarily to work through procedurally as described above. Harries & Sutherland (1998) suggest that textbooks in England and possibly also maths teaching do not pay enough attention to the use of all forms of external representation as discussed by Tall. They conclude that:

> *English pupils are often introduced to a wide variety of*
> *mathematical ideas and ways of solving problems without*
> *being presented with any support to make links between these*
> *ideas. We conjecture that when this approach is used it must*
> *be very difficult for all but the most exceptional pupils to*
> *make sense of and thus learn mathematics. (Harries &*
> *Sutherland, 1998, p. 33)*

These arguments are returned to in the conclusion to the chapter. In the following section, we consider pupil attitudes to school and to the teacher and the possible link between these and classroom culture and achievement.

Attitudes to Schooling, Motivation, and Achievement

Analysis of the pupil questionnaire and group interview data with a sub sample of 96 children from the QUEST study suggested that while the sample of children from both countries felt generally positive towards school and towards their teachers, there were nevertheless striking differences in their perceptions of what it means to be a pupil. From the classroom observation data there was clear evidence that in English classrooms the teacher typically made much more effort than was observed in France to motivate children through arousing their interest, protecting their self-esteem, and avoiding negative feedback. Nevertheless despite experiencing a typically more formal and authoritarian classroom, French children were more strongly positive about their relationship to school, more likely to see teaching as helpful and useful to them and apparently more highly motivated towards educational success and academic goals. Our findings also suggested that the personality and personal characteristics of the teacher were of less concern to French pupils, while having a teacher who makes children work hard was perceived as more important. The French pupils in the study were much more likely both to understand and to share the teachers' values and to see school as a place where one expects to work hard, whereas English children often emphasised the social purposes of school and also expected to have fun at school.

In France there appeared to be a shared value system between teachers, pupils, parents and the wider society based on a common understanding of the organisation and content of schooling and an appreciation of its importance. Since this wider cultural context appears to be more supportive of education in France, the teacher's role is in many ways a more straightforward one. The children already understand the potential usefulness of education to their future as our data show. This clear awareness of a national 'ladder of progress' linking the various stages of schooling was reflected among French children in their clear targets for the future compared to English children's typically much more vague notions of the future and their own goals. We suggested that one explanation of these differences was a clear delineation between work and play in French schools, a clear focus in school culture on academic learning, and the relative absence of a negative pupil peer group opposed to the culture of the school. There appeared to be a close link between these shared notions of the purposes of schooling, of what teaching and learning mean, the common commitment of teachers and pupils to getting through to the next scholastic level, and the readiness to employ learned, authoritatively-taught algorithmic and formulaic strategies in mathematical and language tasks.

In England, by comparison there was a greater diversity of values about the function of school. English teachers had a far more multi-faceted conception of their teaching role, and pupils saw the purposes of schooling in an equally multi-faceted way. English pupils demonstrated more individual variation and independence in both their general attitudes to schooling and in their response to specific mathematics and language tasks, especially in the areas of problem-solving and creative writing.

Findings

Perhaps the most important general finding of the study was that there was no clear 'winner' in the comparison of overall outcomes of English and French pupils' achievements in these two key areas of maths and language. However, there were significant national differences in pupils' levels of confidence and their willingness to 'have a go' and to take risks. English pupils were much stronger in this respect, whereas French pupils seemed to be constrained by their desire to avoid making mistakes and to refer constantly to authority. The detailed comparative analysis of the pattern of errors made revealed that the source of these differences in *orientation*, as well as *performance*, could be traced back through differences in pupils' classroom experiences, as well as to the particular traditions and assumptions about education of the two national cultures. In France, the approach may be characterised as one of 'induction' of pupils into the established bodies of knowledge; a process that Sharpe (1993) refers to as 'catechistic'. Teachers are often 'drillers', their model of the goals of education largely a convergent one. This French emphasis on correct performance was reflected in weaker pupils not always knowing which approach to take in order to solve a particular problem as well as demonstrating a fear of getting a wrong answer by not answering questions to which they did not know the answer.

By contrast, the established pedagogic tradition in English primary schools has been one that emphasises discovery and the search on the part of each pupil for a solution to a given problem. Pupils have been encouraged to think for themselves and their efforts have been valued in these terms. The effects of these different emphases, which of course vary in degree from teacher to teacher and school to school, are reflected in maths, for example, by the finding that some English children tried to develop their own strategies to do long multiplication tasks involving decimal points. High achieving children in particular were able to develop their own efficient strategies in number and investigative maths. They also had a better sense of the correctness or otherwise of their answers than French children. However, one less desirable consequence of this stance was the tendency to use non-standard, inefficient methods for procedures in relation to numeracy and, more generally, not being able to distinguish between efficient and inefficient methods.

The findings suggest that, at the level of the individual pupil, task engagement and overall achievement may not be directly linked with particular pedagogical contexts. However, the success of French pupils in computational skills may be related to the French teachers' dominance in the traditional *leçon*, with its emphasis on structured progression and repetition at each stage until each principle is thoroughly learned. This French emphasis on correct performance was reflected in weaker pupils not always knowing which approach to take in order to solve a particular problem as well as demonstrating a fear of getting a wrong answer by not answering questions to which they did not know the answer.

Conversely, the individualised and differentiated pedagogy of English teachers may place English pupils in a better position to develop the strengths they display in problem-solving skills in maths and in creativity in writing.

Implications for Policy

The research provides strong support for the conduct of more 'diagnostic' comparative studies which use detailed analyses of pupils' test performance in different national settings both to explore the relative strengths and weaknesses of a particular educational system and to link these to the content of the curriculum and teachers' classroom practice. However, it is important to stress too, that pupils are not a 'tabula rasa' but rather that they come to the classroom with expectations and attitudes rooted in their broader cultural experiences. By their nature, such cultural experiences cannot easily be influenced or changed. Rather it is important to recognise them as a 'given' in the educational process which both affects the way in which individual learners respond to particular teaching strategies and colours the collective life of teachers and pupils in the classroom. It is equally important to recognise that teachers, too, are heirs to such cultural traditions and are likely to share the same broad expectations and assumptions about education as their pupils. Thus, particular pedagogic strategies and their consequences cannot be conceived as absolutes. The way in which the content of the curriculum and particular teaching approaches impact on pupil learning outcomes also needs to be understood as culturally specific. Thus the following conclusions and their implications for national policy need to be approached with both caution and understanding concerning the extent to which they may be generalised.

Our study suggests that English primary education is still very different from that of other countries. Despite the introduction of a national curriculum, at the time of the study, in 1996 and 1997, it still seemed to be characterised by relatively less overt direction and commitment to providing a common educational experience in practice. However, this may be beginning to change as a result of the influence of the National Literacy and Numeracy strategies. Furthermore, the choice of curriculum content and pedagogic strategy, in maths in particular, appeared to be more grounded than in France in an individualised and differentiating approach, rather than in social constructivist theories of learning. They appear to reflect the assumption that if pupils are interested and busy, learning will follow.

Thus where other countries provide children with a clear vision of the journey in which they are engaged and a map describing how it is intended they will get to their destination, this is less easy to discern in the English curriculum, which has been criticised for being overcrowded and lacking in any unifying rationale. This, however, may change in line with recent announcements concerning the primary curriculum. Equally, in England, every effort is made to make the learning experience in maths as entertaining as possible for pupils – lively lessons, colourful and attractive books – but these may well disguise the lack of a clear rationale concerning the contribution of a given task to the overall journey. The evidence from our analysis of pupil strategies suggests that English teachers may be overly concerned with arousing intrinsic motivation and therefore may underuse the potential of extrinsic motivation such as marks and grades. A balance between these two approaches may be more appropriate.

The current emphasis on differentiation is also a significant and rather different characteristic of English education. The French education system is informed by the pervasive commitment to equality which is deeply rooted in French culture. This is translated into the reality of a common educational experience for all pupils. It is also clear that the association of curriculum coverage with particular year groups, rather than levels, assumes that there is a common goal for all pupils. Moreover, the French emphasis on effort, rather than ability, as the explanation of differences in performance helps to prevent pupils being discouraged from trying at an early stage in their school career.

The Teaching of Language and Maths

The study highlights the importance of linking pedagogic strategies to an understanding of how children learn in a social context and the factors that influence this. However, our analysis suggests that in maths teaching, English pupils might benefit from a systematic approach to teaching which emphasises differentiation less and which sets common expectations for all pupils. Such an approach might well provide help for lower achieving pupils, in that they would be less likely to be allowed to fall behind and more likely to have a clear understanding of the goals to be achieved, and of what they needed to do in order to achieve them.

The performance of English pupils in language, particularly in reading, would suggest that English methods and styles of teaching are relatively successful, although in language too, teachers need a clearer theoretical understanding of what they want pupils to achieve, so that the strengths of the more open-ended pedagogy can be maximised in learning. It also demonstrates the importance of a more sustained attempt to understand the source of pupils' motivation to learn in terms of teacher activity, peer influence, pupils' understanding of their learning goals and their self-concept; and to consider how issues of motivation can be addressed among those pupils who become disheartened.

The Testing of Language and Maths

The French National assessments are conducted at the *beginning* of the key stage and their purpose is to provide teachers with diagnostic information about their pupils' strengths and weaknesses. They are not 'high stakes' in the way that the English Key Stage 2 national tests are. Their timing and purpose therefore allow them to be constructed primarily to provide information for national monitoring on the one hand and for informing classroom instruction on the other. However, although their timing and purpose would allow them to introduce more emphasis on problem-solving and creativity, this opportunity is not taken.

By contrast, the high stakes nature of the English tests means that reliability has to be at a premium. This makes it difficult to assess and to adequately reflect the full range of English pupils' 'strengths', in particular their greater willingness to take risks in learning, their problem-solving skills and their creativity in writing, all of which arguably are significant lifelong learning' skills.

The French maths tests used more traditional items than the English national test. This both reflected and reinforced the French pedagogic and curriculum emphasis on practising the application of number skills. In order to improve English children's computational skills, there would seem to be a case for incorporating into the English maths test a mixture of both the investigational items currently used and some more traditional, conventionally laid out items in which the emphasis is on correct application of the procedure indicated rather, than as at present, requiring the pupil to find out which procedures could be applied.

These conclusions highlight the powerful potential of detailed comparative studies of pupils' learning strategies and achievements which are linked to relevant data on other aspects of the educational system. They suggest that diagnostic comparative studies of performance have a valuable role to play in identifying the factors informing national profiles of strengths and weaknesses and can help to guard against 'quick-fix' policy borrowing which may well not work in the way intended. Their value in helping to guide both policy-makers and professionals concerning how to improve standards speak for themselves.

Acknowledgements

The study reported here was funded by the Economic and Social Research Council, whose support is gratefully acknowledged. Further analysis of pupil learning strategies was funded by the Qualifications and Curriculum Authority. Some parts of this chapter were originally written for the report to Qualifications and Curriculum Authority (QCA).

Notes

[1] The members of the QUEST team are Patricia Broadfoot, Marilyn Osborn and Claire Planel, University of Bristol, and Keith Sharp and Brigitte Ward, Canterbury Christchurch College. The support of the ESRC for this research is gratefully acknowledged.
[2] (Kruskal-Wallis ANOVA).
[3] (Kruskal-Wallis ANOVA $p = 0.012$).

References

Broadfoot, P. & Osborn, M. with Gilly, M. & Paillet, A. (1988) What professional responsibility means to teachers: national contexts and classroom constants, *British Journal of Sociology of Education*, 9, pp. 265-287.

Broadfoot, P., Osborn, M., Gilly, M. & Brucher, A. (1993) *Perceptions of Teaching: primary school teachers in England and France.* London: Cassell.

Harries, T. & Sutherland, R. (1998) *A Comparison of Primary Mathematics Textbooks from Five Countries with a Particular Focus on the Treatment of Number.* (Qualifications and Curriculum Authority Final Report).

Osborn, M. & Broadfoot, P. (1992) A lesson in progress? Primary classrooms observed in England and France, *Oxford Review of Education*, 18, pp. 3-15.

Planel, C. (1998) Qualitative analysis in comparative international testing, paper given at ESRC seminar on Comparing Pupil Achievement, 3 March.

Planel, C. & Osborn, M. with Broadfoot, P. & Ward, B. (1998) A *Comparative Analysis of English and French Pupils' Attitudes and Performance in Mathematics and Language,* report to Qualifications and Curriculum Authority.

Pollard, A. & Triggs, P. with Broadfoot, P., McNess, E. & Osborn, M. (forthcoming) *Policy, Practice and Pupil Experience: changing English primary schools.* London: Cassell.

Sharpe, K. (1993) *A Double Ethnography of French Primary Schooling,* final report to ESRC.

Tall, D. (1993) The transition from arithmetic to algebra: number patterns or proceptual programming, in *Proceedings of 2nd Annual Conference on Teaching and Learning,* London.

Tall, D. (1996) Can all children climb the same curriculum ladder?, in *The Mathematical Ability of School Leavers,* Gresham Special Lecture, Gresham College, London.

APPENDIX

[In this version of the Test papers some questions have been typeset and their layout has changed. The complete set of orginal papers is available in Planel et al, 1998.]

LANGUAGE 1

READING COMPREHENSION A

Tom had been living with his grandfather, Sir Gregory, as he was known to the local people, since he was ten years old. So he had been on the estate for nearly five years. A series of quite straightfoward events had brought him to this isolated spot, cut off from the rest of the world.

Tom had spent his early childhood at Greenthorpe, a town in the Midlands, with his parents, the Westons. Mr Weston was an official in the Forestry Commission. The family were both happy and comfortably off until Tom fell ill at the age of nine.

For a period of several weeks the boy's health improved but then he suffered several relapses. The doctor and his parents were worried. It was decided that Tom should be entrusted to his grandfather in the hope that a spell in the healthy air of the wild and open countryside would cure him.

Marilyn Osborn & Claire Planel

Read the passage above, then answer all the questions.

1. What is the name of the main character in the story?

2. Which of the titles below is the correct one?

Put a tick in the box which matches the title you have chosen. You can only give one answer.

The Westons Move House   ☐
An Easy Life   ☐
Life Had to Change   ☐
Tom on Holiday   ☐

3. a) Who did Tom live with when he was a little boy?
   b) Who did he live with afterwards?

4. Draw a line between 2 of the dots to show the family relationships:

a)
               • Sir Gregory's father
    Mr Weston is •   • Tom's uncle
               • Tom's father
               • Tom's grandfather

b)
               • Mr Weston's son
    Sir Gregory is •   • Mr Weston's grandfather
               • Tom's father
               • Tom's grandfather

READING COMPREHENSION B

A REPORT FROM OUR TRAVEL WRITER, GITA GUPTA, WHO VISITED THE BOKEHAM MANOR ANNUAL BOOKFAIR.

There's only one thing worse than a wet holiday weekend – and that is a hot one. If it is wet we can laze about at home, playing video games, watching T.V. and reading. There's no rush, no routine or stress.

So you can imagine my reaction when Mum announced that, as it was sunny, we were all going out to visit a bookfair at a place called Bokeham Manor. I wished that the skies would open.

284

Getting to Bokeham was a slow, stifling journey, as we inched our way along the A1 in the usual holiday jams. We had forgotten that sitting in traffic on hot holiday weekends was a national hobby.

Once we arrived, however, it did not take me long to warm to the place. For a start, Bokeham is not like the ordinary type of stately home with cases of dusty vases, wall-to-wall paintings and old-fashioned furniture. The Manor actually recreates life in the 16th century. You don't have to tiptoe about in hushed silence. Bokeham is a lively, noisy place where you can touch and feel everything, and if you want to, you can dress up in Tudor costume and take part yourself.

The main event was a 16th century bookfair. Papermakers, printers, bookbinders and illuminators were all demonstrating their skills. No one could fail to enjoy trying their hand at these crafts or any of the others that were being demonstrated that day.

Visitors in wheelchairs and people with babies had a difficult time, as getting these in and out of the buildings was not easy. In some places it was impossible. I'm not a regular visitor to stately homes, but I'm really pleased that I was taken to Bokeham. It was a great day out and I'd recommend it to most people.

Questions about Gita Gupta's report

1. What was Gita's opinion on first hearing about the family outing to Bokeham?

2. Which words tell you this?

3. How had Gita's opinion changed by the end of the report?

GRAMMAR

Can you find where the words

'they're'
'there'
'their'

should go in the passage below?

1. In the house at the bottom of our road ....
are four dogs. .... all black labradors and
.... names are Billy, Blackie, Brutus and Bongo.

In the same way, where would you put
'where'
'were'

'we're'?
Choose carefully and write one word in each box.

2. The house .... the black dogs live is a bit strange and scary. .... always daring each other to knock on the door and make the dogs bark. When we .... there last week we got caught.

What about
>'to'
>'too'
>'two'?

Write the correct word in each box.

3. A man opened the window and shouted, "What are you .... doing?" But we were .... scared .... answer. We ran home.

PUNCTUATION AND HANDWRITING

Some of the punctuation in the following paragraph has been left out. Can you correct it?

Read this passage.

the thunder storm lasted all night the thunder rumbled and rolled darkly and endlessly over all the land the lightning struck a pine tree which split and crashed to the ground

Write it out in your neatest handwriting, putting in the missing full stops and capital letters. You will be given a mark for your handwriting.

ALPHABET

Look at the envelopes on the next page.

Put the surnames on the envelopes into alphabetical order. The first one is ARMSTRONG: so there is a 1 written in the circle under the envelope. Can you continue? Write under each envelope the number which you think shows the alphabetical order of the surnames.
Be careful: do not use the same number more than once!

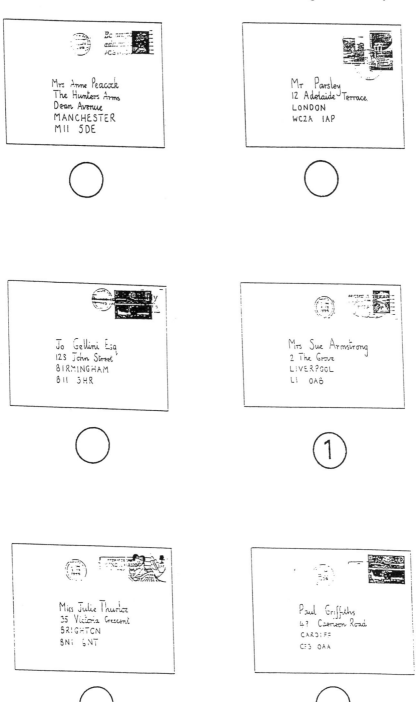

Mrs Anne Peacock
The Hunters Arms
Dean Avenue
MANCHESTER
M11 5DE

Mr Parsley
12 Adelaide Terrace
LONDON
WC2A 1AP

Jo Gellini Esq
123 John Street
BIRMINGHAM
B11 3HR

Mrs Sue Armstrong
2 The Grove
LIVERPOOL
L1 0AB

Miss Julie Thurlow
35 Victoria Crescent
BRIGHTON
BN1 6NT

Paul Griffiths
43 Caerwon Road
CARDIFF
CF3 0AA

A Door Opens

"What's in the room I have never entered?

What's behind the door I have never opened?"

Write a short story about what happens when you open the door.

MATHS A

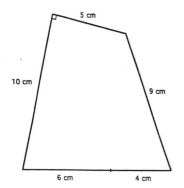

4. a) Read the sentences below. For each sentence circle in pencil the words TRUE or FALSE according to what you think is correct.

Two of the sides in the shape are at right angles.   TRUE   FALSE

Two sides in the shape are parallel.   TRUE   FALSE

Two sides in the shape are of the same length.   TRUE   FALSE

The middle point in the length of one of the   TRUE   FALSE
sides is shown in the geometric shape.

4. b) Write down how many sides the shape has ....

5. a) What is the perimeter of this shape?

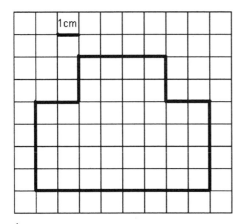

Answer .... cms

5. b) Can you work out the area which is covered in grey?

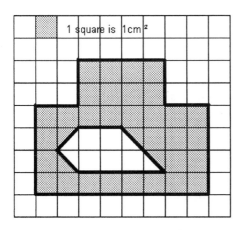

Answer ....cms²

4.   Here are some picture frame sizes.

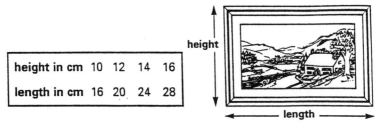

height in cm	10	12	14	16
length in cm	16	20	24	28

For each frame, the length is **twice** the height, **subtract 4**.

What is the **length** of a frame which has a **height** of **36cm**?

cm

MATHS B

5.   This is what it costs to visit a castle.

Allington Castle
Cost per person

Adults	£2.45
Children (11 and over)	£1.30
Children (under 11)	95p

Helen is 10 years 9 months old.

5a. How much will it cost Helen to visit?

On one day the number of visitors was

Adults	4
Children (11 and over)......	16
Children (under 11)...........	12

Here is a graph to show the number of visitors.

5b. Complete the scale for the axis called 'Number of Visitors'.

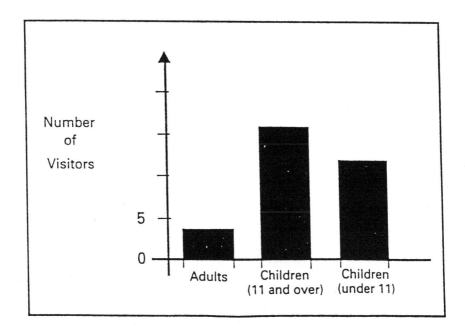

This is what it costs to visit a castle.

**Allington Castle
Cost per person**

Adults	£2.45
Children (11 and over)	£1.30
Children (under 11)	95p

5c. How much will it cost for
18 children (under 11) to visit the castle?

You **must** show your working.

MATHS C

You will need to spend about 20 minutes on this Maths problem.

Some children investigated what answers they got when they did sums with odd and even numbers. They made these comments on what they found.

David
When I add two odd numbers together I always get an even answer. For example, 3 + 5 = 8 and 9 + 11 = 20

Sarah
When I add an odd number to an even number I always get an odd number for an answer.

Megan
I think that an even number multiplied by an odd number might sometimes be even and sometimes be odd.

Farshad
Taking away an odd number from an even number always gives me an odd answer. For example, 12 − 9 = 3

1. Which of these children do you agree with and which do you disagree with? Say *why* you think they are right or wrong.

2. What other general statements could you make about calculating with odd and even numbers? Say why you think they are true.

Commentary

DAVID HAWKER & GÉRARD BONNET

The value of the seminars on which this book is based lies in part at least, on the mixture of perspectives represented in the papers presented and the subsequent discussions. It is appropriate, therefore, that we should close this third and final section of the book with the policy-makers' perspective.

Résumé of Comments Made by
David Hawker, Qualifications and Curriculum Authority

In the end, educational research can only help to shape policy, not to make it. In this context its role is to help answer the questions:

- Are we getting efficiency and productivity from our education system?
- Are children reaching the highest possible levels?
- Are they learning the right things (curriculum issues)?
- How competitive are we as a country?
- What are the likely social consequences of our current policies?

If children are the same everywhere, differences in attainment must be a product of other variables. What are these? Teaching quality, teaching conditions, social conditions and the requirements of the education system are some of the more obvious sources of difference. Pupil attainment has to be linked to other analyses. Squeezing any one country's system into an international framework for comparison is difficult and we recognise that the resultant data can be nonsense. The latest OECD study of 32 countries' performance in reading, literacy, maths and science highlights this problem of validity. There are different national perceptions of both benchmarks and how to reach them. Performance can be qualitatively different. It would be useful to combine a range of perspectives – examinations and qualifications on the one hand; and the more qualitative results of inspections and bilateral studies on the other.

All this needs to be thought through in the light of what we want to get from international comparative studies. First and foremost this is likely to be a consideration of how far we are achieving:

- threshold minimum standards of performance in basic skills – literacy, maths, science, and Information Technology. A common basic entitlement is the foundation of equity and we need to see how well we are achieving this and narrowing the gap;
- the key skills needed for employability – those needed by young people as a 'passport' in a flexible labour market and to function effectively in the workplace;
- the creation of social cohesion and equipping young people to be effective members of society.

Policy-makers want answers, not questions. They need to make decisions. They have a right to good quality data, intelligent analysis and sensible pointers concerning what should be done in their own context as well as advice against jumping to conclusions too quickly. There is a danger from 'cultural implants', thus we need to internalise the lessons we learn in order to make them work in the English classroom.

Résumé of Comments Made by
Gérard Bonnet, Ministère de l'Education, Paris

There are clear problems associated with international comparisons of pupil achievement. The Quality in Educational Systems Trans-nationally (QUEST) project's approach (see Broadfoot and Osborn & Planel in this volume) would seem to be more promising and to avoid some of the pitfalls. ISCAT (see Steedman in this volume) can be no more than a compromise and can never provide a proper tool for measuring outcomes between two countries. Studies such as the Third International Mathematics and Science Study (TIMSS) and the International Adult Literacy Survey (IALS) have similar problems and are disappointing in not being able to explain what is going on. The 'league tables' to which these results have been put have made matters worse. To draw policy indicators from a purely research project is not wise. The international surveys also do not measure what they set out to measure since they do not take into account local culture. Pupils' attitude to a test is important – not just their ability to do it and this may be influenced by cultural factors. Worries of this kind have been more consistently expressed in the United Kingdom – perhaps because the results of international surveys tend to be acted upon by policy-makers. In France, policy-makers have tended not to take data into account when deciding upon policy!

What then should we do about international comparisons if we accept that they are here to stay? The challenge is to invent new ways of measuring achievements among countries. When comparing very different countries (e.g. Germany and Zimbabwe) what use is it to reduce data to common denominators? Large studies are also very expensive. We need to find a way of conducting smaller, less costly surveys that produce usable policy indicators in a short time-scale, not five years later. One way is the QUEST method which involves keeping the study small and looking in detail at the 'ideology' of the system. Another way is to use original data produced in each of the countries using their own indigenous instruments – having decided that they are comparable. This would take into account the cultural specificity of each of the countries.

Postscript

PATRICIA BROADFOOT

Comparative education is something of a cornucopia when it comes to methodologies. We can choose from complex statistical analyses based on huge quantitative data-bases at one extreme through to intensive ethnographic studies on the other. All arguably have a place, the quality of each being determined by its fitness for the purpose in question. But whatever the methodology employed, it must be rigorously executed and subject to the application of the same high standards of procedure that would characterise any scholarly field. These are rightly called 'disciplines'. They represent the cumulative wisdom concerning how best to pursue truth which has been built up patiently and painstakingly through the development over the years of a particular subject specialism.

It is when academic disciplines break out of the safe closet of scholarly enquiry to engage with the powerful and urgent agendas of policy-making that they are likely to encounter both their greatest opportunities and their greatest challenge. To be fruitful, such a development requires a degree of collective maturity which permits accommodation to these new opportunities within the discipline. It also requires the clear and confident assertion of those theoretical and methodological principles that are the foundation of high quality research in the field.

Comparative education has arguably never before been presented with such potentially fruitful avenues to contribute to international and national policy debates. One of the developments to which the seminars on which this volume is based represent a response, is the heightened profile of international educational comparisons in UK national policy and in the work of international agencies such as the European Union, OECD, and the World Bank, especially in relation to test scores, school effectiveness, economic competitiveness and educational development. Such developments represent a heady cocktail of opportunity, financial incentive and potential glory for the researchers involved. There are already many examples illustrating the potentially dangerous effects of over-indulgence. As Robinson suggests, in his chapter 'The tyranny of league tables', "what could be a sober and informed debate about English education is in danger of being drowned out by simplistic and often shrill rhetoric which seems to dominate policy-making in education". Reeling from one set of data to the next, the policy-maker is likely not to recognise the need for a solid foundation of careful technical work, sustained attention to the validity of the comparison being made and its relevance to fundamental national ideals. Thus, as comparativists, we are challenged, as Steedman suggests, in her chapter 'Measuring the quality of educational outputs', "to work to improve the quality of the information base used to establish educational equivalence and the transparency with which such work is undertaken".

Comparative education is at a cross-roads in its long history. If we take the right road we may find ourselves on a major new highway. If we do not, we shall find ourselves trapped in a blind alley from which there may be no escape. If the ESRC seminars themselves and the series of publications arising from them contribute in even a small way to the envisioning of the future for our field, they will have done a major service not only to the continuing fertility of comparative education but to education itself. As the millennium approaches, with all the changes that it represents, there can be no greater challenge.

Notes on Contributors

Robin Alexander is Professor of Education and Director of the Centre for Research in Elementary and Primary Education at the University of Warwick, United Kingdom.

Julia Betts is a researcher in international education at the Department of Educational Studies, University of Oxford, United Kingdom.

Gérard Bonnet is adviser to the director of development and planning at the Ministère de l'Education Nationale, Paris, France.

Patricia Broadfoot is Professor of Education at the Graduate School of Education and Dean of Social Sciences elect, University of Bristol, United Kingdom.

Robert Cowen is Reader in Education at the Institute of Education, University of London, United Kingdom.

Maurice Galton, formerly Professor and Dean of Education at the University of Leicester, is now at Homerton College, Cambridge, United Kingdom.

David Hawker is Head of the Curriculum and Assessment Division at the Qualifications and Curriculum Authority, London, United Kingdom.

Marilyn Osborn is Senior Research Fellow and Co-Director of the Centre for International and Comparative Studies in Education, University of Bristol, United Kingdom.

David Phillips is a Fellow of St Edmund Hall and Reader in Comparative Education at the University of Oxford, United Kingdom.

Claire Planel is a Research Fellow in the Graduate School of Education, University of Bristol, United Kingdom.

David Reynolds is Professor of Education at the University of Newcastle-upon-Tyne, United Kingdom.

Notes on Contributors

Peter Robinson is Senior Economist, Institute for Public Policy Research, London, United Kingdom.

Jürgen Schriewer is Professor of Comparative Education at Humboldt University, Berlin, Germany.

Michele Schweisfurth is Lecturer in International Education at the University of Birmingham, United Kingdom.

Hilary Steedman is Group Leader, Labour Markets Programme, Centre for Economic Performance, London School of Economics, United Kingdom.

Joseph Tobin is Professor of Teacher Education and Curriculum Studies at the University of Hawaii, Honolulu, USA.

Stephanie Wilde is conducting research in comparative education at the Department of Educational Studies, University of Oxford, United Kingdom.